HCI Remixed

HCI Remixed

Essays on Works That Have Influenced the HCI Community

edited by Thomas Erickson and David W. McDonald

The MIT Press
Cambridge, Massachusetts
London, England

For information about special quantity discounts, email special_sales@mitpress.mit.edu.

This book was set in Sabon by SNP Best-set Typesetter Ltd., Hong Kong, and was printed and bound in the United States of America.

Library of Congress Cataloging-in-Publication Data

HCI remixed : reflections on works that have influenced the HCI community / edited by Thomas Erickson and David W. McDonald.
  p. cm.
Includes bibliographical references and index.
ISBN 978-0-262-05088-3 (hardcover : alk. paper)
1. Human-computer interaction. I. Erickson, Thomas, 1956–. II. McDonald, David W., 1964–.
QA76.9.H85H4125 2008
004′.019—dc22 2007005537

10 9 8 7 6 5 4 3 2 1

Contents

List of Works Covered

Work	Essay Author	Chapter	Page
Beach, K. 1993. Becoming a Bartender: The Role of External Memory Cues in a Work-directed Educational Activity. *Journal of Applied Cognitive Psychology*, 7 (3), 191–204.	Churchill	38	235
Berlin, L. M., Jeffries, R., O'Day, V., Paepcke, A. and Wharton, C. 1993. Where Did You Put It? Issues in the Design and Use of a Group Memory. *Proceedings of the SIGCHI Conference on Human Factors in Computing Systems*, 23–30. ACM Press.	McDonald	21	129
Card, S. K., English, W. K., and Burr, B. J. 1978. Evaluation of Mouse, Rate-Controlled Isometric Joystick, Step Keys, and Text Keys for Text Selection on a CRT. *Ergonomics*, *21*, 601–613.	MacKenzie	48	289
Card, S. K., Moran, T. and Newell, A. 1983. *The Psychology of Human–Computer Interaction.* Lawrence Erlbaum.	Ehrlich	46	281
DeMarco, T., and Lister, T. 1999. *Peopleware: Productive Projects and Teams.* Dorset.	Thomas	41	253
Dreyfuss, H. 1955. *Designing for People.* Simon and Schuster.	Winograd	31	193
Englebart, D. 1968. The oNLine System (NLS) demo. *The American Federation of Information Processing Societies' Fall Joint Computer Conference.* Retrieved from http://unrev.stanford.edu/.	Ju	5	29

Work	Essay Author	Chapter	Page
Fitts, P. M. 1954. The Information Capacity of the Human Motor System in Controlling the Amplitude of Movement. *Journal of Experimental Psychology*, *47*, 381–391. Reprinted in *Journal of Experimental Psychology: General*, *121*, 1992, 262–269.	G. Olson	47	285
Forsythe, D. 1999. Ethics and Politics of Studying Up in Technoscience. *Anthropology of Work Review*, *20* (1), 6–11.	Cherny	33	205
Francik, E., Rudman, S. E., Cooper, D. and Levine, S. 1991. Putting Innovation to Work: Adoption Strategies for Multimedia Communication Systems. *Communications of the ACM*, *34* (12), 52–63.	Palen	22	135
Furnas, G. W. 1986. Generalized Fisheye Views. *Proceedings of the SIGCHI Conference on Human Factors in Computing Systems*, 16–23. ACM Press.	Resnick	30	185
Galloway, K., and Rabinowitz, S. 1980. *Hole-In-Space.* Mobile Image Videotape.	Harrison	25	155
Gibson, J. J. 1966. *The Senses Considered as Perceptual Systems.* George Allen and Unwin.	Gaver	44	269
Gould, J., Conti, J., and Hovanyecz, T. 1983. Composing Letters with a Simulated Listening Typewriter. *Communications of the ACM*, *26* (4), 295–308.	Schmandt	24	149
Greenberg, S., and Marwood, D. 1994. Real-Time Groupware as a Distributed System: Concurrency Control and Its Effect on the Interface. *Proceedings of the 1994 ACM Conference on Computer Supported Cooperative Work*, 207–217. ACM Press.	Edwards	19	119
Hiltz, S. R., and Turoff, M. 1993. *The Network Nation: Human Communication via Computer.* MIT Press.	Kiesler	11	69
Hollan, J., and Stornetta, S. 1992. Beyond Being There. *Proceedings of SIGCHI Conference on Human Factors in Computing Systems*, 119–125. ACM Press.	Smith	23	141
Jacobs, J. 1961. *The Death and Life of Great American Cities.* Random House.	Erickson	14	87
Kidd, A. 1994. The Marks Are on the Knowledge Worker. *Proceedings of the ACM SIGCHI Conference on Human Factors in Computing Systems*, 186–191. ACM Press.	Whittaker	28	173

Acknowledgments

The first editor would like to thank his management at IBM—Wendy A. Kellogg, in particular—for both encouragement and support in pursuing this project. IBM as an organization was supportive as well: indeed, the "official" declaration that I was going to do a book (made via creating an entry in an internal database) invoked an archaic part of IBM's organizational DNA that resulted in a letter granting me a certain percentage of time to perform said work along with the "clerical support" that was once-upon-a-time intrinsic to the production of any book. Although clerks and typing pools have gone the way of the typewriter, it's the thought that counts!

Both editors would like to recognize their colleagues, both proximal and distal, who make working in the field of HCI such great fun. Without the members of this community, who we were sure would write reflective, passionate and engaging essays, we would never have embarked on this project.

We'd also like to thank the folks at MIT Press. Doug Sery, our editor, was unflagging in his enthusiastic support for our somewhat unusual project, and guided us through the publishing process with patience and aplomb. Judy Feldmann's careful editorial work on the manuscript improved its clarity and coherence. Thanks to both.

And finally, we'd like to express our deepest appreciation for the support, encouragement and patience of our partners, Katie Solomonson and Lisa McDonald.

Tom and David

Introduction

This has been a wonderful project. We've watched with delight as essays arrived from friends, colleagues, and complete strangers. We've read through them with interest, leavened by moments of surprise and amusement. And in some cases we've been deeply touched. We've remembered things we'd forgotten (once upon a time no one knew what flaming was), and learned things we didn't know (Ivan Sutherland had to work hard to make Sketchpad's circles look right because pixels weren't square). And we've gotten a lot of different takes on fundamental issues in human–computer interaction (hereafter HCI), from the value of qualitative investigations to cognitive modeling.

But we're getting ahead of ourselves.

Our beginning should serve to put you, dear reader, on notice that you are about to dip into something that is rather different. This is a book of essays. The essays are short and personal, and each is about a particular piece of work that is at least ten years old. We asked contributors to select a paper, book, or other piece of work that had an important impact on their view of HCI. We did not require that the work be about HCI. Nor did we require that it achieve any particular external standard of importance. People could choose a work from the informal HCI canon of great works, or they could choose a forgotten gem that they wanted to rescue from obscurity. We received essays of both sorts, and also some of other sorts. We prohibited contributors from writing about their own work (famous contribution or forgotten gem), and succeeded in discouraging them from writing about their advisors' work (so, advisors, don't be offended by your former students' choices!).

Why did we do this? Here are two origin stories. This is the one that we told MIT Press when we sent them our proposal:

As a field, HCI is almost three decades old. While this is not old as disciplines go, it is old enough that those who were present at the beginnings of HCI are moving into retirement, and it is old enough that "fourth generation" HCI researchers and practitioners are entering the field. During this period HCI has produced a rich and varied array of literature. As newer researchers come to the fore, and as the volume of literature grows, the newer literature increasingly becomes the focus of attention. Older contributions that have shaped the trajectory and character of the field may soon be lost or forgotten.

The premise of this project is that there is value in reconsidering earlier work in HCI, and in reflecting on how it has shaped research, practices, our community, and individual perspectives.

The other story involves alcohol, a crowded reception and a chance European dénouement. One of us (identification is left as an exercise for the reader) was describing the recent rejection of an article in which a reviewer (fortunately anonymous) commented that the paper's references were "rather old." As those readers who are versed in the art of attending conference receptions can imagine, this was a promising starting point for a rant. And, as they also might imagine, the implication that the paper was rejected solely because of "old" references was not accurate. But that didn't matter—the important point, for the purposes of the rant, was the implication that references, like milk, bread or cheese, would somehow go bad after a certain amount of time. The rant was sympathetically received by the other editor-to-be, who then responded with a radical proposal: Why don't we do something about it! Why don't we ask people to write about old work, and the impact it had on them, and, perhaps, what it still has to say to us today? This led, through a variety of events, to the note to MIT Press, and ultimately to this book.

Both of these stories are true. We make a point of telling both because they illustrate one thing we are trying to do in the book. The first story is the official story—the front-stage story—the rationale that we craft for our audience. The second story is the back-stage story. It tells what happened behind the scenes, how things "actually" played out in the somewhat haphazard and idiosyncratic fashion of daily interpersonal interaction. What we're interested in, in this book, is the relationship between these types of stories, the interplay between what goes on behind the scenes, and what goes on front stage.

As researchers and practitioners we write papers and give talks and do demos. If our efforts succeed, we receive citations and applause and other sorts of public attention. And if they fail—well, do they ever *entirely* fail? What sort of life does our work have behind the scenes, even if the audience's applause was half hearted? While the institutions that undergird our discipline require metrics, and while overall popularity is probably as good a metric as any, it seems evident that the work we do has impact at the personal level. A demo, a book, a paper, has its effect on the individual: it can solve a problem, illustrate the utility of a new method, or catalyze a shift in perspective. It can change the course of a career or spawn a new line of research. And these effects may be, and sometimes are, independent of popularity. One of our hopes, in assembling this collection, was to get glimpses of how this comes about.

We'll now move firmly to the front of the stage (yes, yes, we're both big Erving Goffman fans). Although the initial idea for the book was quite simple, as we talked it through and discussed how to proceed, it grew more complex.

As we've mentioned, we see valuable older work fading from our discipline's working memory. We are interested in bringing back that work in a way that reflects the diversity of the field's influences, and the idiosyncrasies of the individuals who constitute the discipline. One consequence of this is that we very quickly decided that we were not trying to produce a definitive "best of HCI" collection, or some sort of overarching summary of where the field has been or how it has evolved. And indeed we haven't. Although you'll find some famous pieces of work discussed here, many equally famous works are not covered. What is notable in the set of works covered here is not their stature, but their diversity. The field of HCI has become what it is not because we are intellectually inbred, but because we bring what we have experienced, read, and understood from other areas back into our field.

Also, in line with our earlier comments, we wanted the essays to have an element of the personal in them. We hoped to preserve our essayists' voices, and to allow their enthusiasm, wit, and style to come through. One pleasure of working in such a dynamic, multidisciplinary field is our relationships with our colleagues—this is why we go to conferences, and why we end up talking in the hallways, at receptions, and afterward in the pub. We hope that the essays in this book will provide a bit of that conversational flavor. Perhaps these essays will prompt you to strike up a chat with one of the essayists, building on your existing relationship, or starting a new one.

As disciplines grow, as they become established, and as the existing arguments become well known, it can be hard to figure out where to begin, where to enter the field. One hope is that this book may provide an entrée to those who are new to the field, or to those whose focus has been on practice but are curious about what research has to say (if anything) to them. By focusing on individual pieces of work, and their impacts on particular people, these essays provide a sense of how research can be meaningful in the context of an individual's work. Furthermore, as our essayists describe how various works affected them, we get a clearer picture of the many different paths that people follow when entering HCI—yet another token of our diversity.

Perhaps our principal hope for the book is that it provide a forum for a type of discourse that is unusual in HCI, at least in the literature. It seems to us that the dominant discourse—in papers, in reviewing, in teaching—is critical and analytical. Reviewers are encouraged to look for flaws in submitted work, and students and other readers often address a work critically, carefully examining its suppositions and claims at a fine-grained level. This is a necessary and worthy approach, designed to refine and elaborate work that is in an early stage. However, we are interested in supporting other ways of engaging with work that are more syncretic. We believe that for an interdisciplinary field like HCI, the ability to take a positive, syncretic approach to engaging with work is as important as the critical, analytic work that we are trained in doing. How can we, as a discipline, come to appreciate and value the work of those who came before us? How can we see the good in a piece of work—work that may use different methods and may be based on different assumptions—and appreciate what it has to contribute?

And that is the question we set out to explore by assembling this collection. We asked our contributors not just to choose a work that had an impact on them, but one that they were enthusiastic about. We asked them to let their enthusiasm show, and to articulate the value they saw in the works they chose. This is not to say that our authors were prohibited from being critical, but rather that we urged them to approach their works with the intent of identifying strengths. Our hope was that by reflecting on the strengths of a work, and by seeing the ways in which it has had personal influence, the essays could provide us with more syncretic ways of engaging with our literature.

And that is the sort of work of these essays do. They look positively and appreciatively at contributions by others, often by others whose views are very different from those of the essayists. We hope that some of the essays will inspire you to seek out the original work. And we hope, as well, that the essays will serve to remind you that your own work, whether widely known or a not-quite-forgotten gem, may have an impact on others, and thus move our field forward.

I

Big Ideas

As disciplines go, HCI is young: as a distinct field its history spans a couple of decades. You'll find essays about "historical" work scattered throughout this volume, but this section and the next focus specifically on older work. Here you'll find essays that cover work by people who were pioneers, people who did what we would call HCI before it was called HCI. Often they built the technology from scratch, or worked out the concepts before there was technology. Each of the systems described in this section embodies some "big idea" that, at the time, was not fully recognized for its foundational contribution to the emerging field of HCI. And, as we will see, the importance of this work is not just in the articulation of ideas, but also in its impact on those who encountered it.

We begin with Bill Buxton's essay, set in the early 1970s. It shows how his career was shaped by involvement with a revolutionary system that few have heard of; we also learn a bit about the importance of mentors, and of bribery. In the next essay, "Deeply Intertwingled," we see Dan Russell getting excited by Ted Nelson's vision of hypertext, and how that set him on his course. The next two essays, Ron Baecker on Licklider's vision of human augmentation, and Joe Konstan on Sutherland's Sketchpad, offer reflections on the original ideas, and on how they have shaped the authors' conceptions of the field and their multiple engagements in it. Finally, Wendy Ju's essay is an examination of one of HCI's most significant persuasive devices: the demo. In it she describes her experience of watching the video of Englebart's famous NLS demonstration and reflects on her appreciation of its different layers through successive exposures to it.

1

My Vision Isn't My Vision: Making a Career Out of Getting Back to Where I Started

William Buxton
Microsoft Research, Toronto, Canada

J. K. Pulfer, 1971: "Man–Machine Interaction in Creative Applications"

Blame it on my stepbrother. It was around 1971. I was an undergraduate studying music, happily puttering around in the new electronic music studio at Queens University. Stan, on the other hand, had discovered computers. With that discovery came a missionary zeal.

I was not an easy convert. Perhaps this was the result of my being a preacher's kid. If my father couldn't convert me, Stan sure as hell wasn't going to. I just wanted to make music. Also, I couldn't imagine why I should care about computers, or what they could possibly have to do with music.

But then, my music composition professor, Istvan Anhalt, told me about a new project at the National Research Council of Canada (NRC 1970). It seems they were developing some kind of digital music machine. NRC was up in Ottawa, about a ninety-minute drive from Kingston, where I lived. Still, Istvan's endorsement was not enough. That is to say, not even my respect for him was sufficient to get me to look beyond the electronic music studio that had become my second home. I had helped build it, I knew it, and I was happy there. Why not? I had never seen a computer. Why should I have had any reaction other than "So what?"

What tipped the scales—big time—was Mabel. Since I know you are wondering, Mabel was Stan's highly customized BMW R69S motorcycle. Now that was technology that I *could* wrap my mind (and the rest of me) around. Even music paled in comparison. The reality was, I lived to drive that thing. When Stan would let me, that is.

So here is how he made a believer out of me. If I would go to NRC and try out the computer music system, he would let me take Mabel back and forth to Ottawa. With that as bait, I didn't hesitate for a second. Truth is, with that on the table, I would have gone up there to play a kazoo!

So, with Istvan's help, I made an appointment, and was off at the first opportunity. My life has never been the same.

When I arrived I was shown around an air-conditioned room with what appeared to be about eight whirring refrigerators in it. It turned out to be an SEL 840A computer with a phenomenal 8 kilowords (24 K) of core memory! Sitting in the middle of all of this was a pretty interesting guy, Peter Foldes. He was ensconced watching what appeared to be a rather sketchy TV show. I eventually figured out that the "TV" was actually a graphics monitor, and what he was watching was a segment from a creation of his—one of the first (and still) great computer animated films, *La Faim/Hunger* (Foldes 1974, which won the Prix du Jury—Court Métrage at the 1974 Cannes Film Festival and an Academy Award Nomination).

Interesting. So this thing can do animation as well as music (see Burtnyk and Wein 1976; NRC 1971a). Who would have thunk? My curiosity was piqued, and I started to pay attention.

Foldes had the day shift. I had graveyard duty. I would come in just as he was finishing, and then spend the night with my new mistress—the music machine. And in a week she and I finished the music for a film soundtrack—my ostensible objective in going up there in the first place.

So let me tell you about her—this beautiful music machine.

You can see her best half in figure 1.1. At the console am I (with hair), writing music using common music notation, which is viewable on the graphics screen.

Figure 1.1
The right half of the NRC music machine.

What you can't see is that the music could have up to four voices, each with its own composer-specified timbre. You could work on one melodic line at a time. On a second monitor above, the current voice was shown in one color and the other voices in another. (Red and blue—I can't remember which was which. The miracle, looking back, is that they had color at all.) To my right is an organ keyboard on which I was able to enter music in real time. And further to the right you can see a professional half-inch Ampex four-track audio tape recorder that was under computer control, which enabled me to record my music—as it was digitally synthesized in real time.

Given that I only made the entrance requirements for piano the week before graduation, I did not use the keyboard much. Instead, I did something that I am often (wrongly) credited with being the first to do (as opposed to study): use two hands in graphical interaction.

Just to set the record straight, I picked up on bimanual input from what I learned at NRC. They picked it up from Engelbart and English (1968), who picked it up from Sutherland (1963), who picked it up from uncommon sense—his appreciation for what we do in the everyday world. Therein lies another lesson that I learned from my NRC experience: our most creative work usually turns out to be the recognition and subsequent refinement of other people's good ideas. There is honor in this, not shame, despite today's obsession with "original invention" (Buxton 2004, 2005b).

Getting back to NRC, figure 1.2 shows me in the typical stance assumed in interacting with the system. Like in the system by Engelbart and English, my left hand is on a chord keyboard (see figure 1.3 for a detailed view). Each button specifies a certain note duration. From thumb to "baby" finger, the durations were: whole, half, quarter, eighth, and sixteenth notes, respectively. If I pushed any of the buttons simultaneously I got the sum of their durations. Thus, if I pushed the buttons under my "ring" and "baby" fingers together, I entered a dotted eighth note. The toggle switch by the thumb enabled the mappings to be halved. If I pushed the button under my baby finger in this mode, for example, a thirty-second note would be entered. Finally, there was a larger diving-board type surface that lay under the palm of my hand. It was used to enter bar lines.

So much for the left hand and entering note durations. How about specifying where in pitch and when in time those notes were entered? This was done using the right hand, and there were two devices that one could use for this.

The first was the block of wood shown in figure 1.4. It was about the size of a bar of soap and had two wheels mounted at right angles underneath. It was a carbon copy of the original mouse made by Bill English for Doug Engelbart.

Figure 1.2
Two-handed graphical input in 1971.

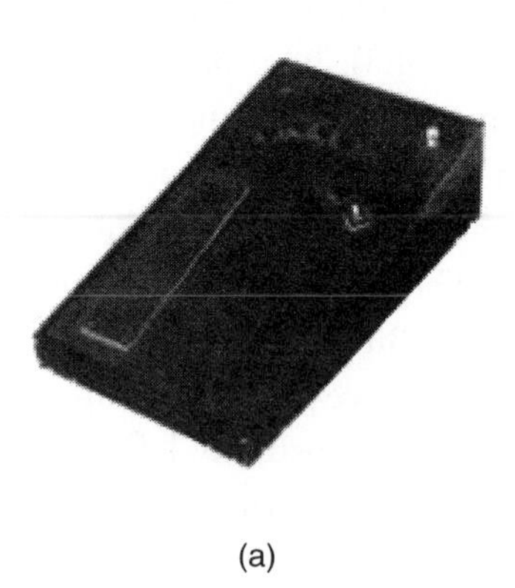

(a)

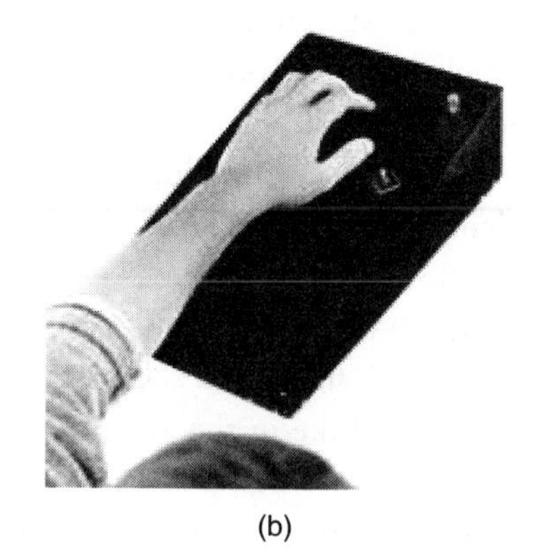

(b)

Figure 1.3
The NRC chord keyboard.

Figure 1.4
The NRC mouse in use from 1968 to 1972.

I didn't use it much.

For what I was doing, I preferred to use two large (circa six-inch diameter) wheels that were oriented horizontally and vertically with just their edges exposed. In a way, they were like a big upside-down version of the mouse, but flush-mounted to the surface of the desktop. For those old enough to remember, they could also be described as a big version of the thumb-wheels found later on the Tektronix 4014 graphics terminal. For those who are younger, they were like a large trackball, but where one had fine-grained orthogonal control along the two axes—which is why I preferred them to the mouse. You can see the vertical wheel under my right hand in figure 1.2. (My right thumb is simultaneously on the horizontal one—you just can't see it in the photo.)

With the horizontal wheel I could scroll left–right through time in my music, and with the vertical one, up–down to specify pitch. Pushing the chord keys entered a note of that duration at that point in time. As notes were entered, you could hear them synthesized through speakers connected to the computer, and at any time you could "proof-listen" to what you had written.

Along with all of this were full editing, recording, and printing facilities. To see many of the user interface features that I have described in action, see the short film, *The Music Machine* (NRC 1971b). Now remind yourself when this was: two years before the first Xerox Alto, eleven years before the Xerox Star, and thirteen years before the Macintosh! Yet all of this functionality was within the grasp of a motorcycle-riding, mathematically illiterate (I still don't know calculus) hippie musician. After a few hours of coaching, I was able to comfortably work independently, and then needed only intermittent help to learn new features or to have some problem explained.

And that is the point, the wonder, and the importance. The system was designed from the ground up with technologically naive users in mind. Furthermore, there was constant involvement of expert users throughout the system's development. To the best of my knowledge, the only other examples of this kind of thing at that time came from Lincoln Lab (Buxton 2005a), and in particular, Ron Baecker's *GENESYS* system (Baecker 1969), which was built for animators. (Pretty good karma given my later and long-standing relationship with him.)

One thing that I want to emphasize is that the real objective of the system's designers was to study human–computer interaction, not to make a music system. The key insight of Ken Pulfer, who spearheaded the music project, was that to do this effectively he needed to work with users in some rich and potent application domain. And he further realized that music was a perfect candidate. Musicians had specialized skills, were highly creative, what they did could be generalized to other professions, and perhaps most of all—unlike doctors, lawyers, and other "serious" professions—they would be willing to do serious work on a flaky system at all hours of the day and night.

I am convinced that the team that built this system knew more about HCI and designing for nontechnical users in 1971 than most "professionals" did for the next twenty years. And yet, virtually nobody has heard about the system or Ken Pulfer (1968, 1971). And, only a few have heard about Peter Tanner (1971, 1972a,b), who programmed a lot of it as an NRC student intern from Waterloo University.

There are reasons for this. The project published little, and what was published did not do a great job of capturing the real essence of what was there. Pulfer's 1971 paper, "Man–Machine Interaction in Creative Applications," for example, hints at it, but misses the mark. To me it gives no sense of the real impact that the system had on those of us who had the privilege and pleasure of working with it. Reading it today, I confess that had I not been there, I would not be able to appreciate its true historical significance either. But the work's significance transcends the publications. For example, for any graphics or HCI student who has come out of the University of Toronto, this work is a significant part of their heritage—whether they know it or not. In fact, the music and animation systems developed at NRC provided one of the key catalysts to Canadian strength in HCI, computer music, and computer animation—and I certainly don't mean just through me.

This was a golden time. My experience with this system surpassed even the motorcycle ride up to Ottawa—including those glorious hilly curves through the countryside. And given my relationship with Mabel, that is no faint praise. But truth be told, even this is an understatement. I am *still* striving to be worthy of the folks who gave me this, my first introduction to what has become my career. And, as the title of this essay suggests, since then, a huge part of my professional life has been an attempt to get back to where I started. My only hope is that I succeed. I at least owe them that. And the recognition. And thanks.

2

Deeply Intertwingled: The Unexpected Legacy of Ted Nelson's *Computer Lib/Dream Machines*

Daniel M. Russell
Google, Mountain View, California, U.S.A.

T. Nelson, 1974: *Computer Lib/Dream Machines*

It was a time of dreaming big cybernetic dreams—a time when the MITS Altair 8800 computer was on the songline of every budding computer science student, and a time we spoke in excited tones about hypertext, hypermedia, transclusion, and artificial intelligence. These were heady days, when everything impossible seemed just beyond our reach; there was an undeniable sense that if we just pushed a little bit harder, we could wrestle reality itself into the computational box. It was also a mythic time, when computers were expensive, mostly large and incomprehensible, with an aura of shifting power toward centralized authority and away from the individual. In this time, a liberating book appeared.

Computer Lib/Dream Machines was my Genesis, the place where it all started. Although I don't remember where or how I bought this self-published book in pre-Amazon.com 1974, I have the distinct memory of it suddenly appearing in my high school days when I was pondering what to do with my future. I knew I wanted to do some kind of science, but what kind? I loved biology in all its many forms and knew I wasn't about to be a chemist or a mathematician. I had fun fooling with electronics, wiring up this and that, playing with whatever IC chips I could get my hands on, so there was an early bent toward the computational.

Then Nelson's manifesto showed up and I absolutely devoured it. The type was tiny, the images cut-and-pasted from a thousand sources, the sketches and section headings hand-drawn. All that didn't matter. With its loose, almost haphazard layout and energized writing it was more a zine than a scholarly tome. But the ideas! The writing! It was breathless! Excited! Human! Enchanting! It had the Renaissance attitude that everything isn't in neat, separable categories, but is all deeply "intertwingled."

And it forever convinced me that there really was something to all this computer science business. More to the point, it convinced me that I should dedicate my studies (and what has since turned into three decades of work) along the path of the dream machines.

Since those early days I've carted my oversized copy of *Computer Lib/Dream Machines* (third printing) around with me from office to office as I've worked my way in various labs throughout Silicon Valley. I still look at it from time to time, if only to rekindle the excitement of what computing really can be. The book is a paean, a love song, a screed, and a manifesto—a fulminating reminder that we shouldn't rest lightly on the work we've done thus far—the really exiting stuff is yet to come. And more: it's the life coach in the corner reminding us that there is a higher purpose for all this technology. There's a handwritten cry on the cover: "You can and must understand computers NOW!" We, as a culture, still don't have our minds wrapped around the capabilities and promise of computation. Nelson's book rants at us to keep upping the ante, reset the bar and wrestle these things into serving the higher goal, the almost sacred purpose of being uniquely human-facing, letting us all think and write in ways that only gods and demigods could before.

We're not there yet. Rant on. Remind us that we need to always aim higher.

HCI Remixification

A pervasive theme in the books is one the HCI community resonates with easily: Computing is technology for the people to use to do great things; it's not just its own *raison d'être*.

Nelson got much of his scholarship right: he points to many of the early HCI researchers and influences in the text. People we now recognize as seminal in their work—Licklider, Engelbart, Evans and Sutherland, Baecker—they're all captured in the book. Long before HCI was popular and recognized, they're wrapped in glowing praise with the confident assertion that *this* is going to be the work that will set computing on the true and proper path to intellect augmentation.

Many of the components of HCI are here as well: computer graphics, information architectures, augmented reality, volumetric displays, input devices, simulation environments, information retrieval, computer-aided design, text-to-speech, voice recognition, brain–computer interfaces, to name just a few.

What strikes me now, looking at *Computer Lib* so much after the time it was written, are the trail markers Nelson left for his readers. You cannot help but be impressed that in his version of computing, human interfaces are of primary importance, as they are the direct coupling of human intelligence to computer support.

His sentiments about systems complexity are also well placed: "Any system which cannot be well taught to a layman in ten minutes, by a tutor in the presence of a responding setup, is too complicated." To put this in perspective, at the time of writing, programmers often used punched cards with incredibly bizarre job-control languages that were apparently designed for ease of writing the parsers, not for anything like human ease-of-use. Although human factors had been an important part of systems design, the tradition to that point had been primarily ergonomic rather than conceptual simplicity and usability.

He also warns us of *cybercrud*—esoteric terms and practices used to hide the straightforward reality of what's going on in computing. But "warn" is perhaps too relaxed a verb: Nelson extols, cajoles, and alarms us with the dangers. And rightly so, for it was also a time of great confusion and not a little intentional obfuscation. There's a political undertone here, a populist sentiment that computers are *not* all that hard to understand, and that it is incumbent on everyone to really understand what's going on in the computational realms. Nelson hammers home what came to be a truism—with great capability comes great capacity to abuse, both directly by making things more confusing than needed, but also indirectly through the abuse of computation by centralization and usurpation of personal control.

In this way, education is central to the *Computer Lib/Dream Machines* ethic. Not only is understanding computation important, but so is seizing control of one's own educational destiny, for it is only through *knowing how things work* that users can comprehend both what's personally possible and what's socially compelling. The reader not only needs to learn about computers, but also about the future of education as seen through the lens of computing. To his credit, Nelson does not portray educational computing as the universal solution for all educational crises; it is construed instead as a tool, a way or a method by which personal control can be exercised. If computation is to give power to the individual, it also needs to reconceptualize and restructure human thought processes themselves. This inevitably leads to the vision of the ultimate repository of human thought, and all the mechanism needed to cross-link and cross-reference: hypertext.

Hypertext/Hypermedia

Ted Nelson is best known as the evangelist for hypertext in its earliest days, when the idea of universal linking seemed a little outrageous. Since reading the book was so influential for me early on in my career, it was only a natural thing for me to join up with the Notecards project at PARC to work on a *real* hypertext system.[1] Remember, this was the late 1980s, before the World Wide Web was a reality, when all of us were trying to make some version of Nelson's Xanadu vision into a reality, most often by writing our own hypertext systems from the ground up (see Russell, Moran, and Jordan 1988).

It was a challenge to reach the Nelsonian vision of "tools to augment the intellect." We had so much base technology to develop first in order to build a decent platform, before we could begin living the grand and glorious vision. There's a natural tendency to get bogged down in the details. What seems simple and straightforward from the outside turns out to be intricate and complex.

But this was a cultural movement, as much as anything else. Hypertext fiction began to appear and become popular. I was working at PARC to use hypertext systems to structure and organize thoughts for education design—a trope I'd picked up straight out of Nelson—the highest calling and the most potent application we could imagine.

And it all pretty much worked. At least until the Web happened and ate the lunches of closed, non-interoperable hypertext systems. All those beautiful hypertext systems were stranded as jellyfish ashore on the desiccated sands of history. Lessons were learned—to wit, openness is a great and glorious good, interoperability matters, simplicity of interface and content encoding beats academic completeness, and search is really, truly important. In so learning, we all moved, a little helter-skelter, into the age of the all-encompassing Web.

Sure, the World Wide Web lacks many of the features of the Xanaduic conception, but it truly is a world-wrapping content-interweaving system, one with such breadth and depth as to radically transform both scholarship and day-to-day life.

And as such, hypertext is a large and hugely successful idea. Such ground-cracking ideas always have many fathers. But everyone recognizes that Nelson's book provided a huge amount of the vision and evangelism to motivate the masses. At the time, nobody was writing about hypertext with the depth and clarity of *Computer Lib/Dream Machines.*

But in many ways, like computing itself, hypertext was, for Nelson, merely a means to an end: the real goal is nothing short of a transformation of reading and writing paradigms, and implicit in that, human thought. Surely this links to Nelson's deep model of transformed education, but his key argument is that the hypertextualization of thought itself can change the way people think. From the perspective of the mid-1970s this seemed an unattainable dream and a bit outré. Today's Web, with search engines providing ever new capabilities for concept-chunk-finding and reference-following for ideas grand and trivial, when combined with the ease of authoring to create even more cross-linking, that dream is becoming the day-to-day.

Of course, the unanticipated downside of an ever refined Web of cross-linked content is the shallow gloss and mere collections of links that adds no particular value. The brilliant, the sublime, and the absurd all exist in the Web equally well, requiring new kinds of skills to navigate to what's worthwhile. The future—even the Xanaduic future—is not without dark, sharp edges.

Seeing the Future

One of the deepest memes of Nelson's book is the one that lasts the longest and is still often understood in the breach: Everything is deeply intertwingled. It's just as true today as then. But only now, perhaps, with the perspective of thirty years, do we understand how deeply true that statement is for our own field.

None of these areas is neatly separable from any other. Human–computer interfaces remain one of the great arenas of interdisciplinary thought. At our conferences, we commonly see experts from many domains working together to try to craft the future of simple, understandable, usable interfaces. As the title suggests, "humans" "computers," and "interaction"—and all that those terms imply—need to come together and commingle in a deep intertwingling.

Nelson's book also portrays a future when computing would be deeply personal—one-to-one, one-human-to-one-computer—and that we need to understand how it all fits together. How do brains, perception, social systems, theater, writing, and thought all bind and inform each other? What are their ineluctable connections? How can we make it all work?

The lasting value of Nelson's book is not the particular predictions he made about the future of computing, but his insight about key directions in which the industry would move: toward a personalized, human experience and away from incomprehensible, central systems. The vision is not yet realized. Computers today *are* more approachable and robust, but we still have light-years to go before our culture remixes the lessons of computation, hypertextual content, and deep knowing in ways that were previously unthinkable.

Note

1. In Nelson's notion real hypertext has double-ended links of different types with specific location anchors and authorship annotations for reference and authorship management, as opposed to the World Wide Web architecture, which has much looser versions of these.

3

Man–Computer Symbiosis

Ronald M. Baecker
University of Toronto, Toronto, Ontario, Canada

J. C. R. Licklider, 1960: "Man–Computer Symbiosis"

I am a knowledge media designer. I conceive of novel tools that incorporate computational and communications technology in order to help people think, learn, create, communicate, and collaborate. The work proceeds best when based on deep understandings of how people work and learn.

How did I choose this career? I became inspired to think about interactive computing by a seminal J. C. R. Licklider (1960) article entitled "Man–Computer Symbiosis," an Anthony Oettinger 1965 course at Harvard entitled "Technological Aids to Human Thought," and good fortune—joining in 1966 a group at MIT Lincoln Laboratory[1] that was the birthplace of the new field of interactive computer graphics.

The central idea was Licklider's (everyone called him Lick) vision of interactive computing as a synergistic coupling of human and machine capabilities. In a now famous passage, Lick draws an analogy between the symbiotic relationship of the fig tree and the *Blastophaga grossorum*, the insect which pollinates it, and man–machine systems: "The hope is that, in not too many years, human brains and computing machines will be coupled together very tightly and that the resulting partnership will think as no human brain has ever thought" (1960, p. 4). Noting that the then-current generation of machines fails to facilitate this symbiosis, he goes on to postulate requirements for achieving his vision:

> One of the main aims of man–computer symbiosis is to bring the computing machine effectively into the formulative parts of technical problems. . . . To think in interaction with a computer in the same way that you think with a colleague whose competence supplements your own will require much tighter coupling between man and machine . . . than is possible today.

He then suggests how computers could facilitate thinking and problem-solving, concluding (p. 6):

If those problems can be solved in such a way as to create a symbiotic relation between a man and a fast information-retrieval and data-processing machine . . . it seems evident that the cooperative interaction would greatly improve the thinking process.

The remarkably prescient second half of the paper catalogs problems whose solutions are prerequisites for realizing human–computer symbiosis. These include bridging the speed mismatch between humans and computers (his solution is time-sharing, since conceiving of ubiquitous and inexpensive personal computers in 1960 was too big a stretch, even for Lick); memory hardware improvements by many orders of magnitude; innovations in the way memory is organized and accessed; more powerful languages for communicating with machines; and input and output equipment, including desktop displays and controls, computer-based wall displays, and automatic speech generation and recognition.

Where did these brilliant insights arise? Licklider's history[2] suggests the influence of six interacting sources: Trained in psychology, math, and physics, Lick became an accomplished scientist and psycho-acoustician. He interacted with and was in turn influenced by pioneering cognitive psychologists. He also came under the influence of radical new ideas in cybernetics, information theory, and neuroscience that were being developed by amazing MIT mathematicians, scientists, and engineers. At Bolt Beranek and Newman Corporation he consulted on military, scientific, and engineering challenges such as command and control. In doing science, he was both experimenter and model builder, using analog computers and, by the 1950s, digital computers to analyze data and build models. Today he would be described as a hacker,[3] as he spent long hours working directly with early machines. Finally, he had the good fortune to experience and use extraordinary early interactive computers such as Whirlwind, TX-0, TX-2, and the first PDP-1s.

Licklider's influence on the development of computers and ultimately on the field of human–computer interaction was profound. This was not simply due to "Man–Computer Symbiosis," but also to a remarkable range of other activities. Important publications include "On-Line Man–Computer Communication" (Licklider and Clark 1962), which expanded his list of five research challenges to the achievement of man–computer symbiosis to a longer list of ten prerequisites; a seminal book entitled *Libraries of the Future* (Licklider 1965); and other writings on human–computer communication (Licklider 1968; Licklider and Taylor 1968).

Yet in 1962 he found himself in a quite different role from that of scientist and scholar. He was asked to lead the new Information Processing Techniques Office (IPTO) of the Advanced Research Projects Agency (ARPA) of the U.S. Department of Defense. In his two years in this position, with a budget of roughly $10 million per year, he initiated a significant expansion and deepening of computer science research and education in the United States. This included funding pioneering work on time-sharing, knowledge augmentation environments, interactive computer graphics, artificial intelligence, cognitive information processing, and the theory of computing. Lick funded the work of visionary computer scientists such as Doug Engelbart, Dave Evans, Ed Feigenbaum, John McCarthy, Marvin Minsky, Allen Newell, Alan Perlis, and Herb Simon at universities including Berkeley, Carnegie Mellon, MIT, and Stanford.

He termed his growing ARPA community the Intergalactic Computer Network, by which he meant ARPA researchers and graduate students, and also the emerging concept of a self-evolving "information utility" (Licklider 1970) that was prototyped by the Arpanet and that later evolved into the Internet. Lick stayed at ARPA only two years, but he and successors Ivan Sutherland, Bob Taylor, and Larry Roberts, along with talented scientists and engineers such as Paul Baran, Vinton Cerf, Bob Kahn, and Leonard Kleinrock, invented the technology of the Internet. Lick's leadership and vision got it all started.

More generally, work in these labs and at Xerox PARC—the intellectual by-product of Lick's ARPA community—did pioneering work on areas of critical importance to modern HCI such as information-processing models of user interfaces; tools for document processing, artistic expression, and scientific modeling; search engines; and systems to support real-time collaboration and virtual communities.

I am a living embodiment of Lick's vision. In aiding users of computers "to think as no human brain has ever thought," we needed to develop and to document in teaching materials a craft of user-centred interactive system design (Baecker and Buxton 1987; Baecker et al. 1995). We also needed to create centers such as Toronto's Knowledge Media Design Institute (KMDI 2006) dedicated to transforming computers into tools to help people think, learn, create, communicate, and collaborate.

My early work on picture-driven animation (Baecker 1969) allowed animators to deal with motion as effectively as they could deal with still images, and to see their creations come to life instantly on a CRT screen, something that had never previously been possible. I then worked on creating software visualization systems (Price, Baecker, and Small 1993) and exemplars (Baecker 1981; Baecker and Marcus 1990), seeking to empower programming students and software engineers to be able to see, for the first time, their programs come to life in vivid computer animations and other graphical representations.

My research on collaboration technologies (Baecker 1993) and collaborative writing tools was fueled by a vision of distributed student writers thinking and working together synchronously. Research on multimedia authoring and Web publishing systems (Baecker et al. 1996) empowered filmmakers to create video documents with structure as rich as that of text documents, and to Webcast and publish multimedia presentations on the Internet so they could be viewed anywhere, any time (Baecker 2003). Finally, I have begun a new effort to envision, design, create, and evaluate electronic prostheses to combat the ravages of cognitive decline and to preserve as well as possible our abilities to think as we age (Baecker 2006).

In summary, I have tried to achieve effective human–computer symbiosis through the design of novel knowledge media. I hope what I have accomplished is worthy of Lick's vision.

Notes

1. For an introduction to the work and culture of interactive computer graphics at Lincoln Lab, see http://www.billbuxton.com/Lincoln.html/ and http://epresence.tv/mediaContent/website_archived.aspx/.

2. For more detailed accounts, see Fano 1998; Waldrop 2001.

3. Like a good interactive system builder, Lick used and learned from his own tools. I once heard him speak about how some ARPA contractors, finding it difficult to reach him to discuss their projects, began sending him reports with an early email system to enable some measure of communication. Soon Lick was greeted each morning with teletype paper cascading all over the office.

4

Drawing on SketchPad: Reflections on Computer Science and HCI

Joseph A. Konstan
University of Minnesota, Minneapolis, Minnesota, U.S.A.

I. Sutherland, 1963: "Sketchpad: A Man–Machine Graphical Communication System"

Sutherland's SketchPad system, paper, and dissertation provide, for me, the answer to the oft-asked question: "why should HCI belong in a computer science program?" I first came across the paper "SketchPad: A Man–Machine Graphical Communication System" from the 1963 AFIPS conference nearly thirty years after it had been published (Sutherland 1963). I was nearing completion of my own dissertation in which I was exploring a variety of techniques for constructing user interface toolkits. At the time, the paper seemed little more than a handy reference in which I could trace the lineage of constraint programming in user interfaces—from Sketchpad, through Borning's ThingLab (Borning 1981), to my own work, with various hops and detours along the way. I guess I was young and in a hurry. It was only a few years later when I started to teach this material that I realized how much of today's computing traces its roots to Sutherland's work.

What was this tremendous paper about? A drawing program. Not just any drawing program, but one that took full advantage of computing, a million-pixel display (albeit with a slow pixel-by-pixel refresh), a light pen, and various buttons and dials to empower users to draw and repeat patterns, to integrate constraints with drawings so as to better understand mechanical systems, and to draw circuit diagrams as input to simulators. Indeed, by placing constraints on drawings, the user could readily link shapes together or constrain them. Ignoring the advent of color and images, one can readily argue that deployed drawing programs didn't surpass SketchPad until the early generations of computer-aided design (CAD) software packages. Indeed, although several low-distribution CAD systems became available over the next two decades, in many ways the widespread availability and use of sophisticated CAD tools can be traced back to the founding of AutoDesk and the release of AutoCAD in 1982.

For me, however, the importance of SketchPad lies in its implicit argument that HCI and advances in the science of computing are so closely intertwined. I'll provide just a few examples.

Pointing with a light pen A substantial part of Sutherland's work related to the use of a light pen as an input device. What's impressive about this work is not simply the engineering needed to make it work, but Sutherland's awareness of the human need to point *at* things rather than generically at the display. His pseudo pen location—a semantic mapping of the pen's location into drawing space—is the predecessor of modern pointing and dragging operations that snap to object attachment points and grids (see, e.g., Bier and Stone 1986). The taming of the light pen is a multifaceted triumph. First, it is no mean feat simply to find the pen in the first place (a task that requires that the user point to an illuminated pixel on the screen). Sutherland's explanation of "inking up" and the provision of a default illuminated space helped here. But more important, precise pointing was exceedingly difficult, as a result of both natural hand movements and the occlusion of the target by the pen and the user's hand. Having a pseudo pen location addresses these issues by identifying points where the user is most likely to be interested in pointing. Thus, the user needn't point exactly at a line to select it (merely close enough) and can connect ends of segments together by simply moving one close enough to the other.

Rendering of lines, circles, and text As a new faculty member, I was assigned to teach computer graphics. Of course, this meant that I had to *learn* computer graphics. One of the first areas to excite me was two-dimensional rendering—particularly, incremental algorithms for rendering lines and curves. Imagine my surprise when seeing that Sutherland had anticipated much of this work (if without some of the later elegance of efficient integer algorithms). Even more impressive is the care he evidently put into making sure that the circles would look right. He did this in the straightforward way (by identifying points around an eighth of a circle, and then replicating those points around the circle), but I haven't found earlier work laying out the algorithm. Similarly, he already had font tables for display of text and numbers, which greatly increased the capabilities of the display for engineering drawings, particularly since it allowed labels to be rendered at different angles.

Constraints and their display Constraints were the reason I found SketchPad, but in the end I was more impressed with the fact that Sutherland had already anticipated the need to display constraints over the drawings to which they were applied. His constraint language is certainly not for the novice, but then again, neither was his system. He supports a full range of position, orientation, and shape constraints that make it possible to, for example, create a regular hexagon by constraining the six lines of the hexagon to be the same size, and constraining the vertices to lie on a circle. The famous example of a modeled bridge with stresses on it gives additional insight into the power of the constraint systems, though its power becomes most apparent in the appendix to his dissertation where he lists all the constraint types. And the visualization of those constraints, though not necessarily a scalable solution, made it possible to at least begin to understand the network of forces that were acting on your drawing behind the scenes. As a constraint programmer myself, I found that even applications with only a few dozen constraints could quickly overflow my head and force me to grapple with the complexity. How I would have liked to have a visualization tool such as Sutherland's.

The data structures, algorithms, and programming structures As I see it, SketchPad anticipated object-oriented (OO) programming (in ways that would later be extended through other user interface–centered research), and contains within it a collection of interesting data structures and algorithms. The ring buffers and inheritance structures developed to make SketchPad programmable have much of the functionality of early class-based OO inheritance systems. Fundamentally, SketchPad anticipated over fifty years ago many of the programming ideas that are still with us today.

As I pull together these examples and think of the paper as a whole, the paper presents the first answer to the question posed above. It loudly asserts that HCI belongs as part of computer science because the needs of innovative interfaces drive forward the science of computing. Indeed, computer science has always been advanced through attempts to solve hard problems. Much of what we've learned about reliable computing and software engineering has emerged from trying to solve aerospace problems. Today we are advancing our theory of formal languages by solving problems in gene and protein bioinformatics. But the broader challenge of making a computer that can interact with humans in a manner supportive of human creativity—this is a challenge that has pushed forward nearly every aspect of our field, from graphics (for interfaces) to operating systems (for responsive multiprogramming) to speech recognition to networking and beyond. Sutherland's quest for a "man–machine graphical communication system" advanced interactive computing immeasurably, and our continuing quest to make computers serve as effective tools and partners with humans continues to drive the field forward. To me, this is the key argument why computer science as a discipline must embrace applications-oriented computing in general, and HCI in particular.

What lesson can we draw from Sutherland's SketchPad work about the challenges that remain for HCI and computer science? I find three lessons here:

There is still a great amount of work to do on computing systems designed to serve as tools for expert users. HCI researchers, especially in the first decades of the field, focused substantial effort on novices, on walk-up-and-use interfaces, and on "knowledge workers" whose knowledge was channeled into fairly generic tools. Less work has been done on the potential for computing systems that may involve custom hardware and extensive investments in training. There are, of course, notable exceptions, including some of the work done on systems for CAD, air traffic control, intelligence analysts, and others. But too often our textbooks and our widely promoted techniques fail to reach beyond to generic knowledge worker. Just to mention one simple example from SketchPad, I'd like to see more dials and buttons!

Basic computing hardware and software has advanced to the point where few of us need to invent much to create new interfaces; but how often are we handicapping ourselves by accepting whatever today's desktop computer has to offer? There is a wealth of exciting research that breaks this mold, adding everything from touch sensors to new displays to location awareness into our devices and applications. Some of this research is grounded in application ideas, but much of it is "for its own sake" technology. As a field, we need to bring together the creativity behind these new interaction ideas with concern for users and applications. Sutherland created SketchPad as a way to think about computers for users—it is hard to believe that the details of interaction would have come out right it he'd thought of himself as a researcher exploring pixel displays and light pens for their own sake.

It is critical to keep a presence of HCI within computer science—critical to both HCI and computer science. It is wonderful that there are many venues where HCI is advanced. Just in the academy, it has homes in cognitive science, design, information science, and various social science and engineering disciplines. There are good reasons for all of these connections, and they can help HCI move forward. However, it would be a big mistake if HCI migrated out of computer science departments entirely. From the perspective of HCI, it would cut us off from the venue where the future capabilities of computing are being developed. If we're not there to help set the agenda, the next generations of networking, software tools, handheld computers, and development techniques will not be to our liking or particularly supportive of user experience. At the same time, computer science departments need us. They need someone "on the inside" who understands and promotes the importance of the human–computer connection. Failing that, it is too easy to imagine the field being driven by the wrong problems and focusing too much on computation and not enough on communication.

These ideas bring me back to Sutherland. I use the SketchPad paper at the start of my graduate seminar on HCI (which attracts a wide range of students), and for many years it has helped to bring home the importance of HCI in shaping computing. The last time I taught this course, however, this paper elicited puzzled reactions. "Isn't this how computers just are?" asked one of the students. Sutherland's ideas have been in the core of computing for so long that we now have a generation of computer scientists who take them as a given. That's a great success for our field, but also a reason to make sure that we're regularly nurturing the next SketchPads out there.

5

The Mouse, the Demo, and the Big Idea

Wendy Ju
Stanford University, Stanford, California, U.S.A.

D. Englebart, 1968: "The oNLine System (NLS) Demo"

The Mouse

I first saw Doug Engelbart's oNLine System (NLS) demo video as an undergraduate in college. The video[1] is a recording of a demonstration Engelbart gave to the Fall Joint Computer Conference on December 8, 1968. One day, Terry Winograd wheeled a TV on a cart into my human–computer interaction class, and we spent that lecture session just watching the video. At least, I think we watched the whole video; after Engelbart introduced the mouse that he and Bill English invented, I was so electrified that I could hardly sit still in my chair. I just saw the birth of the mouse! Sure, it was giant—a wooden index card box with buttons and a cord—and yet it was instantly recognizable as the progenitor to the thing I used each day. It was not unlike the wonder you might feel at discovering photos of your grandparents as small, sometimes petulant children.

Growing up in Silicon Valley, I tended to take the computer completely for granted. Both of my parents worked for IBM, and we had a personal computer in the house from the time I was eight. I didn't think of myself as having a particular interest in working on computers. Sure, I enjoyed using the ol' beige box when producing family newsletters, programming digital versions of choose-your-own-adventure novels, making parameterized versions of favorite cookie recipes in Lotus 1-2-3, and making dot-matrix-printed greeting cards with fonts and clip art I found on bulletin boards. But I associated working *on* computers with green-and-black retinal burn-in, and finger ache. I liked working with my hands, on things, in space. I liked taking things apart and putting them back together to see how they worked. So when I got to college, I was happy to break with my Silicon Valley upbringing to focus on mechanical engineering and product design.

Seeing the beginnings of the mouse made me reconsider what it meant to work on computers; I didn't necessarily have to write code or design chips. I could work on physical, mechanical objects that changed what you could do with the computer. I had always admired the mouse. I was particularly keen on the rumors I heard about haptic mice, which could help you navigate the graphical interface by registering letters as ticks, and the edge of the window as bumps. Sometimes, daydreaming in class, I would sketch ideas for devices that could be attached to the computer—heck, even "smart" devices that had computers in them. But seeing the Engelbart video made me finally realize where I was heading all along. I could not escape the computer—but I could dramatically change the way it worked.

The Demo

The next time I saw the Doug Engelbart NLS video was roughly four years later, when I was a Master's student at the MIT Media Lab. The Lab has a fairly infamous "demo-or-die" culture. Project development schedules revolve around the biannual sponsor events, but popular projects were demoed more regularly. My project, an interactive kitchen counter that guided users through cooking recipes, was popular. Some weeks I had to demo every day, even multiple times a day. For those who have never been on the performing end of a demonstration, know this: they are time-consuming energy sinks. So it was discouraging to learn that these efforts were not respected in the rest of the academic community. Even before attending a single academic conference, I knew from talking to other graduate students how the Lab and its demo culture were perceived; the word that kept resurfacing was "hype."

Every time I grew disillusioned with the demo culture at the Lab, or weary about the popularity of my CounterActive demo, my advisor Michael Hawley tried to put this practice in perspective: "Everybody deserves to understand these ideas a little," he'd say. "The true role of research is to flip bits in people's heads."

Finally, one day, he said, "How long has it been since you've watched the Engelbart video?"

"You mean the mouse video?" I asked, happily.

Mike looked at me strangely.

Rewatching the video, with Doug Engelbart's image once again floating ghostily against the image of the document being edited, was a shock. The demo was so familiar, and yet, this time, completely captivating. I was rooted from beginning to end of the video, even though it was over an hour long. I don't know if I paid much attention to the words that were being said, but as a veteran of so many demonstrations, I was a lot more appreciative of how the ideas were illustrated. There was a power to seeing the cursor on the screen move, and Engelbart organizing his grocery list, creating categories like produce, and sticking the bananas and apples into it. I was transfixed, watching Bill Paxton's head in a corner as he worked jointly with Engelbart on a document. He dragged a word across the blank page and placed it where he wanted—drag-and-drop! He didn't even call attention to the fact that they had just implemented drag-and-drop! Even such little missteps made by the presenters were gripping, because they served to reinforce that the demo was not faked; all these amazing things were actually happening in real time.

The NLS demonstration is often described as "The Mother of All Demos." There are echos of the NLS demonstration in every presentation of new technology, from the unveiling of the Mac on. The demo is a powerful, democratizing thing. The problem is, a successful demo creates converts; people are not just knowledgeable about your ideas, they are sold on them. This is why the demo gets its bad rap in academic research. The NLS demonstration balanced these concerns admirably. Engelbart's presentation was incredibly compelling, and obviously highly produced. However, Engelbart himself was incredibly plainspoken and earnest, as far from a huckster as could be. It was the demonstration that sold the ideas. Seeing this again renewed my faith in the power of the demonstration, and gave me a model to aspire to: A great demonstration is not hype, but proof.

The Big Idea

I naively assumed that, since the recording of the demonstration ends with standing ovation, and because almost all of the ideas that Engelbart presented in the NLS demonstration had come to pass, Engelbart's ideas were embraced and championed at the time. In fact, Engelbart had real difficulty getting an audience for his ideas, even after the triumphant NLS demonstration.

> It wasn't that my ideas were so radical by then, but that they didn't fit with either of the prevailing schools of research at the time. Back in the 1960s and 1970s the hot topics were Office Automation and Artificial Intelligence. . . . They were impressed by our demonstration, but couldn't see how it fit with their thinking. Office Automation was all about making secretaries more efficient but what we showed wasn't secretarial work. Artificial Intelligence was about teaching the computer to do the work for you, so while what we showed was very nice the people from that school felt that the computer should do those things automatically. So they applauded our work, but if anything it became even harder to find money to continue the work. (Engelbart, quoted in Cringley 2004)

Despite the fact that Engelbart stated again and again that his central goal in this research was augmenting human intellect, most who watch the demo come away with a memory of the mouse. Others come away with the feeling that they've witnessed an amazing performance. Only a few fully understand Engelbart's complicated and somewhat circular statement of intent to create a sample augmentation system that would augment computer system development, and his articulation of design principles to develop augmentation systems. People like me, who were captivated by the mouse, only understood the seed of Engelbart's vision.

And yet that seed contained the crucial elements of the Engelbart's Big Idea, and it has taken root. The state of the art today is not so very unlike the one Engelbart described in 1968. We have display editing, view control, collaborative remote authoring tools, linking, and object addressing. We are a lot closer to the model where the computer acts as a tool to empower humans than to either artificial intelligence or office automation. And this realization has spurred me on in my latest viewpoint on the NLS demonstration.

Imagine that we were transported back to 1968, and held a press conference to explain to people the technologies that had developed by 2006 and what we were using them for. People would likely think we were kooks. That was exactly the situation Douglas Engelbart was in. His Big Idea gave him a new perspective on the world, took him radically different directions from his peers, and in doing so, made him a time traveler, a Silicon Valley Yankee in a 1968 King Arthur's Court. If, as Arthur C. Clarke says, "Any sufficiently advanced technology is indistinguishable from magic," then it must also be said that any sufficiently advanced vision is indistinguishable from madness.

Engelbart was not wholly prophetic; his obsession with viewing the human as an information processor, for example, keeps him even today from appreciating the mouse's value for its ease-of-use.

> He sighs, and this time the weary frustration is obvious. "I guess what I really want is that conscious pursuit of the whole system of methods and skills and languages." So the world will be changed, and man's power extended. Augmented.
>
> He looks down at the implacable mouse to the right of his keyboard. The mouse that has won the pointing device sweepstakes, the mouse that has taken the thunder from the marvelous whole system of augmentation he has spent a lifetime to develop and promote.
>
> "Now you might understand," Engelbart says, "why I wrinkle my nose so much when I hear that a mouse is 'easy to learn and natural to use.'" (Levy 1984)

But this is part of the power of the Big Idea. It doesn't even have to be right. It just has to compel us want to go out and do stuff, stuff that is different from what everyone else wants to do. It can make our work valuable to those who only have the vaguest inkling at what we're getting at. Time will sort the good from the bad. And, sometimes, when all is said and done, our Big Ideas might just buy us a slice of immortality.

Note

1. Available online at http://unrev.stanford.edu/.

II

Influential Systems

How does HCI get invented? And how do its ideas get picked up and passed along, changing over time? Our current conception of the graphical user interface was not always with us. Once upon a time no one questioned that the way to interact computers was by issuing commands. The forward march of HCI was from punch cards to teletype with paper tape, and then to terminals with screens. Then things changed. Our notion of direct manipulation, and the concepts of icons, folders, and desktops were invented, designed, and implemented. Today they are so familiar that we scarcely remember that their names and appearances were carefully chosen to help users build a conceptual bridge between the unfamiliar and ungrounded digital world and the familiar workaday world. In the same way, computers, once viewed with trepidation by office workers accustomed to filing cabinets and typing pools, are now an unremarkable feature of the workplace landscape. Yet once again, technology is changing, and we are challenged anew to develop, design, and build novel ways of interacting with computers.

The section begins with Henry Lieberman's essay on Pygmalion, the system that introduced the notion of icons and programming by demonstration and developed the notion that the concrete and manipulable nature of icons is a better way to interact with a system. The Star, addressed in a pair of essays by Sara Bly and Susanne Bødker, is a touchstone for much of our thinking about graphical user interfaces. The Star established the "desktop" as a metaphor for how we organize our interaction. Bly discusses some of the underlying principles of the design of the Star, and Bødker reminds us of its continuing freshness, as well as how ordinary it all seems today. The section concludes with essays that explore the move away from the familiar terrain of the desktop. Norbert Streitz introduces Weiser's notion of ubiquitous computing, describing the migration of computational capacity into whiteboards and ultimately walls and furniture. And Anind Dey, reflecting on another strand of ubiquitous computing, discusses the first active badge system, foreshadowing a world of networked sensors and ambient intelligence.

6

A Creative Programming Environment

Henry Lieberman
MIT Media Lab, Cambridge, Massachusetts, U.S.A.

D. C. Smith, 1977: "Pygmalion: A Creative Programming Environment"

Flashback, 1978. I'm a young researcher at the MIT Artificial Intelligence Lab. For the preceding several years, I had worked with Seymour Papert's Logo group, trying to make computer programming accessible to young children as a way of teaching them to think, and give them an environment in which they could explore, hypothesize, experiment, and understand what math and science were really about by experiencing the process themselves. What we were trying to do, essentially, was make a *Creative Programming Environment*. Remember those words.

I had become somewhat frustrated with Logo and wanted to push programming for beginners in a new direction. While graphics, using the famous Logo turtle, was a linchpin of our strategy for getting kids engaged with learning programming, Logo itself was still a textual programming language, and I wondered about the possibility of using graphics itself directly for programming.

I discussed my interest with a researcher visiting the lab, and he handed me a copy of a 1975 Stanford thesis. "You ought to read this."

Ought to, indeed. The title: "Pygmalion: A Creative Programming Environment." A *Creative Programming Environment*, huh, OK, sounds up my alley. The author: one David Canfield Smith. Never heard of him. But hey, his advisor was Alan Kay. Good sign. Kay, like Papert, was one of the greats in promoting programming as a medium for children to learn and express themselves.

It was a rather strange document. It was supposed to be about a programming environment, but he didn't really even start to talk about the programming environment until page 67. The writing before that was filled with sections entitled things like "The Nature of Creativity" and "The Computer as an Artistic Resource." Was this a thesis in computer science or in philosophy? As it turns out, both.

Much later, Smith recounted to me his first meeting with his advisor Alan Kay. Kay handed him a big stack of books. "Oh, great," Smith thought, "a bunch of books on operating systems and programming methodology." Instead, it was books like Gombrich's *Art and Illusion*, Arnheim's *Visual Thinking*, and Koestler's *The Act of Creation.* Smith credits Kay for inspiring his own approach to creativity.

It took me a while to get into reading the thesis, but once I did, I tore through it in a single sitting, and emerged dazzled and stunned. This is fantastic! I went around in a daze, blabbing about it to every person I met. "Well, what's it about?" someone would naively ask. I didn't have a good answer. "It's about . . . well, a new programming language, but um . . . not really a language, but a new way of doing programming . . . but it's really about the creative process . . . um . . . well . . . you gotta read it. . . ."

The next year, I found myself making my first trip to Silicon Valley. I vowed to look up the author of the document. Arriving at the famous Xerox Parc, I asked a secretary for him. She said no one of that name worked there. Are you sure? After asking around, she said, "Oh yeah, he works across the street, in, um, kind of . . . another part of Xerox." I went to an unmarked building, where I was led to his office. The low-key approach, I now know, was because Smith was by then working for a very secretive Xerox division charged with developing the hush-hush Xerox Star project. Star eventually became the first modern iconic file system, which Steve Jobs then famously "borrowed" for the Macintosh. It is not an exaggeration to say that we owe this man all of today's modern graphical interfaces. If you don't believe me on this last point, see his article (Smith et al. 1982a), which shows how the programming icons of Pygmalion could be transformed into metaphors for office objects.

Smith was welcoming and modest, seemingly flattered that someone would take the interest to look him up because of his thesis. I gathered it had not received a great deal of attention after it was completed. He had not published about it in any major conference or journal. The thesis itself was published only as a book by an obscure publisher in Switzerland (Smith 1977).

"Would it be possible for me to actually see Pygmalion running?" I asked. He said he would try. He hadn't touched it in a long while, and he needed to revert the microcode of the Alto machine on which it ran to an older version compatible with the program. He reached up to the top shelf, dusted off an old disk-pack, and fired it up. It ran, though a little slowly, and he demonstrated how to do Factorial of 3, that *E. coli* of programming language demonstrations. Then he said, "and now we'll try Factorial of 6." And it crashed. The disk had a head crash. There

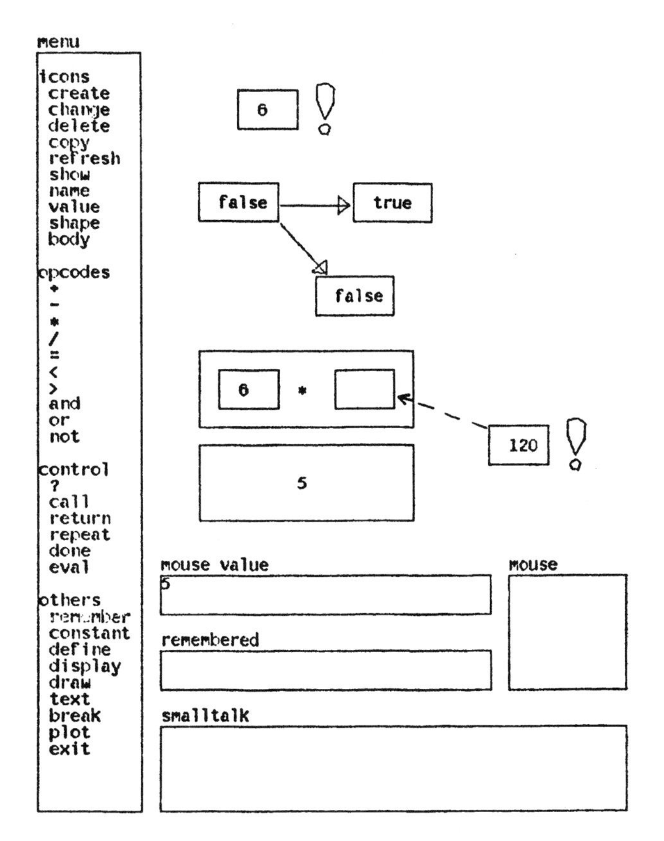

Figure 6.1
Pygmalion, computing Factorial of 6. (From Smith 1975.)

were no backups. I believe I am the last person (other than Smith himself) ever to actually see the program live. (See figure 6.1.)

But I got the idea. And it transformed me.

Pygmalion's Innovations

Pygmalion innovated in so many ways, it's not funny.

It is generally credited as the first system to introduce the modern notion of icons. At that time, the author even felt the need to explain what an icon was: "Communication between human being and computer is by means of visual entities called 'icons,' subsuming the notions of variable, reference, data structure, function, and picture" (Smith 1977).

It was certainly the first true iconic programming language. Every other attempt at graphical programming languages until then had been essentially the same as a flowchart, and even today the notion of graphical programming language is too often what I call just "icons on strings." Here not only were icons used to represent switches that invoked functions, but containment of icons represented containment in the programming language. It was probably the first system to introduce drag-and-drop as a way of passing arguments to functions. The thesis quite explicitly talks about the semiotics of the role of icons as symbolic representations of concepts, and the differences between textual and graphic representations. The eye-opening discussion of these roles still applies to all graphical interfaces today.

It conceived of programming as a process of animation, using successive states of the graphic display to represent successive states of the program. It understood the differences between static and dynamic representations, again a valuable principle applicable to all of today's interfaces. You could both write your program and test it at the same time.

Most important, it introduced the idea of *programming by example*, a revolutionary idea that I believe is still underappreciated today. It identified one of the major obstacles to making computers easy to use as excessive abstraction. Programming involves languages that talk about abstract concepts, but it is hard for most people to visualize how these abstract concepts relate to the concrete behavior of the computer in an actual example; or how to achieve some desired behavior in concrete examples by specifying abstract concepts. Programming by example is the idea that the user can just show the computer an example of what they would like to do, demonstrate the steps of the procedure on the concrete example, and the computer can record the steps, and *generalize* them to a program that can work in analogous situations.

Inspired by Pygmalion, programming by example (PBE) has since become one of my major research topics. I went on to develop PBE systems like Tinker, Mondrian (Cypher 1993), Grammex (Lieberman 2001), and Creo/Miro (Faaborg and Lieberman 2006). I was a coeditor of the first book on the topic, Allen Cypher's *Watch What I Do* (1993), and in 2001, I edited the book, *Your Wish Is My Command* (Lieberman 2001). I thus owe a significant part of my career to the inspiration provided by Smith's work.

But what I liked best about the thesis was that each detail presented about the system was directly motivated by the desire to support creativity: *visual programming* because the creative process is intensive in diagramming and visualization; *programming by example* because the creative process works by making analogies that allow old ideas to be employed as metaphors for new situations; *interactive techniques* like drag-and-drop and immediate execution because the creative process depends on quick tinkering for experimentation.

Lessons from Pygmalion for Today's HCI

What lessons can we learn from Pygmalion for contemporary research in human–computer interaction? Above and beyond the specific innovations of the thesis, some of which have been thoroughly absorbed by the community (icons), others of which have yet to be fully appreciated (programming by example), I think Pygmalion can teach us, by example, how to have the courage to do HCI research that is truly innovative.

Don't let the big questions scare you Let's go back to the title: *A Creative Programming Environment.* What chutzpah to think that your thesis could make a significant dent in the age-old problem of creativity! Yet there is a real problem there. The creative potential of computers should be obvious, yet there was (and is) no easy-enough way for a person to tap into it. Why the hell not? Get indignant about the field's failures. Fix 'em.

Think globally, act locally Yes, the thesis attacked big and important questions, but it didn't stay completely at the philosophical level; otherwise it really would have been a philosophy, not a science, thesis. Even though you can't entirely solve the problem of creativity in general, think about how creativity works in the domains you're interested in. Build a system. Show people what things would be like if your vision were realized. Try it out. Reflect on the experience. Tell others what they should learn from seeing it. At my lab, now, the MIT Media Lab, our motto is: Demo or Die.

Hunt for the good stuff, even in out-of-the-way places The reason I tell you the story about how I discovered Smith's work is to say that sometimes the most innovative work might be ignored by the mainstream. You might find it in long-forgotten theses instead of the Best Paper at CHI.

Teach by example Finally, let the work speak for itself in making the point you're trying to promote. The work on Pygmalion was a fantastic example of creativity in its own right. It amply supported its own ideas with rich visualizations, and deep thinking about what it takes to support the creative process. It made a firm case for programming as a medium for creativity.

Conclusion

Could something like an article on Pygmalion get accepted to the CHI or Interact conferences today? Sadly, probably not. The reviewers would find a million things wrong with it. No user-centered requirements gathering or prototyping prior to implementation. No user testing after implementation. Only works on small examples. Won't scale up. You can imagine the criticism.

Too much of today's HCI is incremental, another-brick-in-the-wall work. Well-designed experiments, diligent implementation and testing, but ultimately, work that won't change things very much. But there should always be a place in HCI for the revolutionary, almost crackpot, work that at least holds the possibility of profoundly transforming the field. This is the story of one such work. Now go do some more.

7

Fundamentals in HCI: Learning the Value of Consistency and User Models

Sara Bly
Sara Bly Consulting, Oregon, U.S.A.

The Xerox Red Book: *Star Functional Specification*, Revision 5.3 for Star-1, 1981

I pretty much came of age along with the coming of age of HCI. I finished my dissertation on a user interface in 1982 and presented it at the first ACM Computer–Human Interaction conference in Gaithersburg that year. Frame buffers were fairly new and computer graphics was booming. My research work extended the notion of multivariate data display from visuals to sounds; my user interface focus was on how to present information rather than how to design user interactions. Several CHI '82 papers that year did focus on user interactions; many were concerned with command names and how users remember them. The individual workstation with bitmapped display and pointer was not yet widespread.

Those were the days when the Xerox 8010 Information System, called the Xerox Star, was fairly new on the market. For someone with an interest in user interfaces, Xerox was the place to be, and I was thrilled in 1984 to get a job working in the Xerox Star Systems Development Division. The successor to the Star, Viewpoint, was underway and was to be based on the same design principles as the initial Xerox Star. One of the first and most important pieces of documentation I received was the Xerox Red Book.

The Xerox Red Book is a functional specification that details the user interface for the first Xerox Star workstation. Formally called the *Star Functional Specification,* revision 5.0 was completed August 1, 1979, and revision 5.3 that I was given was released in May 1981. Consisting of over four hundred and fifty pages in a red loose-leaf notebook, it was known internally as the "Red Book." Although the Red Book is currently only available through the Xerox archives or PARC library, there is an effort to get it released publicly, and several detailed articles have been written about its content (Lipkie et al. 1982; Johnson et al. 1989; Smith et al. 1982a; Smith et al. 1982b).

The book is organized around two main categories, *document creation* and *document management*. The first contains sections on documents, text editing, formatting and layout, frames, graphics, and tables. The second contains sections such as document filing, directories, electronic mail, printing, and removable storage media. Although the Xerox Star represented an integration of many advances in user interfaces, there are three aspects of the Xerox Red Book that have had a particularly important impact on me. The first is that the user interface was specified before the development of the workstation hardware and software; the user interface was considered of primary importance to the design, not as an afterthought or window-dressing. The second is the way in which consistency was used advantageously; it was not a constraint that cut out innovation but a well-considered framework. The third is the desktop metaphor; it offered users a conceptual model that is all too often missing from interfaces today.

User Interface Specification

The Xerox Star workstation was the first commercial personal office workstation intended for office workers more interested in accomplishing their own tasks than in delving into computers. Although planning began in 1978, Star drew on research from a number of places, including the Xerox Palo Alto Research Center (PARC) and the Stanford Research Institute (SRI). It combined a number of innovations at the time—the notion of personal computing, a graphical user interface, a mouse input device, the office metaphor, email, windows, and the local area network. As described in a wonderfully complete retrospective on the Xerox Star development (Johnson et al. 1989, p. 24):

> To foster uniformity of specifications as well as thoughtful and uniform design, Star's designers developed a strict format for specifications. Applications and system features were to be described in terms of the objects that users would manipulate with the software and the actions that the software provided for manipulating objects. This "objects and actions" analysis was supposed to occur at a fairly high level, without regard to how the objects would actually be presented or how the actions would actually be invoked by users. A full specification was then written from the "objects and actions" version. This approach forced designers to think clearly about the purpose of each application or feature and fostered recognition of similar operations across specifications, allowing what might have seemed like new operations to be handled by existing commands.

It's notable that the Xerox Red Book set forth both a formal specification for the Star user interface and a set of concepts for user interface design that are still valuable today.

Consistency

A fundamental principle of the user interface design was the notion of selection and action. The rule was that an object was first selected and then an action was performed on that object. By first selecting the object, a user always had the option to decide not to perform an action. Furthermore, no "accept" command was necessary since invoking the operation was the last step in the sequence.

Consistency was applied across domains: an object could be a word (or sentence or paragraph) in a document, a line or other graphic object in a drawing, a document on the desktop. Selection was done with the two-button mouse, the left button to *select* an object and the right button to *adjust* (shorten or lengthen) the selection if desired. Pressing down on the mouse button was separate from releasing the mouse button so that a user could see what was selected before completing the selection itself.

A set of basic actions appeared on an extension to the traditional typewriter keyboard, a set of "function keys," such as MOVE, COPY, DELETE, and SHOW PROPERTIES. Note that these actions provided a range of capabilities. I might *move* a document from one folder to another or I might *copy* a document to the out-basket to send it as mail or to a printer to get a paper version. Furthermore, the notion of properties applied to both objects and actions. A property sheet allowed a user to specify the parameters of a selection; an option sheet allowed a user to specify the parameters of a command.

The beauty of the Red Book "rules" such as these is that they are basically simple to follow but extremely powerful in use. Once the object-action paradigm and the basic actions are set, both the designers and the users do not have to wonder how to proceed. Of course there are exceptions, particularly given the complexity of functionality in workstations and laptops today. But the notion of consistency in underlying user interface guidelines remains an important principle.

Desktop Metaphor

The Star workstation interface design was based on standard office functions and artifacts. The "desktop" presented office information in a recognizable and easily remembered way. Documents (e.g., reports, presentations, memos) were the most common objects. They could be grouped into folders and folders put into file cabinets. There were in-baskets, printers, and a wastebasket. Although the metaphor clearly would break at times (an UNDO action is generally not possible in the physical office), it provided an extremely straightforward way in which to introduce office workers to the use and functionality of the workstation. More important, I think it offered users a conceptual model that is too often missing today. Knowing how to think about something that is otherwise unfamiliar is a helpful first step in learning.

The Xerox Red Book Today

Can we learn from the Red Book today or is it only important as a historical document? The aspects of the Red Book that most influenced me are only a part of the value of the Red book to the user interface (UI) community. Clearly the details of the user interface functionality make the Xerox Red Book important as an archival document. More significant, however, are the overall principles on which the user interface design was built. Although these are not called out specifically in the Red Book, there was an internal paper that set the basis for the design methodology (Irby et al. 1977). Subsequent papers (Smith et al. 1982a; Johnson et al. 1989) provide complete explanations.

In addition to consistency and a user's model, there are six other principles that specifically directed the design: seeing and pointing versus remembering and typing, what you see is what you get (WYSIWYG), universal commands, simplicity, modeless interaction, and user tailorability. The graphical interface supported seeing rather than remembering, that is, one knew what had been selected or what action was occurring. It was a WYSIWYG interface so that creating a document meant seeing it unfold, as it would ultimately appear on a printed page. The universal commands applied to almost all interactions as described in my view of consistency. Simplicity introduced progressive disclosure in property and option sheets. I learned the value of modeless interactions through the object-action model so the user didn't have to keep track of or know the state of the system. The importance of good graphic design was taught through the careful and systematic use of icons on the bitmap display, the manipulation of which provided one way for users to customize the system to their own use.

For me, the Xerox Red Book not only provided an important guide for developing user interfaces for new Star functionality, it was a textbook on user interface design. Note that in *Principles of Interactive Computer Graphics*, the chapter entitled "User Interface Design" was introduced in the second edition of 1979, not in the first edition of 1973 (Newman and Sproull 1979). *The Psychology of Human–Computer Interaction*, an early UI textbook, did not come along until 1983 (Card,

Moran, and Newell 1983). From the Xerox Red Book, I learned many fundamentals of good UI design. When I moved into research at Xerox PARC in 1986, I took a firm foundation in the best of HCI with me.

Though I grew to embrace the value of ambiguity in design and the inherent inconsistencies in human behavior, I still find the Xerox Red Book provides an important grounding for user interface design. As a document, it articulated the amazing foresight and imagination of the Xerox Star designers and today is still a valuable guide for basics in UI design.[1]

Note

1. The Xerox Star Red Book would not have been a reality without the vision of a number of designers and developers at Xerox Corporation in the 1970s, including David Smith, Charles Irby, Ralph Kimball, Eric Harslem, and Bill Verplank. Thanks to them and thanks to Robyn Mallgren and Terry Roberts for their part in Xerox user interface design and their comments on this essay.

8

It Is Still a *Star*

Susanne Bødker
University of Aarhus, Denmark

D. Smith, C. Irby, R. Kimball, B. Verplank, and E. Harslem, 1982: "Designing the Star User Interface"

People need a way to quickly point to items on the screen. Cursor step keys are too slow; nor are they suitable for graphics. The Star . . . use(s) a pointing device called the mouse.
—Smith et al. (1982a)

Think about it—in 1982, people didn't know what a mouse was! Engelbart invented it, and Star was a first attempt to put it to commercial use. Today it is a given, and often we forget that there are other possible pointing devices. Microsoft decided that we would never need more than one cursor control at a time, which is a problem for attempts to experiment with two-handed interaction. This is an excellent example of how, for good and bad, a very experimental design has become totally taken for granted.

I have recently become interested in the taken-for-grantedness of the desktop metaphor, and in how computer applications today are based on a particular version of the (computer) desktop. When I try to discuss the current desktop design with my first-year students, I point out that we have a trashcan on the desktop, that we can basically only work on one document at the time, and so on. And they just don't get it: "that is just how things are—what is strange about that?"

To see what's strange, lets look back to the origins of the desktop, and one of the original presentations of designs that led up to the desktop as we know it: Smith et al.'s "Designing the Star User Interface" (1982a).

The Star User Interface

Historically, there was a time before the current version of the desktop, and the Star design illustrates this. Star was the first to make available a desktop as we know it, with documents presented directly on the screen—documents that could be "clicked on" (a new term then), "dragged" to folders (new too, in the context of the computer screen), and so on. Star used *concrete*, *visible design* elements *that were recognizable* and could be *copied and modified* directly, rather than the alien command syntax that was common at the time.

The Star designers used eight user interface (UI) principles, including a familiar user's conceptual model (the desktop, with icons and windows); the infamous "what you see is what you get" (WYSIWYG); universal commands; consistency; and simplicity. Until the Star (and the experimental predecessor, the Alto), users would create and edit a representation that looked like a computer program, and then compile the result in order to produce drawings or page layout. With Star, users worked on a direct representation of what would appear on the printed page.

The Smith et al. paper illustrates that some of these UI principles required a lot of work to realize; that choices were made; and that some of them, such as *consistency,* are self-contradictory. The paper nicely discusses how printing by moving the document to the printer icon could work (consistently): should the document disappear, move back to where it came from, or be left in the printer? That is all a matter of what kind of consistency is given the highest priority.

The principles led to a unique design, many elements of which are still with us. However, though we may still throw documents in the wastebasket, we generally don't activate functions by dragging and dropping, the way Star mailed or printed documents by dragging them to the out-box or printer. We work with documents that can open in various applications, which has certain advantages. Yet I don't really remember seeing a discussion anywhere of what was gained and what was lost when that change came about.

Beaudouin-Lafon (2000) and others have pointed out how the number of menu items and the depth of menu hierarchies increase for each new version of (e.g.) Word. Similarly, documents get hidden away in deeper and deeper file/folder hierarchies. We probably have more documents and functionality on our PCs today than anybody ever thought about when Star was designed. It seems that the principle of *simplicity* has long been lost.

When I show a screen dump of the Star user interface to my students, they all seem to notice how crisp and orderly it looks. The desktop is gray, icons and windows stand out. It is organized as an array of one-inch squares. An icon can be placed in any of those. Star centers an icon in its square, hence lining up icons. Windows fill out the space of a U.S. letter page, with icons on either side. Today, depending on your favorite operating system, we are haunted by either overlapping windows and random dumping of icons, tabs, and the like, which aim to provide an overview but do not allow users to see the contents of several windows at the same time. None of these operating systems allows the user to focus on more than one document in more than one application. We have only one locus of cursor control. It seems that the desktop interface has moved toward being the one-document-at-a-time interface, more than was necessary and desirable.

The Star Design Process

The shifts away from Star's design are worth paying attention to, because Star was not designed casually. Actually, Star was designed though an exemplary systematic design process, where state-of-the-art methods were applied. Smith et al. 1982a and Bewley et al. 1983 are reminders that innovation is not a strike of luck, but involves both hard work and a concern for future use.

According to Smith et al., the Star design process developed around the following principles:

1. User interface first.
2. Iterative design and throw-away prototypes.

User interface first meant: design the user interface before the software and hardware. It meant the development of a conceptual understanding of what was to be achieved. Bewley et al. (1983) discuss how the choices made were not straightforward at all. Combinations of empirical tests and keystroke level analyses were applied in iteration with redesigns of the interface. Selection, using one, two, or three mouse-buttons, was compared in seven different selection schemes. Seventeen distinct sets of icons were developed for Star, and tested for recognizability and the time required to pick them. In hindsight, it is comforting that so much work was put into developing the fundamental interface mechanics that we still live with. At the same time, the community at large often seems to forget that icon design is hard work that includes concerns for recognizability by users, comparability across icons, and so on, and not just common sense.

Iterative design and throw-away prototypes: The Alto was a valuable prototype for Star, and it had been developed and used for about eight years when the Star process started. At PARC "dozens of experimental programs were written for the Alto" (Smith et al. 1982a). Until that time it was most common among software design practitioners and researchers to use the "waterfall" model—a strictly sequential, non-overlapping series of stages—as their ideal design process (Raccoon 1997).

However, statements like the above were fueling the debate about iterative design in the (emerging) software engineering community.

By setting up PARC and letting researchers work for eight years or more on something whose commercial value was not immediately recognizable, Xerox took a lot of risk. Star was a first attempt to make PARC results commercial, and it failed as commercial success, for Xerox at least (whereas Apple and Microsoft managed to harvest from the effort later on). My point here, however, is more general: Making commercial successes out of groundbreaking research is done neither overnight nor through direct pipelining of research into products.

To return to my own research, the following anecdote serves to understand why throw-away prototyping of human–computer interaction became an essential element of participatory design. In 1983, I worked on the UTOPIA project (Bødker et al. 1987), where we collaborated with workers from the graphical industry on developing page layout technology that would utilize and develop their skills rather than make them redundant, which was the trend in graphics production then. Indeed we knew that WYSIWYG text processing was at their doorstep. Yet it was difficult to get access to, so as to be able to show it to the typographers. Accordingly, we *described* to one of our collaborators what it would mean to change type fonts directly by selecting, choosing, and so on. His experience was with computerized typesetting within a LaTex-like system. He listened to our explanations of how you would directly see the change of font size on the screen. And then he commented: "But you forgot to tell me what the code structure is like." In other words, he could not fully understand the most essential aspect of WYSIWYG typography—that there were no codes—without seeing it and trying it out.

As a consequence of this sort of experience we started working with cheap mockups; we invested in our first workstation, and we decided to understand better why hands-on experience was necessary for user involvement in design (Bødker et al. 1987). Although the UTOPIA project had severe problems achieving commercial success through its innovative product design, the design methods have lived on with us and are still being developed.

Looking Backward, Looking Forward

Generally, I believe that we need to keep reminding ourselves of how, and why, our everyday technology came into being. In that sense HCI has reached a stage at which it is not only a science pointing ahead. It needs to be aware of its history too, in order to be better at pointing to the future.

Indeed, whether *the conceptual model* of Star (the desktop) is familiar to users is hardly an issue today, because the computer desktop has come to have its own life. Hardly anybody is a total novice. However, we continue to introduce new conceptual models that may or may not be familiar to users, and indeed, as designers we need to understand what can and cannot be taken for granted. Looking back on historical papers and designs is one way of guarding against taking the current designs of computer technology for granted.

9

The Disappearing Computer

Norbert A. Streitz
Fraunhofer IPSI, Darmstadt, Germany

M. Weiser, 1991: "The Computer for the 21st Century"

"The most profound technologies are those that disappear. They weave themselves into the fabric of everyday life until they are indistinguishable from it." This opening statement in Mark Weiser's paper "The Computer for the 21st Century" in the September 1991 issue of *Scientific American* (pp. 66–75)[1] has been a source of inspiration for me. When it was published fifteen years ago, it was "for the Twenty-First Century"—now we are "living in" it! Reading it back then, I found Weiser's ideas startling and familiar at the same time. Startling, because he proposed a challenging vision of how the role of computers would change when made available in a ubiquitous fashion; familiar, because the underlying philosophy of "making the computer disappear" was in line with ideas (e.g., minimizing the "interaction problem") I was contemplating around that time when reflecting on interactive problem solving, human–computer interaction, and cognitive ergonomics (Streitz 1986).

The introductory section of the article is followed by a description of examples of ubiquitous computers categorized by Weiser as tabs, pads, and boards. I still remember vividly when I was a visiting scholar at Xerox PARC in 1990 and witnessed the first "live board," a wooden cabinet with a large interactive display, later known as the LiveBoard and marketed by the spin-off company LiveWorks. It was rolled into a special room where only people with confidentiality clearance had access, and there we had the chance to try it out. Although the wooden frame was intended to make it look different from a traditional computer, it was still a big box: it didn't really "disappear"; rather, it attracted attention. But it did provide new ways of interacting with information. This was owing especially to the pen-based mode of interaction, modeled after the "traditional" interaction with a felt pen on a whiteboard. This, in combination with the large display area, made the

LiveBoard different from traditional desktop computers even though it had no more resolution than a workstation display at that time.

From LiveBoard and Tivoli to DOLPHIN

Having the opportunity to experience firsthand one of the major components of the ubiquitous computing approach at its birthplace, I was fascinated and set out to continue and extend this line of research. After my return to Germany at IPSI in Darmstadt, I started negotiations with PARC about getting LiveBoards. It was quite a process to get the handmade LiveBoards out of Xerox, but I was successful. Finally, two boards (color units) with serial numbers 007 and 008 were shipped and arrived in Darmstadt in January 1993—the first examples that existed outside of Xerox.

Building on our previous work on cooperative hypermedia systems in, for example, the SEPIA system (Streitz et al. 1992), we developed the DOLPHIN system (Streitz et al. 1994) for supporting group work in an electronic meeting room. The setup involved a LiveBoard and four workstation-like computers that were physically integrated into a meeting room table. Our DOLPHIN software used the pen-based interaction hardware of the LiveBoard and combined it with our multiuser cooperative hypermedia system. DOLPHIN supported scribbles, gestures, and annotations, as did the Tivoli software developed in parallel at PARC. By combining it with a CSCW (computer-supported cooperative work) and hypermedia system, we were able to support group work such as brainstorming and idea generation, creating and processing informal structures as well as formal argumentation structures, and shared document processing across all devices in the meeting room.

From Human–*Computer* Interaction to Human–*Information* Interaction and Human–*Human*–Interaction and Cooperation

After some time, working with the big and somehow clumsy LiveBoard boxes no longer satisfied us. Although enabling people to stand and interact with a large vertical display was an important step in the right direction, it was still a large box. Going back to Weiser's original vision of "disappearing" technology, we thought of making the technology disappear even more.

It became obvious to us that the phrase "human–*computer* interaction" could lead us in the wrong direction. Normal users are actually not very interested in interacting with *computers*. They are interested in interacting with *information* and with *people* in order to communicate and collaborate with them. Thus, the field we want to explore should be called "human–*information* interaction" and "human–*human*–interaction and cooperation," terminology that implies that the computer should disappear from the scene.

Two Types of Disappearance

The goal of making the computer disappear described in Weiser's opening statement can be achieved in different ways. Disappearance can take different forms (Streitz 2001):

Physical disappearance refers to the miniaturization of devices and their integration in other everyday artifacts as, for example, in clothes, so that they become invisible.

Mental disappearance refers to the situation in which the artifacts, though they may still be large, are not seen as computers but rather as ordinary objects that are now interactive, such as "interactive" walls or "interactive" tables. That is, the technology disappears from our perception and moves mentally into the background.

This raises some core questions: How can we design human–information interaction and support human–human communication and cooperation by exploiting the affordances of existing artifacts in our environment? And, in doing so, how can we exploit the potential of computer-based support to augment these activities?

From LiveBoard to DynaWall and Roomware

These considerations resulted in another extension of the seminal work at PARC: increasing the display size, moving beyond "boards" and toward the notion of "walls." At the same time, we wanted to integrate other everyday artifacts like tables and chairs into the overall UbiComp setting. This resulted in our Roomware® components DynaWall, InteracTable, CommChairs, and ConnecTables (Streitz, Geißler, and Holmer, 1998), developed in several generations (Streitz et al. 2001). They were part of the i-LAND environment, an interactive landscape for creativity and cooperation (Streitz et al. 1999). For the realization of the DynaWall, a 4.5 × 1.10 meter interactive wall, we departed from the original LiveBoards and integrated three dismantled SmartBoards into the architectural environment, replacing a major part of a wall. Instead of having a big box in front of a wall, we had a large *interactive wall* very smoothly integrated with the rest of the architecture—approaching what we call "mental disappearance." While the Roomware components were one achievement, further appropriate software was needed for dealing with the constraints and exploiting the affordances of such a large interactive area. This motivated our gesture-based approach of interaction, which was modeless as a result of an incremental gesture recognition realized via the BEACH software (Prante, Streitz, and Tandler 2004). It allows users to throw, shuffle, and rotate digital information objects (e.g., on the DynaWall and the InteracTable) as one would do with real objects in the real world. At the same time, it was a cooperative, truly synchronous multiuser, multiple-devices system connecting all Roomware components, not just in one room but between remote locations as well.

From Sal's Home and Office to Cooperative Buildings and Smart Environments

It is interesting to revisit the scenario at the end of Weiser's article describing parts of a day in the home, on the road, and in the office of Sal, the main actor in the scenario on the role of computers for the twenty-first century. One is shown a world where comfort is provided; everything is calm and working smoothly. Annoying occurrences like traffic jams are remedied by warnings that enable a driver to take the next exit and stop for a cup of coffee. In the office, the existence of fresh coffee is indicated by a telltale at the door. Although not explicitly called "smart environment" or "ambient intelligence," this is the view conveyed here. Combining sets of sensor data with inference engines and other artificial intelligence methods should allow adaptation to the many possible situations. Without entering into the philosophical discussion of when it is justified to call an artifact "smart" or what we consider "smart" or "intelligent" behavior in general, we propose the following distinction (Streitz et al. 2005).

System-Oriented, Importunate Smartness

An environment is "smart" if it can carry out certain self-directed (re)actions based on continuously collected information about its constituents, and surroundings, including the humans staying within its reach. In this version of "smartness," a space would be active and in control of the situation, making decisions on what to do next and executing actions without a human in the loop. Some of these actions could turn out to be importunate.

People-Oriented, Empowering Smartness

This can be contrasted with a perspective where the empowering function is in the foreground, summarized as *smart spaces make people smarter*. This is achieved by keeping *the human in the loop*, thus empowering people to make informed decisions and take actions as responsible people in control.

Of course, these two points of view will not often exist in their pure distinct forms. The challenge is to find the right balance for combining both approaches. The overall design should be guided by having the human in the loop and in control as much as possible and feasible.

Conclusions

Fifteen years later, the influence of Mark Weiser on the field of ubiquitous computing is at its peak. For many years now, his 1991 article has been the standard reference when people refer to the origins of ubiquitous computing.

It took some time before the major conferences in this field got off the ground. Two events advanced these views in a systematic fashion: the symposium entitled "Handheld and Ubiquitous Computing" (HUC'99) initiated by Hans Gellersen and held in Karlsruhe in September 1999 (Gellersen 1999), which evolved into the Ubiquitous Computing conference series.

One year before, I initiated the First International Workshop on Cooperative Buildings (Cobuild'98) (Streitz, Konomi, and Burkhardt 1998) held at IPSI in Darmstadt, followed by the Cobuild'99 event held at Carnegie-Mellon University in Pittsburgh. It was a pleasure for me to invite Mark Weiser to be the opening keynote speaker for CoBuild'98. It was one of his last public international appearances before he passed away in April 1999, much too early and much too young.

Unfortunately, Weiser could not witness the lasting impact his work had. These two events marked somehow the beginning of the "revival" of ubiquitous computing. In 1999, the "disappearing computer" idea became also a theme for the European Commission. As part of the Information Society Technology (IST) program, the proactive research initiative "The Disappearing Computer (DC)" (www.disappearing-computer.net) was conceived by the Future and Emerging Technology (FET) unit. Being involved in the planning activities of the initiator Jakub Wejchert, it was great to see how quickly it proceeded. Seventeen projects were selected and started in 2001, lasting for around three years until 2004. They were complemented by the "DC-Net" activities of the DC Steering Group (which I had the honor to chair), facilitating exchange and cooperation between projects. A particular venue for communicating the work in the Disappearing Computer initiative was the special issue "The Disappearing Computer "of *Communications of the ACM* published last year (Streitz and Nixon 2005) where we related the work in Europe and the United

States and the edited volume *The Disappearing Computer* (Streitz, Kameas, and Mavrommati 2007) covering the highlights of the DC initiative. I am sure Mark Weiser would have loved to observe how his ideas were taken up by the different research communities in Europe, the United States, and Asia, and I am sure he would have wanted to get involved.

Note

1. Weiser's article is often referenced with wrong page numbers (pp. 94–104), probably because similar page numbers (pp. 94–10) are quoted on the UbiComp webpages (http://www.ubiq.com/hypertext/weiser/UbiHome.html), interestingly enough with "10" and not "104." Having the original issue at hand, I can confirm the correct page numbers are pp. 66–75.

10

It Really Is All About Location!

Anind K. Dey
Carnegie Mellon University, Pittsburgh, Pennsylvania, U.S.A.

R. Want, A. Hopper, V. Falcao, and J. Gibbons, 1992: "The Active Badge Location System"

It is often said that the cardinal rule of real estate is that everything depends on "location, location, location." In computing, we are also seeing a trend toward interactions where location is paramount. We can use search engines that leverage our location information (e.g., Google Maps, MSN Search Local); use GPS (global positioning system) devices for hiking, boating, and even treasure hunting (Sherman 2004); use tour guides to enhance our museum experiences (Abowd et al. 1997); and locate friends, family (Charny 2002), and packages (e.g., UPS, FedEx). Today, these applications are called *location-based services*, or LBSs. It is estimated that by 2015, the revenue from LBS will be €135 billion (Swann, Chartre, and Ludwig 2003). The number of mobile phones in use with the ability to locate themselves is currently in the millions, and this number is expected to grow to 1.5 billion by 2015. I personally use LBS for providing my location to family members (as I'm tracked by my GPS-enabled cell phone), finding gas stations in unfamiliar locations (thanks to an in-car navigation system), and locating my car when I thought it was stolen (using the car's LoJack vehicle recovery system).

Fifteen years ago, this was all unimaginable. We had no commercial positioning systems available for either indoor or outdoor use. This is what makes the work of Roy Want, Andy Hopper, Veronica Falcao, and Jon Gibbons all the more exciting. In 1992, they published a paper entitled "The Active Badge Location System" on an indoor positioning system developed at Olivetti Research (Want et al. 1992). It was the first location-based system and one of the first in a series of efforts to fulfill the ubiquitous computing vision proposed by Mark Weiser (Weiser 1991) being undertaken at Xerox PARC, Olivetti Research (later, Olivetti and Oracle Research and then AT&T Research), and EuroPARC. Ubiquitous computing or ubicomp was first introduced in 1988 by Weiser, as a third wave of computing, beyond mainframes and personal computers. In this third wave, computing devices would be so numerous and so embedded in our everyday lives, they would seem invisible to us. These seminal writings have had great impact on my research career, helping to establish a research path that I have followed for over ten years.

Less than two years after this vision was first articulated, Want et al. developed and deployed an indoor location system, in February 1990. At that time, existing positioning systems included swipe badges and pagers. Swipe badge systems, still commonly used today, allow users to swipe their badges through readers to gain access to or leave a defined zone. Users can be located and granted access to resources on a per-zone basis. With pagers, someone trying to locate the user could page him or her, causing a signal to be sent to the user's pager creating an audible beep and delivering the callback number of the caller. If the user returned the call, the caller could then ascertain the user's location by directly asking him or her.

Instead the Active Badge location system presents a location system that really allowed users to be located without having to do anything other than wear the Active Badge itself. Each Active Badge sent out a short unique infrared signal every fifteen seconds. This signal was picked up by any sensors that were within six meters of the badge and had a direct line-of-sight to the badge. Sensors were cheap enough that reasonable coverage of a space was not prohibitive. Sensors were placed high on walls, on ceiling tiles, and at entrance and exit points. Sensors detected and reported unique badge identities to the workstation they were connected to, and this information could be shared with other Active Badge networks and users via an Ethernet network.

While the paper focused on the novel technology developed, it also presented an application that was built on top of the Active Badge location system. To aid the receptionist at Olivetti Research, an interface was provided to help them route phone calls to extensions closest to the person being called. The interface displayed a table consisting of each user's name, the closest telephone extension, the physical location of the extension, and the probability of finding the user in that location based on the length of time since the user's badge was last sighted by the Active Badge system.

After a two-week trial period in which all thirty-two employees of Olivetti Research were requested to use the location system, employees continued to use the system. The receptionist's job was made easier and there was a substantial drop in the number of phone calls not reaching the appropriate destination. Users found the phone call forwarding service quite useful and liked that it allowed them to move throughout the lab even while they were expecting a phone call.

An extension made to the receptionist's system distributed badge location information throughout the lab, allowing all employees to use it. Some used the same application as the receptionist, while others used a command-line interface. This latter interface allowed employees to locate a particular badge, find out which other users were with a particular user, determine which users were in a particular location, receive an audio notification when a particular badge was seen next, and view a one-hour location history for a particular user. Over time, additional interfaces were designed for the location system. One interface contained a floor plan of the laboratory overlaid with badge locations and badge identities. A second interface, and the most useful one, textually presented the locations of all users (employees and visitors) and equipment. When a user clicked on a person or a tagged piece of equipment, a list of other people and equipment in that same location was presented along with a list of communication methods for talking with those people. Employees commonly used the system to allow groups of users to find each other easily to have impromptu meetings, and to locate visitors in the lab for security reasons. Over time, numerous applications were built on top of the Active Badge location system, including authentication for doors and resources, delivering printouts to the printer closest to the person who created the print job, and "teleporting" a desktop environment from a computer the user had been using to the one he or she was currently standing in front of.

I first read this paper in 1996, when I was being introduced to ubiquitous computing. Since then, I have read and reread this paper countless times, and I have always assigned it to my students in classes on ubiquitous or context-aware computing. Although I was (and continue to be) inspired by the initial Weiser articles on ubiquitous computing (Weiser 1991, 1993), this paper had a huge impact on me. Weiser laid out the vision, and Want et al. (1992) worked on fulfilling a piece of it in this article. It was the first instantiation of ubiquitous computing. It was the first example I had read of computers that could react to the context of the user. It arguably spawned the field of context-aware computing. This work, among others at the time, had such impact on me that I began to conduct research in context-aware computing, completed my doctoral research on it, and have continued to do research on it, more than ten years later. If citations are a reasonable indication of impact, then it is clear that this paper influenced a lot of people in the same way it did me.

Over time, I have come to gain a new appreciation for this work along two different dimensions: the use of novel hardware to support exploratory research and the depth of the issues addressed in the paper. First, the Active Badge system demonstrated that by developing novel hardware, researchers could effectively time travel into the future and explore novel forms of interaction with their environment. Whereas today, researchers and companies are still working on developing reliable and accurate indoor positioning systems, the Active Badge system allowed researchers at Olivetti Research to live with and experience future technology. This work showed that you did not have to be limited by the technology you have today to experiment with the ideas of tomorrow. It also illustrated the challenges involved in building such a system. After struggling to build a number of similar systems and facing many similar challenges, I chose instead to build the Context Toolkit, an infrastructure that makes it easier to build location-aware and context-aware systems (Dey, Salber, and Abowd 2001).

Second, particularly after having worked on ubiquitous computing systems for ten years, I have gained a real appreciation for both the depth and range of issues discussed in this paper. A tremendous amount of effort went into the design of the Active Badge system to ensure that it was lightweight and small, used minimal power and had energy conservation modes, and was scalable to encompass multiple badge networks. None of these issues was necessary to demonstrate the feasibility of such a system, but all were certainly necessary to conduct a realistic deployment of such a system. Far too often in ubiquitous computing, partially working prototypes are presented that could never be tested in the field to get a sense of the real impact of these systems. More research should follow the example of the Active Badge system, which had, at the time of the paper's publication, over one hundred badges and two hundred sensors spread over a group of five badge networks in Cambridge. Additionally, the authors said that the key contribution was not in demonstrating that they could build a location system but in investigating the question of whether people even want to be part of a location system. This is obviously a question that resonates quite strongly today, when concerns about online privacy are ubiquitous. In this paper, the authors address the issue of privacy head on. They discuss how users could remove the badge to avoid being tracked, how the interface would display a probability of finding the user in a given place and how that probability would decay over time, and how support for end-user control of who has access to a user's location data and logging such access could be helpful. These are issues and ideas that remain important for ubiquitous computing systems today. Although I did not realize it at the time, these issues of usability and evaluation would stick with me over the years, and I have recently begun to focus on supporting basic features of usability in context-aware systems: feedback, control, privacy, and information overload.

Sixteen years after the Active Badge system was built, location-based services are finally becoming a reality outside of the research world. The use of GPS and network services are widespread and available for most of our mobile devices. Time will tell whether the technology of location-based services will become the billion-dollar industry many have predicted. If it does, it will be in part due to the excitement caused and the impact created by the Active Badge system.

III

Large Groups, Loosely Joined

In this section the focus shifts to large groups of people and relations among them. Computers are not just for computation, of course; they serve as powerful communication tools as well. By virtue of computers' ability to mediate communications among people who would not otherwise know one another, computer-mediated communication lays the ground for vast webs of influence. Some of this influence is direct, as when people form virtual groups and talk with one another, and some is indirect, more subtle, as when ideas propagate through a culture or organization.

Our first essay is Sara Kiesler on *The Network Nation*. She relates how her reading of Hiltz and Turoff led to her first experiment on computer-mediated communication, and along the way we meet Mina, an overly informal lab assistant, and have a brief encounter with Allen Newell. Next Danyel Fisher describes how *Cinderella* led him to an interest in how and why stories traveled, and how that, in turn, led to Roger's *The Diffusion of Innovations*. Barry Brown's essay on Zuboff's ethnography, *In the Age of the Smart Machine*, recounts her analysis of the impact of computers and automation on the workplace, and reflects on the value of understanding the complex situations in which technologies are used. Next, in an essay on Jane Jacobs's *The Death and Life of Great American Cities*, Tom Erickson discusses Jacobs's observations of the relationships among strangers, and their implications for the design of online systems. Amy Bruckman recounts Seymour Papert's writings on samba schools as a metaphor and model for education, and reflects on the role of community and culture in learning. The section concludes with Beki Grinter's essay on David Parnas's paper on program architecture, and how it led her to ask why, in spite of modularization, dependencies continue to exist between code modules. Her answer to this seemingly straightforward question involves communication within and across organizations, coordination work and the division of labor.

11

Network Nation: Human Communication via Computer

Sara Kiesler
Carnegie Mellon University, Pittsburgh, Pennsylvania, U.S.A.

S. R. Hiltz and M. Turoff, 1978: *The Network Nation: Human Communication via Computer*

In 1978, some of my current graduate students were born, and, like more than 99 percent of the world's population, I had never used a computer to communicate with another person. That year, Murray Turoff, a computer scientist at the New Jersey Institute of Technology, and Starr Roxanne Hiltz, a sociologist then at Upsala College, published a visionary book on communicating through computers. A few years later, their book, *Network Nation: Human Communication via Computer*, would help set my research and life off in a new direction. My dog-eared copy of the book has disappeared from my office, and I must borrow Jane Siegel's copy. Her book is stuffed with little paper notes that say things like "Xerox pg. 15, 27–28, 30." Jane and I have published several articles together; these faded notes are some of the evidence of the influence of this book on my own work.

Network Nation is a combination of research report and insightful policy analysis. For its time—pre–personal computer, pre-AOL, pre-Web—it was prescient. Teresa Carpenter said in her *Village Voice* review in 1993 that the book laid out "a future when home computers would be as common as the telephone, when they would link person to person, shrinking . . . 'time and distance barriers among people, and between people and information, to near zero.' In its simplest form, the Network Nation is a place where thoughts are exchanged easily and democratically and intellect affords one more personal power than a pleasing appearance does. Minorities and women compete on equal terms with white males, and the elderly and handicapped are released from the confines of their infirmities to skim the electronic terrain as swiftly as anyone else."

The book was not mere lofty Net dreams. In 1971, its computer scientist author, Murray Turoff, designed and implemented the first virtual team—a computer conferencing system, called EMISARI, for Delphi decision making for the Office of Emergency Preparedness. He later designed EIES, a conferencing system to support scientific discussion. EIES was an infrastructure for a virtual online community, consisting of what we now call chat (synchronous communication), discussion boards or forums (asynchronous messaging), and customized news. In 1975, Starr Roxanne Hiltz, a sociologist, began reporting on the effects and social impact of the computer conferencing systems the team was testing. Together, through careful and voluminous documentation of their field tests and experiments, the interdisciplinary team of Hiltz and Turoff defined key problem areas in computer-mediated communication and Internet research that remain today. They were perhaps the first to argue that "to understand computer-mediated communications at all, you must see them as a social process" (p. 27). They grappled with questions of how to create online community, and they noted the paradox that "although the medium seems inherently impersonal, there have been many cases observed or reported by the participants of the most intimate of exchanges taking place between persons who have never met face-to-face and probably never will" (p. 28). They also raised enduring questions about how to manage distributed work teams, what to do about free riders in online groups, addiction or dependence, and information overload (see, e.g., Thompson and Coovert 2006).

How did a social psychologist like me, whose dissertation topic was "gratitude," end up reading a techie book like *Network Nation*? I owe something to President Reagan, whose freeze on social science NSF projects led to my doing some catch-up reading, including Murray Turoff's (1972) paper on Delphi anonymous online decision making. The federal government had supported Murray's research to make decisions more accurate by removing social pressures on the group through computer conferencing. Hiltz and Turoff then published new work marking a change in their thinking. Jane Siegel found the *Network Nation* book and we read it avidly. It wasn't just technology; it was about people who seemed to be forming meaningful groups using computers. Here is a discussion in *Network Nation* that moved us to run our first experiment:

> The emphasis in designing [computer conferencing systems] has been to maximize the amount of task-relevant information that can be shared among the members of a group, while still keeping the medium as "comfortable" as possible. Those who are most enthusiastic about the potential advantages of this form of communication tend to focus on this characteristic, as reported, for instance by Johansen, Vallee and Collins (1977, p. 3).
>
> Computer-based teleconferencing is a highly cognitive medium that, in addition to providing technological advantages, promotes rationality by providing essential discipline and by filtering out affective components of communications. That is, computer-based teleconferencing

acts as a filter, filtering out irrelevant and irrational interpersonal "noise" and enhances the communication of highly-informed "pure reason"—a quest of philosophers since ancient times. (Hiltz and Turoff 1993, p. 28)

At that point Hiltz and Turoff questioned whether computer conferences were impersonal, and whether they would really promote "pure reason." In their conferences, they had found that people felt "free to be extremely frank and open with one another, whether discussing a topic such as a scientific or business problem, or in exchanging information about themselves and their feelings" (p. 28).

They offered examples: "At least one case of a dyadic relationship in which two persons are fairly friendly and cooperative in face-to-face meetings, but in which disagreements and hostility soon surface when they communicate by computerized conferencing"; and "A young woman who exhibited signs of schizophrenia or other severe personality disturbance, communicating in grunts, nods, and monosyllables in a face-to-face condition; within ten minutes of being introduced to CC, she was sending a constant stream of long messages, all signed 'anonymous'" (p. 102). Hiltz and Turoff wrote, "These observations and speculations are offered to suggest our extreme ignorance in this area. We know there are personality factors. At present we have only the skimpiest of insights into what these factors are."

I was trained in the Kurt Lewin tradition, which assumes social forces in all groups. Might there be such a thing as an impersonal group? My background as an experimental social psychologist made running a controlled study an obvious option. Jane Siegel and I decided to compare three-person decision making groups that would work face-to-face and remotely with computer-mediated chat. We hired Mina, an undergraduate, to run a pilot study. Mina quickly proved a disaster, or so we thought. Her face-to-face sessions were fine but her computer chat sessions were a mess. One of her first groups was not able to reach consensus until 2:00 in the morning. Subjects were getting upset with each other, refusing to reach consensus. We went back to training, and asked Mina to follow a strict protocol and to wear more formal clothes so subjects would "take the experiment seriously." We continued to see problems in reaching consensus when participants used chat.[1] Lee Sproull suggested I talk with Allen Newell. He told me, smiling, "Oh, that's just flaming." Jane decided to run the experiments herself, and we began to document carefully the processes that ensued when people had to reach consensus using the computer to communicate. With that began a new program of research, soon leading to a new NSF grant, field studies with Lee Sproull, a new focus on email, and many new and wonderful colleagues.

Roxanne Hiltz had run pilot studies prompting new ways to think about computer-mediated communication. In *Network Nation*, she and Murray described a pilot study of group problem solving in which Roxanne calculated an index of inequality of participation in these groups, reasoning that computer conferencing might reduce the impact of stigmatizing physical attributes (p. 111). Thus we measured inequality of participation in our studies, and later explicitly tested the impact of social status in face-to-face and computer-mediated groups (Kiesler, Siegel, and McGuire 1984; Dubrovsky, Kiesler, and Sethna 1991).

To give a further sense of the prescience of Hiltz and Turoff's observations and ideas and the indirect and direct influence they had on me and others, let's take a look three other examples.

Example 1: Anonymity In Murray Turoff's conferencing systems, participants could choose a pen name, use their real name, or decide to be anonymous. Hiltz and Turoff wrote, "The motivation of the sender of an anonymous message or conference comment is self-protection. However, anonymity can have some very important social consequences for the groups. As [one of our conferences] points out . . . the use of anonymity can promote interaction, objectivity, and problem solving . . . e.g., one would not have to worry about unpopular ideas, etc." (p. 95).

These observations led us to ask in our 1982 grant proposal whether "anonymity caused by difficulty in [identifying] speakers, poor resolution of physical detail, and use of 'alias' options, might prove significant in affective responses," and we raised the matter again in our *American Psychologist* paper (Kiesler, Siegler, and McGuire 1984). Anonymity later became a primary factor in SIDE theory (Postmes et al. 2005).

Example 2: Flaming and candor Hiltz and Turoff quoted from their logs to demonstrate people's openness in computerized conferences. Here is one from 1975:

NUMBER 9269 BY CHARLES AT 1619 ON 11/02/75

well I for one am particularly concerned . . . Come on Iris if you want another conference. Open it up. Don't fuck around with supposedly private ones . . . We hae enough problems without adding to them. Remember I did not sign that promise not to get pissed off at you. (1978, p. 127)

These examples (and Allen Newell's remarks) helped us understand that our observations were perhaps not a fluke, and we made a big point of the "openness" argument in our book *Connections* (Sproull and Kiesler 1991). Lee and I discussed how people could at once express feelings they might not express in face-to-face discussion, and also take on different personas or personalities in different online groups. The reasons for this behavior have since fascinated many researchers, and the issue persists today, not just at the margins of HCI but in the core disciplines (see, e.g., Kruger et al. 2005).

Example 3: Community and citizen participation Hiltz and Turoff foresaw that computer communication would enable people to self-organize without the aid of officials or formal organization:

> Often citizens feel at a disadvantage when participating in the political process because they do not have access to the same knowledge and expertise that government officials and industrial or business groups have. . . . Computerized conferencing would make it possible for citizen groups in different areas to pool the technical and professional talent available to them. This pooling would at least provide the opportunity for citizen groups to get better handles on facts available and the opportunity to take well-informed positions on complex topics. This would lessen the likelihood that well-meaning citizen groups would take unreasonable positions because of a lack of knowledge. (1978, pp. 200–201)

They foresaw the use of computers by citizens to organize during disasters and even to vote.

We agreed with these possibilities for online community in *Connections*. Today, with technical reality catching up to Hiltz and Turoff's vision, the ideas permeate HCI and CSCW (see, e.g., Preece 2000; Postmes and Brunsting 2002).

In 1994, the Electronic Frontier Foundation presented its annual pioneer awards to Murray Turoff and Starr Roxanne Hiltz. I could not say it better:

> Murray Turoff and Starr Roxanne Hiltz are key innovators and the premier theorists of computer-mediated communications. Turoff and Hiltz . . . helped define the electronic frontier: The Network Nation. The term we currently use for online discussions, "computer conferencing," was popularized by Turoff almost a quarter-century ago. The term was no metaphor—it was a literal description of what they had built in the EIES ("Eyes") system—that is, a system that allowed people to "confer" via the computer. Hiltz's notion that computer conferencing could form the basis of communities is a concept that increasingly dominates popular discussion of online conferencing systems. Hiltz and Turoff forecast most of the common uses and conventions of online conferencing systems that we see today. (Electronic Frontier Foundation 1994)

Note

1. A meta-analysis of thirty-six experiments showed that computer-mediated groups had a harder time reaching consensus than face-to-face groups (Baltes et al. 2002).

12

On the *Diffusion of Innovations* in HCI

Danyel Fisher
Microsoft Research, Redmond, Washington, U.S.A.

E. Rogers, 1995: *Diffusion of Innovations*

In 1997, I took a folklore course from Alan Dundes, at UC Berkeley. I was excited by the field, and by the work being done: the field of folklore was attempting, piece by piece, to understand how stories were passed on from person to person. I read Dundes's (1988) *Cinderella* collection, fascinated, as it described how the story had moved across the world and changed along the way.

And yet something was missing. Folklore saw itself as a liberal art, not a science. Folklorists had collected hundreds of specimens of stories, recording where they had been collected; researchers had thoroughly indexed how themes from a story told in one place were related to parts of a different story in a different place. Folklore theorists tried to interpret stories.

What seemed to me to be missing was the next step, of figuring out *how* stories traveled, and *why*. Could we predict whether a given European story would show up in China? Could we read a folktale and connect it to a particular culture, or a particular set of ideas? Which people would tell, or retell, or rewrite these stories?

I was frustrated. I had done some research on stories being passed from person to person, updating some classic "faxlore" work to the age of email and Usenet. Much to my surprise, I had found that even online, stories were being retyped and changed: a simple formulaic joke would exist in several different but similar phrasings. Copy-and-paste might have been possible, and many joke recipients had clearly just forwarded the original, but not all had. Neither the fallibilities of memory and cultural adjustment (as folklore would put it) nor the degrading quality of repeatedly faxed images (as faxlore would have it) could account for these changes to a digital, perfectly reproducible medium.

Much of my frustration also came from interdisciplinary differences. I was working on a computer science graduate degree; I built things—image recognition algorithms, compilers, machine learning tools. I wanted the field to provide me with the instruments to build a folktale—or, failing that, to measure it.

Not long after that class, I stumbled upon Everett Rogers's *Diffusion of Innovations* (1995). Rogers takes those pieces that I had found scattered in the folklore field, and organizes them. He summarizes, in one volume, a century's research on the ways that ideas and innovations were presented, adopted, and spread. By the time I was finished, a sleepless night later, the book was a colorful forest of sticky notes and I was inspired.

I would suggest that this volume should be an important part of the HCI bookshelf.

Diffusion Research

Rogers lays out a framework that is simple, thorough, and easily reusable: the book looks at the innovation itself, the way the innovation is communicated, the potential adopters who pick up the innovation over time, and the social system in which they are all embedded.

Research into the diffusion of innovations, as told by Rogers, has its origins in agricultural research. Unlike folklore, where stories are easy to tell and retell, convincing a farmer to innovate in agriculture had been a matter of some difficulty. Scientists had developed tools to improve crop yields, but needed to find ways to convince farmers to use them. Under what circumstances would a farmer adopt a new type of seed corn, plowing method, or tractor? Diffusion research has since broadened to other areas; the book draws from work in public health fields, product development and marketing, and education.

After presenting the area's history, Rogers is direct about the ethical and social challenges faced by diffusion research: researchers may have a strong pro-innovation bias, and may be inclined to blame non-adoption on recalcitrant individuals. Here he echoes the HCI dictum: do not blame the user for your poor design!

Subsequent chapters in the book examine the factors that drive adoption: first at the process of generating innovations, then of adopting an innovation. Next, the book examines the innovativeness of adopters, and follows this by a review of the networks between adopters. Later chapters examine the people who drive the innovations and the ways that innovations diffuse within organizations. The book concludes with a discussion of the second-order effects of diffusion, and wrestles with what happens when different groups have varying access to innovations.

Social Networks and Diffusion

The part of the book that compelled me first was the work on social networks. Rogers uses networks to model exposure and awareness in order to predict adoption in different circumstances. His former student Tom Valente has extended this work, detailing models for diffusion across networks (Valente 1995). Increasingly, social network analysis is growing as an analytical and design approach in computer-supported collaborative work (CSCW); this book is a way to understand the value of those analyses. There are, from the diffusion of innovations perspective, real differences between the well- and the poorly connected: not only will they be exposed to different information, but they may make different decisions about what to adopt. Connectedness is related to a proclivity to adopt, but not simply: a person with many laggard friends is less likely to adopt than a person who is close to just a few early adopters.

Communication and Diffusion

Early on, the book discusses different media for communication, but it tends to discuss communication as either mass-media broadcast or face-to-face. Indeed, one theory discussed suggests that mass media are efficient for communicating information about innovations, while personal contact is superior for convincing people to adopt. With the rise of the Internet, we have broader access to different media: blogs, mailing lists, and newsgroups can present information to a much smaller—or more carefully selected—group of people than a mass-media magazine can, providing some of the authority of the opinion leader while achieving some of the broadness of the mass media.

Web page links, email messages, and peer-to-peer file sharing are all contemporary networks that allow us to trace how ideas spread and are communicated online in ways that were once not possible. Today, such tools are commonplace: we can monitor spread with Technorati and similar Web services, but also by analyzing the hits on Web server logs.

Types of Adopters

Their degree of network connectivity is only one aspect of the people who will adopt the innovation. Perhaps the most famous section of the book is Rogers's division of users into four categories. "Early adopters" are leaders; they take to new products quickly and spread the word to others. They are followed by the "early majority," who are eager to try but want to be secure in their decision; the "late majority" who follow only when the way is well trodden; and finally the "laggards," who adopt only when absolutely sure that the innovation is right for them.

Just a year after I read the book, the dot-com boom peaked in San Francisco, and the word "early adopter" was everywhere in dot-com marketing language. Would the early adopters think you were cool? Would they tell their friends? Could you get a free version into their hands fast enough for them to play with?

Rogers's book tells us what to look for in an early adopter: they are likely to be wealthier (and thus more able to afford both the innovation and any costs that may result from its not working), better-educated, and younger than those who do not adopt. Yet an innovation that is targeted too narrowly to these early adopters might not diffuse further: the system must be useful to the later adopters, too.

Characteristics of the Innovation

In the long term, the part of the book that has been most useful to me is its discussion of the ways that characteristics of innovations help drive adoption. The problem of how people choose to use, or not use, innovations is one that the CSCW field has wrestled with on a fairly constant basis. Grudin (1994), for example, found that users must have a reason to use a system; the benefit of others is not sufficient to drive adoption.

This notion, called "relative advantage," is the first criterion in the list of reasons of why someone might adopt. An innovation is also more likely to be adopted if it can be tried out, and possibly rejected; if it matches the adoptees' needs and beliefs; if it seems reasonably simple; if its effects are observable; and if it can be "reinvented," or customized by the user.

This framework is a useful one for designing technologies. It explains why a new operating system might be very hard to diffuse: even with a high perceived benefit, it might not be easy to try out, and would have a very high perceived cost if it fails. Conversely, it helps explain why many users' computers have many small applications installed: they are perceived as low-cost to install, and are fairly easy to "unadopt," simply by not using them.

I have used this framework when considering how to deploy trial applications and design participatory experiments. It is always valuable to ask, "why would users install this? What might they be afraid of happening? How will they know it has worked, and how will they show it to their friends?" To the extent that these questions can be answered, the better is the likelihood of a choice for adoption.

These points are not entirely new: a good designer takes many of these factors into account automatically, and each of these points has been brought up in the research. What is unusual in Rogers's book is the clear placement of these ideas together and in context; it works very neatly as a predeployment checklist.

Putting *Diffusion of Innovations* on the HCI Bookshelf

My own experience with Rogers's book helped me focus my graduate work: reading it convinced me that I should begin to learn more about social networks, which, in turn, led me to HCI in general and CSCW in particular. I remain convinced that *Diffusion of Innovations* belongs on the well-stocked HCI bookshelf.

First, the timeline for adoption that Rogers presents—from introduction of the innovation up through the decision to adopt out to confirming the adoption—can help put HCI adoption and use studies in context. The question should be not "is three weeks long enough" but "what stage of adoption did users reach?" We should look for the signs of adoption to understand whether a diffusion has been successful: are users reinventing the technology, telling their friends, and so on?

Second, understanding the attributes of innovations—as outlined above—is critical for designers in trying to understand who will use their innovation, and why. Again, these questions are basic, but they compose a useful checklist.

Last, Rogers's persuasive discussion of social networks and communication media should help researchers understand the roles of online communication and the ways that ideas travel across the Internet, which is of critical importance if we are to function well in today's online environment.

13

From Smart to Ordinary

Barry Brown
University of Glasgow, Glasgow, U.K.

S. Zuboff, 1988: *In the Age of the Smart Machine*

A computer science degree has many redeeming features. When I was studying computer science at Edinburgh University in the early 1990s, much of my (productive) time was happily concerned with what went on inside computers. Computer science can give you a deep appreciation for how computers work and, what's perhaps more important, how to make them do interesting new things. If, in Arthur C. Clarke's words, any sufficiently advanced technology is indistinguishable from magic, computer science dispels that magic by revealing the boring, difficult, but at times exciting work involved in getting troublesome machines to do desired tasks. Like most computer science courses, those I took at Edinburgh taught me very little about how computers are actually used outside in the world. Indeed, even though PCs were beginning to drop onto every desk and into every home, the consequences of all the stuff we were being taught was nearly completely absent from our courses. The focus was on the "science of computational processes," and seldom on anything as mundane as the actual use of computers. One joke we had was that the degree name was going to be changed to "computer science science"—since the lecturers seemed to like the idea of its being a *science* so much.

While working on my degree I read Zuboff's *In the Age of the Smart Machine*, and it had a strong impact on me. Published in 1988, Zuboff's book was one of the first book-length ethnographic investigations of how technology is used in workplaces. Even today it is one of the few book-length ethnographies of computer use that covers a range of both white- and blue-collar work. Zuboff studied how technology changed the nature of work in manufacturing plants, paper mills, and steel mills, while it also changed white-collar work in financial institutions. The book is an excellent ethnography, and reading it, as someone who had no idea what ethnography was, opened my eyes to a form of research that took seriously the everyday problems and issues of work. Our dealings in the modern world are such that we often encounter things going wrong or causing frustration—be it at our own workplace, or when dealing with other organizations. Zuboff's method—that of an in-depth ethnographic focus on technology—lets her seriously engage with those kind of problems, and if not solve them, at least understand their source.

Zuboff's book takes seriously the detailed practices of how people and things work together, without attempting to simplify those details to overviews or generality. Zuboff's central argument, one she builds by drawing on diverse evidence throughout the book, is that the nature of work itself has changed with the introduction of new technology. Perhaps the most vivid example from the book is that of a paper pulp mill. The engineers at the mill originally used their "know-how" and "knack" during the paper-making process to produce paper. The engineers would chew the stewing paper pulp to test its consistency and to test if it was ready to move on to the next stage of production. But with the introduction of computers, algorithms now automatically calculated when to move the pulp through the process. While the production of paper was still nominally in the hands of the engineers, much of their work had been coded into the computer. Their knowledge and tacit skills had been automated. Zuboff describes how the process knowledge held by the staff was now encapsulated in computer programs that were actually outside the control of those very staff. For new staff at the mill this meant they were completely dependent on the computers to do the work—they had none of the old process knowledge—and had to rely on the old staff when things went wrong with the new technology.

Zuboff contrasts the automation of the paper mill with the introduction of an electronic bulletin board in a white-collar financial organization. Here computers had not simply automated work, but changed its form by supporting more information-rich discussions around work activity. Rather than simply following procedures, online discussion forums supported connections and discussions of problems across the whole of the company. Zuboff describes what is familiar to anybody using the Internet today: how work was supported and enhanced through electronic communication that took place outside official hierarchical channels. In Zuboff's terms, technology "infomated" the work by supporting richer communication and sharing of information. This is Zuboff's first "grand theme" in her analysis—that the changing nature of work takes two forms, automation and infomating.

The story of the electronic bulletin board also supplies Zuboff with her second theme: how old-style hierarchical forms of command and control are incompatible with the peer-to-peer communications and connections that information technology can support. The online forum she studied was eventually shut down because management was intolerant of criticism by the workers that appeared online. By trying to control the database they eventually killed the very thing that had kept it so relevant to workers—its support of their own nonhierarchical ways of organizing themselves. Indeed, this story is reminiscent of recent attempts to control corporate blogs. Zuboff goes on to argue that technology can support more networked forms of organization, a radical change from the hierarchical corporate forms of old—arguments similar to those of Malone, Yates, and Benjamin (1987).

Looking back on Zuboff's book, and comparing it with the many different ethnographies of technology since 1988, Zuboff is inspirational, if at times a little naive. Zuboff foregrounds how it is that the tools used in work come to infuse the quality and nature of that work itself (ironically itself something of a Marxist argument). While the main impact of Zuboff's book was in information and management science, where it has encouraged a steady growth of ethnographic and qualitative studies, within HCI the book influenced and encouraged the work of those such as the Lancaster school of ethnographers, as well as a growing interest in the contexts in which computers are used.

If the book has one failing it is its "cyberutopia" tone (indeed this proved to be the main critique of the book by others, e.g. Noble 1991). Essentially unsolvable disputes between management and those managed are often optimistically dissolved in the book. As Wilmot (1996) put it, the book suffers from a "conceptual framework that assumes away the contradictory forces inherent within the structures of liberal capitalist economies." As with much American writing on management, Zuboff never questions the roles or rationality of managers themselves. Yet Zuboff does at least document the conflicts and conversations with a clear eye.

These criticisms aside, what is still refreshing about *The Age of the Smart Machine* nearly twenty years later is Zuboff's grand ambition to look broadly at the nature of work and to ally this with solid empirical research. Zuboff takes aim at no less a beast than what we do with all our working hours, our practices of work, putting it into a historical context. Zuboff's ambition is to tell a grand story, yet in doing so she is careful to document her arguments with real examples and descriptions of work. Her narrative is one of how labor has been in a continual process of transformation, particularly one of codification and measurement. Borrowing from the work of others, namely Jo Ann Yates (1989) and Alfred Chandler (1977), Zuboff puts her ethnography into a historical narrative of change. Although this leads much of her argument to be speculative, and at times she overemphasizes change instead of continuity, it remains inspiring. Zuboff's ethnography boldly reaches beyond specificities.

One example of this reach is her exploration of how the monitoring of work is incorporated into computer systems, and how this interplays with work activity itself. Zuboff tells this story through the example of a telephone engineer starting his day—it is worth quoting Zuboff at length:

> Not many years ago entering the building meant reporting in to the foreman and exchanging greetings with several other craftsworkers. The foreman distributed assignments, pertinent information was discussed, and the craftsworkers set to their tasks.... On this morning, the building is empty. The only sounds the craftworker hears as he enters the work area are the low hum of the electronic equipment and his own footsteps moving across the yellowed linoleum floor. He moves towards a computer terminal and enters his password, time and location. Within seconds, the screen is filled with his assignments for the eight-hour workday. The assigned tasks are listed in the order in which they are to be undertaken, and each task is accompanied by a "price"—the amount of time in which it is to be completed.... Sometimes a task will take longer to complete than its assigned time. Usually it is because a very complicated assignment has been underpriced. Managers in the central office want to know how workers perform against the prices they were assigned. The system uses these rations to computer "efficiency ratings" for each worker, rating that are later used to evaluate performance.... Today this worker is concerned. Three of his allocated tasks were complex and required more than the allocated time. Rather than finish the day with a poor efficiency rating, he decides to change the original prices designated for each of those jobs. He feels fortunate to know the foreman's password, which will allow him to enter the system and alter the prices; he wonders, briefly, if anyone will notice. (1988, p. 318)

In this short extract Zuboff puts command and control in its place, covering not only the damaging change in sociability which automation can cause, but also the ways in which essential "work-arounds"—such as knowing the foreman's password—are used. Zuboff's analysis both outlines details yet boldly connects them to broader themes. In my own work, Zuboff imparted to me an aspiration to connect the particular with the generic. As ethnographers, we face a constant dilemma of how much we can connect, and how much we find in the generic speaks to one particular setting (Brown and Laurier 2005). Zuboff's work is a lesson in grounded generalization.

To HCI, a book like Zuboff's presents a clear challenge. The history of HCI has been one of taking more and more seriously the complex situations in which technology is used. Zuboff's work shows how to address, as a whole, the nature of work. While computer science and infomatics departments increasingly seem to be drifting apart, this book is a clear example of what could be lost to computer science. It is not just that computer science would lose an understanding of the changes it brings to the world. Rather the field could become disconnected from the worlds in which technology is used, seriously damaging its chances for innovation and impact. After a career that had at times been hostile to HCI, in his last publication Roger Needham relented. As he put it: “Computing researchers need to climb down from their ivory towers to look at the real-world contexts in which their systems will be deployed” (Needham 2003, p. 1555). *In the Age of the Smart Machine* may not be core computer science, but it is still as relevant to that act of climbing down as when it was first published.

14

Knowing the Particulars

Thomas Erickson
IBM Research, Minneapolis, Minnesota, U.S.A.

J. Jacobs, 1961: *The Death and Life of Great American Cities*

I prefer examples to theories, case studies to experiments. Given a choice between a rich, particular example and an elegant, general theory, I will take the example every time. I prefer the concreteness, depth, and specificity of examples—especially the ways in which they are entwined with their time, place, and history. I am not suggesting that examples are some sort of pure, unmediated form of experience—to be powerful, an example needs to be unpacked. A skillful analyst can lift the example up, draw out its ties to its contexts, reveal the processes that have shaped it, and thus connect it to larger issues in a way that is broadly meaningful.

Among the most incisive analysts of examples I know of is Jane Jacobs, author of *The Death and Life of Great American Cities*. Jacobs's work has inspired me for years. Although the leap from planning cities to designing interactive systems might seem a long one, the gap is not as large as it first appears. I find her examples and analyses a wellspring of inspiration for thinking about the design of interactive systems, and particularly the challenges of moving from systems that are simply "easy to use" to those that are engaging, convivial, and sustainable.

The Death and Life of Great American Cities appeared in 1961. It was a critique, sometimes verging into polemic, of the approach to urban planning that was dominant in the United States in the mid-twentieth century. This approach, sometimes called "urban renewal," involved the wholesale demolition of residential "slums" and "blighted" business districts and their replacement with neat, "modern" homes and buildings. The residents—at least those not dispersed by the disruption of "renewal"—were supposed to be edified and uplifted by their orderly new environment. Jacobs argued fiercely against this approach, writing: "There is a quality even meaner than outright ugliness or disorder, and this meaner quality is the dishonest mask of pretended order, achieved by ignoring or suppressing the real order that is struggling to exist and to be served"(p. 15). Jacobs's aim in *Death and Life* was to reveal the real order beneath the veneer of chaos, to show that it was critical to the effective functioning of cities, and to understand how design might support and strengthen it, rather than suppress it.

For Jacobs, one of the defining aspects of cities is that they are composed of people who are almost all strangers to one another. When you think of it this way—that a city is a concentrated mass of people who share neither ties of kinship nor strong social bonds—it seems like a recipe for anarchy. But in fact, cities are by and large orderly places, and that order is supported by a complex array of social processes, which in turn are entwined with how cities are designed. In the 450 pages of *Death and Life*, Jacobs discusses sidewalks and streets, neighborhoods and parks; she is concerned with residents and shopkeepers, children and the elderly; her analyses range from the ways in which strangers interact in public, to the physical factors that produce a lively and sustainable level of commercial activity; and her recommendations range from the size of city blocks (make them short!) to the design of zoning laws (support mixed uses!). *Death and Life* is too grand in its scope to cover in its entirety, so I shall confine my comments to her discussions of sidewalks.

Sidewalks and streets are, for Jacobs, the basic unit of the city. Everyone must use them: they are where strangers encounter one another and where much of the public life of the city plays out. When visitors speak of a city, commenting on its safety, appearance, and liveliness, they are typically referring to the character of its streets and sidewalks. Jacobs devotes the first three substantive chapters of *Death and Life* to an analysis of sidewalk life. She begins with the question of safety, of how order is maintained amid the constant parade of strangers. She notes that order is not primarily maintained by the police, but rather that "it is kept primarily by an intricate, almost unconscious, network of voluntary controls and standards among the people themselves, and enforced by the people themselves" (p. 32). And, she adds, "Safety on the streets by mutual surveillance and policing of one another sounds grim, but in real life it is not grim." Instead, the production of this order "works best, most casually, and with least frequent taint of suspicion or hostility precisely where people are using and most enjoying the streets" (p. 36).

Although this order is produced by people, it is not immune to the effects of environment. One of Jacobs's primary aims is to describe the ways in which the design of an urban space can facilitate or hinder the production of this order. She argues that to enable the maintenance of order, a city street must have three main qualities: a clear demarcation of public and private spaces, the presence of many "eyes upon the street," and a continuous stream of users. What Jacobs returns to again and again are the relationships among strangers, and the environmental conditions that foster such relationships. She describes the ways in which strangers become familiar with one another, developing nodding acquaintances as they wait at the bus stop together, or patronize the same drugstore, and notes that "It is possible to be on excellent sidewalk terms with people who are very different from oneself . . ." (p. 62).

In Jacobs's view there is *not* an implied trajectory from nodding acquaintance to friendship. The beauty of such public relationships, and in fact a necessary condition for their easy formation, is that they are free of the obligations and "entanglements" of more intimate relationships. Nevertheless, such "weak" relationships are powerful. Even if no familiar strangers are actually present, those who are on good "sidewalk terms" with others have, at a deep level, an expectation of support that will lead them to assist a stranger or to stand ready to help in an altercation. As Jacobs says (p. 56):

> The trust of a city street is formed over time from many, many little public sidewalk contacts. It grows out of people stopping by at the bar for a beer, getting advice from the grocer and giving advice to the newsstand man, comparing opinions with other customers at the bakery and nodding hello to the two boys drinking pop on the stoop. . . . Most of it is ostensibly utterly trivial but the sum is not trivial at all. The sum of such casual, public contact at a local level—most of it fortuitous, most of it associated with errands, all of it metered by the person concerned and not thrust upon him by anyone—is a feeling for the public identity of people, a web of public respect and trust, and resource in time of personal or neighborhood need.

Why should those of us involved in designing technologies be interested in Jacobs's analyses? One reason is that interactive systems are spreading from our homes and offices and into the commercial and public spheres that make up our urban environment. Those involved in designing ambient intelligence and ubiquitous computing would do well to consider the environments that our new technologies are colonizing, and to reflect on the ways in which interactive systems might serve to support (or diminish) the web of public respect and trust. Eric Paulos and his colleagues at Intel (see, e.g., Paulos and Goodman 2004; Paulos and Jenkins 2005) provide one example of researchers who have used a sophisticated understanding of urban behavior to inform their work.

For myself, I find that Jacobs's view of the nature of urban interaction provides a provocative model for thinking about online interaction. Although it has been popular to use "community" as a framework for thinking about many-to-many interactions on the Internet, I've become disenchanted with this as a general approach

(Erickson 1997). Online sites that function as genuine communities are rare. Instead, graphs of the frequency of interaction at most online sites follow a power law: most of the interaction is generated by a very small percentage of the visitors; the large majority are just passing through, perhaps pausing to look or read; and of those who "participate," the majority do so only once. These sorts of interactions seem much more similar to those that occur on a city's sidewalks.

If we think of most online systems as being conduits for flows of strangers—and strangers who would mostly prefer to retain their autonomy and avoid "entanglements"—then Jacobs's observations have much to offer systems designers. First and foremost, users of online systems must be able to see one another. Not that real names or personal details must be revealed, but simply that users must be able to notice one another's presence, have a sense of the foci of activity and attention, and, perhaps, over time, start to recognize others. This has been the primary thrust of my work over the last decade, with the development of the Babble system and its successors (Erickson et al. 1999), and the development of the notion of social translucence, which has to do with the issue of how to find the right balance between individual privacy and the visibility that is essential to supporting the social processes that produce order (Erickson and Kellogg 2003). But Jacobs, in her consideration of behavior in urban environments, goes much farther than this. The questions she asks—What features of an environment support interaction among strangers? What attracts people to a place, and what makes them stay or go? What does it require for a commercial area to become self-sustaining?—and her answers to them provide rich grist for those charged with designing online systems.

Jacobs's book is part of a larger body of work on urban design to which I keep returning. Beginning in the late 1950s and early '60s, there was a remarkable convergence of interest in the ways in which urban environments function. Kevin Lynch, best known for *The Image of the City* (1960), was investigating and writing about urban design during that period. So was the anthropologist William Whyte (mentioned in Jacobs's acknowledgments), although it would be two decades before he produced his best-known (to those in HCI) work, *The Social Life of Small Urban Spaces* (1980) and *City* (1988). And social psychologist Stanley Milgram embarked on a series of experiments and field studies of urban behavior (Milgram, Sabini, and Silver 1992), popularizing the term "familiar stranger" (and verifying it as a quantifiable phenomenon) a decade after Jacobs's description of strangers who were on "sidewalk terms" with one another.

Jane Jacobs died this year, at the age of 89, the last of this group. I've learned a lot from her. Perhaps the most important lesson is one of method. Jacobs was unsurpassed at observing, at finding the telling example that both provided a deeper understanding of the situation and served as a way of making the point to her audience. She was suspicious of theory, and though she did, of course, generalize, she wrote: "but let no one be misled into believing that these generalizations can be used routinely to declare what the particular, in this or that place, *ought* to mean. City processes in real life are too complex to be routine, too particularized for application as abstractions. They are always made up of interactions among unique combinations of particulars, and there is no substitute for knowing the particulars" (1961, p. 441). There is no substitute for knowing the particulars. This is good advice for anyone involved in design of any kind.

15

Back to Samba School: Revisiting Seymour Papert's Ideas on Community, Culture, Computers, and Learning

Amy Bruckman
Georgia Institute of Technology, Atlanta, Georgia, U.S.A.

S. Papert, 1980: *Mindstorms*

In 1980 in his book *Mindstorms*, Seymour Papert presents a vision of what he calls a "technological samba school." At samba schools in Brazil, a community of people gather together to prepare a performance for Carnival. Original music and lyrics are written, lead performers are chosen, and costumes are designed and sewn. Papert writes (p. 178):

> Members of the school range in age from children to grandparents and in ability from novice to professional. But they dance together and as they dance everyone is learning and teaching as well as dancing. Even the stars are there to learn their difficult parts.

Papert suggests that the samba school might serve as a model for a new kind of learning environment where people learn through creative projects with technology. In a "technological samba school," learning is self-motivated, intergenerational, and playful. The broader cultural and community contexts are essential components of the learning environment.

What I find most inspiring about Papert's vision is his basic faith in people—in their intelligence and creativity. It's a hopeful vision. Learning should not be a chore but a joy, and is within everyone's reach.

Papert of course was thinking of a technological samba school as a physical place. But encountering his ideas for the first time around 1990—just at the start of the explosion of the Internet as a popular medium—I imagined it as an online "place." In my research on learning in online communities, I've found that other people provide a ready source of technical support, emotional support ("Oh, I was confused by that at first too!"), accessible role models, and an appreciative audience for completed work (Bruckman 1998).

After years of thinking about this idea, I suppose Papert's original text had almost fallen away—I was left with my own reinterpretations and that oft-quoted line about everyone learning, even the stars. So it was an eyebrow-raising experience when I reread the original for the first time in many years. Rather like rereading the work of John Dewey (see, e.g., Dewey 1938), each time I return to Papert's text I discover new depth and insight. For example, Papert writes:

> Let me say once more, the obstacle is not economic and it is not that computers are not going to be objects in people's everyday lives. They eventually will. They are already entering most workplaces and will eventually go into most homes just as TV sets now do, and in many cases initially for the same reasons. The obstacle to the growth of popular computer cultures is cultural, for example, the mismatch between the computer culture embedded in the machines of today and the cultures of the homes they will go into. And if the problem is cultural the remedy must be cultural. (1980, p. 183)

With the HCI research community's focus on "usability," to what extent have we really addressed the question of the culture of the computational artifacts we create? Papert here is specifically addressing the factors that cause people to choose to embrace computer-assisted learning activities, but the underlying point speaks to the design of computational artifacts more generally. Papert continues (p. 183):

> The gulf must be bridged between the technical-scientific and humanistic cultures. And I think that the key to constructing this bridge will be learning how to recast powerful ideas in computational form, ideas that are as important to the poet as to the engineer.

His analysis here seems prophetic. Many of the computing phenomena that are currently rising in popularity share this bridging quality—humanities disciplines inspire them as much as engineering. When Papert was writing in 1980, a skeptic might have asked, for example, "what does popular music really have to do with computing?" In 2006 we can say, without hesitation: everything. Computers are now central not only to how we make music, but also to how we listen to it and buy it. From animation to theater to architecture, computers are influencing the arts, and the arts are influencing the evolution of computing technology. We have clearly discovered how to leverage these ties for business purposes—convergence is a reality, and media computing is big business. Can we now also leverage them for educational aims?

Taking the Metaphor Literally

Rereading Papert's thoughts on samba schools, José Zagal and I posed a question: What would it mean to take Papert's metaphor more literally? What are samba schools really like? Would a more detailed analysis of real samba schools give us any new insights into the design of successful learning environments? Regrettably lacking the time to go join a samba school in Rio, José instead reviewed the published literature about samba schools. We noted a number of potentially educationally significant features of real samba schools: cultural significance, existence of a public event, flexibility to outsiders, and pluralism of membership. (Zagal and Bruckman 2005). I will summarize those findings briefly, discussing each in turn.

Cultural Significance

Central to understanding samba schools is, of course, understanding samba itself. Samba to Brazilians is rather like baseball to Americans—a popular pursuit that forms part of the national identity. You can imagine that a learning environment designed around love of baseball might start off at a strategic advantage. How can we understand this type of cultural power and try to leverage it in the creation of new learning environments?

Existence of a Public Event

Even if a cultural phenomenon is already as popular as samba, it still must continually remind people of its existence. What better publicity for samba schools could there be than Carnival itself? The annual event is high profile, drawing everyone's attention to the community's work. The annual nature of the event helps create rhythms of life for the community. Could a technological samba school have an annual Carnival equivalent?

Flexibility to Outsiders

Once people are aware of a cultural phenomenon (like samba or baseball), to become involved they need an easy opportunity to join in. It is possible to participate in a samba school's performance simply by buying a costume. Newcomers in costume may dance with the school at Carnival. This legitimate peripheral participation (Lave and Wenger 1991) provides an easy route for newcomers to become involved with the activity of the school and possibly increase their participation the following year. How do we welcome newcomers to our learning environments? How can we create easy routes to gradually increase participation?

Pluralism of Membership (Socioeconomic, Age, Expertise, and Race)

If we are successful in supporting an easy path for people to join a cultural activity, one must still ask, which people are willing and able to participate? Is this just appealing to one socioeconomic or ethnic group, or is the appeal broader? Diversity among learners can be a tremendous asset. For the learner, it's beneficial to learn from someone more experienced. For the teacher, teaching someone less experienced can be a great opportunity to refine one's own knowledge. Yet in most Western learning environments, students are segregated by age. Schools that draw from particular geographic regions also often become de facto segregated by race and socioeconomic status. Samba schools draw members of all ages—families often participate together. Surprisingly, many samba schools also draw members from diverse economic and racial backgrounds. What might it mean to a technological samba school if we could leverage diversity of membership as an asset for all learners?

Learning from Samba

Some readers find Papert's utopian enthusiasm naive. Making these ideas work in real-world settings is challenging, and he often doesn't seem to take the barriers seriously. Many find his writings about school disrespectful in tone. He sometimes seems angry at schools, teachers, and school administrators—as if they are the oppressors of youth. Although these critics raise some valid points, I believe the real value in Papert's work is not in the answers he provides but in the questions he asks. Could education be fundamentally different? What are our implicit assumptions about schooling and learning? Papert shines a light on those assumptions, and asks us to question them and imagine alternatives. He reminds us that learning is not just about cognition, but also about feeling.

In the section of *Mindstorms* about technological samba schools, he asks us to consider the culture of learning. What is the relationship of that culture to popular culture? Could that be more symbiotic instead of oppositional? Who are the participants in our learning environments, and might we all benefit from greater diversity? Why can't learning be more like play? And where in our learning environments is the joy, the celebration? These continue to be as provocative questions in 2007 as they were in 1980.

16

The Work to Make Software Work

Rebecca E. Grinter
Georgia Institute of Technology, Atlanta, Georgia, U.S.A.

D. L. Parnas, 1972: "On the Criteria to Be Used in Decomposing Systems into Modules"

David Parnas, though famous for his many contributions to software engineering, has not been accorded the same status within human–computer interaction research. Yet, it is to him that I owe much of what would become my first and longest sustained research interest: the empirical study of the "work to make software work."[1] From his prolific body of work, one paper stands out to me as having direct implications for human–computer interaction but as not having received sufficient attention for its contributions: Parnas's paper on modular programming, "On the Criteria to Be Used in Decomposing Systems into Modules."

In the early 1970s modular programming was already being proposed as an effective approach to designing software systems. Modules were, and remain, units of software that stand distinct, each providing a unique piece of functionality. The argument for modularity was simply that it would lead to less confusion in the code base. It would improve the understandability and evolvability of systems. Yet, prior to Parnas's paper little was known about *how* to divide the system design into these modules, specifically, what criteria to use.

Parnas filled that gap in this paper, and it is for those criteria that this paper is most widely known. Today, we know these criteria as leading to modules that exhibit two critical features. They should have tight cohesion: all the elements within the module should relate to each other. Simultaneously, modules should have low coupling—they should be as isolated from each other as possible—in order to avoid needless intermodule dependencies.

Yet, the criteria are not what drew me to this paper. Along the way to outlining the criteria Parnas makes the following statements:

> The benefits expected of modular programming are: (1) managerial—development time should be shortened because separate groups would work on each module with little need for communication. . . . In this context "module" is considered to be a responsibility assignment rather than a sub-program. (Parnas 1972 p. 1,054)

These statements jumped out at me, for they seemed to be about the relationship between software and people.

Even as an undergraduate at Leeds University I was much more interested in studying people who were developing software rather than building it myself. All the problems that most interested me did not begin with my use of C and assembler, but occurred whenever my project team talked about the code. Even then, I recall finding those discussions more intriguing than coding itself. And, of course, one point of this team-based project work was to teach us how programming is inherently collaborative.

And so I went to the University of California, Irvine, to pursue a Ph.D. in what was at the time the Computers, ORganizations, Policy and Society (CORPS) group.[2] Advised by Jonathan Grudin, John King, and Rob Kling, I began to understand that software was an inherently social endeavor; specifically, the management of the process required considerable coordination. And that's where Parnas comes in.

The contribution that Parnas's work made to my own was to spell out what I had not seen before. In a nutshell, it was Parnas who helped me to see that the division of code was also simultaneously a division of labor. Getting this division of labor "right" was a matter of assigning independent modules to distinct groups. It was this assignment of work that would reduce the need for communication.

At the time, I had been collecting data at small start-up in southern California, during the emerging phenomena that would come to be known as the dot-com era. Parnas's paper made me think about my data in a new way; in particular, despite following observable best practices for modular decomposition, the start-up's code modules still had dependencies. The fact that dependencies still existed troubled me, but I began to see that their presence was often at the root of the work that needed to be coordinated, the work of who needed to collaborate with whom.

Armed with this new perspective, my data began to raise the following question for me (over and over again): what types of coordination problems do the relationships between modules, and consequently between people, produce? Now I saw dependencies everywhere, and I realized that what seemed to change was the nature of how it could be coordinated, in other words the relationships between the individuals.

For example, between individuals working in the same group, dependencies were often handled through the type of knowledge people typically have about what their immediate coworkers are working on, for example, by being able to see into the same code base and identify who was working on what parts of the code.

However, other dependencies require management across working groups, across organizational divisions of the corporation, or between companies, and in these situations the work to make the software work escalates dramatically. Such coordination requires multiple individuals working together to resolve the problem, which typically includes a protracted process of identifying the "right person": someone who knows who is working on the code that yours depends on, or an individual who knows the best way to find out the answer to that question. All of this work to find the other end of the dependency is the work of coordinating these technical relationships that exist within a living code base.

But Parnas's insight also raised a new question for me: why did modular decomposition not remove all these dependencies, despite its goal of achieving independence among modules? My new perspective came with a new challenge, one of explaining the presence of these dependencies in the first place. Again, I turned to the data I had collected. And again, the answers I found reinforced how inherently social the development of software actually is, and how that in turn can have profound implications for the code base.

I found at least three reasons why dependencies exist in the code. First, some relationships get defined during the process of decomposition itself. Despite significant efforts to eradicate them, even the best designs seem to present unavoidable dependencies. Sometimes these dependencies result from competing needs. For example, I watched as developers and their managers chose system performance optimization over a clean separation of two modules.

Second, legacy code complicates the decomposition process enormously. No one I interviewed or observed was working on "fresh" software. While some developers worked on code under five years old, others were working with software that had been developed around the same time that I was in high school (the 1980s). New additions to the code base were being designed to fit into an already existing set of design decisions. Economics, most particularly development schedules, did not permit restructuring the entire code base in order to remove dependencies. Within these code and temporal constraints, dependencies thus emerged.

Third and finally, another truism of software development that has been long known is that, invariably, the first attempt at design and development will not ultimately turn out to be completely correct. In other words, requirements change.

I saw this everywhere I went. I saw a variety of situations that led to software changes midstream—requirements that had been misinterpreted when transferred from the customer into the development organization, changes made midway to accommodate innovations in the marketplace (such as the arrival of new operating systems or new processors), and sometimes revisions made in response to direct feedback from a user. All of these led to changes in the software.

At the end of this intensive data analysis (and often reanalysis), I concluded that the phenomenon of recomposition creates a significant amount of coordination work. I identified recomposition as all the work it takes to assemble a working software system from its constituent parts (Grinter 1998). I chose the word "recomposition" to reflect the direct association that this work has with decomposition. For it is in the process of software decomposition, the process of dividing software up, that the relations of recomposition are defined. Decomposition dictates who will need to coordinate what with whom, based on the dependencies that their collective efforts share. Yet, unlike decomposition, which has received a huge amount of scholarly and professional attention, questions of recomposition have gone largely unnoticed. Integration, it typically seems to be assumed, will simply happen. My field notes suggested that nothing in software development was simple, and leading the way in complexity was integration.

My Ph.D. in hand, I left Irvine for Illinois to join the Software Production Research Department at Bell Laboratories. Shortly after I arrived, James D. Herbsleb joined the same department and soon we discovered that we shared a common interest in understanding the types of coordination work required to produce functionally working software systems. What had been true of my experiences of studying software development until this time was that there was some significant degree of colocation among the people working in the same corporation. In the start-up everyone worked on the same floor; in the larger sites I studied, their efforts were spread across a few buildings on their main campus.

However, a new trend in software development was emerging: "round the clock" development. The idea was that if you spread a development effort across three time zones with largely separate working hours, then you get twenty-four hours of productivity in each calendar day. That was the theory.

But was globally distributed development living up to its promise? Jim Herbsleb initiated and led a project to find an empirical answer to that question and, along the way, to try to solve any problems that this organization of software development work was creating. For me, Jim's project provided a new opportunity to again look at recomposition work. Perhaps unsurprisingly, what I saw was that recomposition work, in the easiest cases, gets much more difficult when the code base is split across time and cultures. Sometimes even the simplest coordination took an agonizingly long time, as people negotiated language, religious (often manifested as needing to know who was on holiday and when), and work rhythm boundaries (Herbsleb and Grinter 1999).

According to Conway's Law, the structure of the code mirrors the communications structure of the organization that developed it (Conway 1968). This law is widely accepted within software research and practice. At the time Conway made this argument (in the 1960s), the majority of code was still being built from scratch each time. What recomposition seems to suggest is that not only is this law true, but eventually, as the code base matures, so the reverse of Conway's Law reveals itself as true. In other words, recomposition explains why the communications structure of the organization has to mirror the structure of the code base. As recomposition shows, without that parity, the code simply cannot function well.

In 2000 I left Bell Laboratories, and after eight years of study, I also exited the world of software development. It was time for a fresh challenge, and I'd begun to notice an interesting trend among teenagers in the United Kingdom. They seemed to have stopped using their mobile phones for voice calls and were now somehow, incredibly, typing on the keypad. I wondered why, but that's another story.

Notes

1. To paraphrase John Bowers yet again.
2. Now known as the ICT group.

IV

Groups in the Wild

A vast amount of work and communication occurs within small, tightly knit groups. This, in turn, raises the question, how do they get things done? An important strand of this work has involved the close observation of groups "in the wild"—that is, real groups doing ordinary things in everyday settings. In this section, we find a variety of perspectives on how groups work—both in the sense of what makes them function and how they accomplish their work, play, and communication. The essays here examine frameworks for understanding groups and group processes, and the systems that support them.

The section begins with Jonathan Grudin, who, overcoming his distaste for the use of acronyms in titles, reflects on McGrath's theory of groups. Grudin considers group behaviors through the lenses of typology and theory, and challenges the importance we currently place on theory. The next two essays, by Saul Greenberg and Keith Edwards, consider how applications and infrastructure can be designed and developed through a better understanding of group activity. Greenberg reflects on the implications of Tang's studies of design teams, and Edwards in turn reflects on Greenberg and Marwood's work on concurrency control. Prevalent issues in the workaday world that have driven much of the research in computer-supported cooperative work motivate the next three essays. Geraldine Fitzpatrick—so struck by her first encounter with the phrase "computer-supported cooperative work" that she rewrote her Ph.D. program application at the last minute—discusses how Schmidt and Bannon's paper on articulation work helped her make sense of her newly selected field. In "Let's Shack Up," David McDonald discusses Berlin et al.'s paper on the design and use of a group memory, and offers reflections on what happens when a "deleter" marries a "saver." Leysia Palen discusses Francik et al.'s paper, "Putting Innovation to Work," reminding us of the remarkable but ultimately unsuccessful Freestyle system from Wang Laboratories, and reflects on the issue of the adoption of groupware systems. This section closes with an essay by Brian Smith on Hollan and Stornetta's "Beyond Being There" that provides a more personal account of the use of technology to support remote collaboration. In particular, Smith challenges us to think about the ways technologies can serve as a bridge across personal and emotional distances.

17

McGrath and the Behaviors of Groups (BOGs)

Jonathan Grudin
Microsoft Research, Redmond, Washington, U.S.A.

J. E. McGrath, 1991: "Time, Interaction, and Performance (TIP): A Theory of Groups"

I don't recall when I first read Joseph McGrath's essay "Time, Interaction, and Performance (TIP): A Theory of Groups." I wasn't impressed. Introducing an acronym in the title? McGrath presented a typology of functions and modes of group behavior, accompanied by a fairly intricate theory. Jung, who introduced typologies into psychology, noted that a typology is neither right nor wrong; rather, it is either useful or not. I didn't see how to use McGrath's typology.

Now I do.

A Summary of McGrath's Article

Writing in 1991, McGrath noted that prior to the 1980s, research into group behavior relied on controlled studies of small groups formed for the experiments. Such groups were typically ephemeral, with fixed membership, no past or future, and little freeloading. A group was given a single task and all necessary resources. Although the approach conformed to a reductionist model of experimental hypothesis-testing, McGrath argued that the results had little bearing on the rest of the world.

Such experimental studies of artificial groups absorb tremendous energy to this day. They can identify phenomena to look for in naturally occurring settings, but McGrath's discussion is a healthy reminder that they prove little. However, his purpose was not to beat up on this tradition, and the value of his essay lies elsewhere. McGrath shifted focus to *in vivo* observations and studies to develop a typology and theory of behavior in what is often called "the real world."

Table 17.1
Group modes and functions

	Production	Group Well-Being	Member Support
Inception	Production demand and opportunity	Interaction demand and opportunity	Inclusion demand and opportunity
Problem-Solving	Technical problem-solving	Role network definition	Position and status attainments
Conflict Resolution	Policy resolution	Power and payoff distribution	Contribution and payoff distribution
Execution	Performance	Interaction	Participation

From McGrath 1991.

McGrath (1991) built on Hackman (1985) to create the typology laid out in table 17.1. Project teams or groups engage in four critical modes of operation: inception, problem-solving, conflict resolution, and execution. Inception encompasses the activities that surround taking on a project. Groups reexperience this mode whenever they take on a new project. Execution comprises the activities directly related to project goals. Problem-solving and conflict-resolution cover tangential activities that may arise along the way. (When problem-solving or conflict-resolution *is* the task, incidental problems or conflicts trigger these modes. For example, in Spike Lee's bank heist turned hostage negotiation film *Inside Man*, the law enforcement agents played by Denzel Washington and Willem Dafoe are in conflict-resolution mode when quarreling over tactics and in execution mode when quarreling with the hostage-takers.)

Each mode comprises activities in support of three functions: production, group health or well-being, and member support. Production activities focus directly on getting on with the project. Group well-being is the goal of a morale-building event to strengthen empathy and trust among team members, for example. Promotions help ensure that members get what they need as individuals. To see the difference between group health and member support, consider a team that works together well but breaks up because one member can't afford to continue participating, and another team, such as a successful but dysfunctional rock group, pulled apart by animosities despite everyone's being personally rewarded. Non-production functions are not directly tied to a group's task, but in the long run they contribute to accomplishing it.

Over half of McGrath's essay and ten of its twelve propositions elaborate TIP, a "theory of groups" focused primarily on temporal aspects of project activity: how we schedule and synchronize work, match activities to available time, manage task-duration ambiguity and conflicting priorities, handle commitments and deadlines, address assignment inequities, and so on. For example, a team that takes on a highly familiar type of project can move from inception to execution with negligible problem-solving or conflict resolution. McGrath regarded TIP as his principal contribution, but I find the typology more broadly useful.

The Typology

"At any one time, a group will be engaged in activities . . . having to do with all three contribution functions." This statement is the key, although on first encounter it seemed an exaggeration. I came to understand it to mean that although a group may avoid a mode of interaction, it cannot avoid attending to all three functions. This is important to emphasize because activities that address group well-being and member support are easy to overlook. In fact, it's difficult *not* to overlook many of them.

Our ancestors lived in groups for millions of years. Like perceptual and cognitive behaviors that are shaped by genes interacting with environment, our innate social behaviors don't require conscious attention. We constantly, intuitively address status, motivation, and other aspects of group health and member support. Some people are more skilled at it than others, but even skill is largely unconscious. Not only are these activities taken for granted, discussion of them may be avoided, such as status concerns in cultures that emphasize egalitarianism.

As a result, we don't see or understand effects of technological and behavioral innovation on these activities, leading to many an unsuccessful outcome and misunderstandings of why failure occurred. To address this, it's advisable to assume that group well-being and member support activities are always present—even when group members are sleeping!—and look for them.

Consequences of Ignoring the Typology

A rational approach to supporting project activity is to ask "what are these people trying to do and how can we help them?" Unfortunately, this leads to an exclusive focus on the execution mode of the production function: performance. How can we increase the rate of production, reduce errors, and increase quality? Attention fixates on the lower left cell in table 17.1.

This is often reflected in an obsessive concern with metrics and proof of ROI, return on investment (Grudin 2004). Of course, when we are marketing or introducing an innovation, we would like to know that its effects on performance will be positive, but it's often impossible to tease out short-term effects of a change, much less subtle long-term effects. Too often, the result is a grim combination of grasping for straws, wherein flimsy data are taken out of context and exaggerated, and looking under lampposts because the light there is better, measuring anything that can be measured easily whether or not it is of great significance.

Examples

Many experiments were undertaken in vain efforts to show measurable benefit from adding video to audio in distributed problem-solving groups. These experiments focused on performance measures, the lower left cell. Then Williams (1997) found evidence that video is consulted more when groups are in conflict situations or are not native speakers of the same language, activities in two of the other production cells. Also, studies reported that participants *liked* video, which could contribute to group well-being and/or member support, with positive long-term consequences for real groups (Poltrock and Grudin 2005).

Electronic meeting rooms (also called group decision support systems or group support systems) show remarkable performance benefits in controlled studies, yet after decades of research and fifteen years of commercial availability, adoption is minimal. Why? Consider this example from Nunamaker et al. (1997, p. 174):

> The founder of a very successful medical technology firm called together key personnel from multiple levels in the organization for a GSS session. Thirty minutes into the meeting he turned red in the face and stood up. Pounding a fist on his PC for emphasis, he shouted, "I want to know who put in the comment on the problem with the interface for the new system. We're not leaving this room until I know who made that statement!" He glared around the room waiting for a response. Everyone greeted his outburst with silence. (The founder then terminated the meeting.)

This executive had been convinced that the technology would improve performance, but the potential loss of status from being openly challenged was more important to him. In general, effective use of these systems often requires a behavioral facilitator and a technician, who become a focus of attention at the expense of the organizer. Enhanced performance comes at the expense of activities in other cells. (See Dennis and Reinicke 2004.)

I've seen managers try new technologies that they believed would increase productivity or enhance their status as innovators, but a manager who appeared helpless in the face of a breakdown would not try a second time.

Another example is workplace use of instant messaging. Measurable time savings from use may be far too few to build a case for the technology, but the pleasure of quick yet minimally intrusive interaction can serve non-production functions that ultimately serve the group and organization.

The Theory

TIP details could be useful as social psychology or in designing workflow or other complex group support systems, but first-time readers might prefer to skim the theory lightly and spend more time thinking about the typology. The theory won't appeal if the typology doesn't.

Those more familiar with natural sciences might be advised, in approaching TIP, that in the social sciences "theory" can be interpreted broadly. Natural sciences followed a path from description to identification of patterns, and then, often centuries later, useful theory. Social science is in more of a hurry. Erickson (2000) is an elegant, humorous critique of the use of theory.

Centuries of observations of animals preceded Linnaeus's taxonomy and conceptual hierarchy. Much later came Darwinian theory. Similarly, centuries of identifying elements preceded Mendeleyev's periodic chart. Later came Bohr's model and theory of atomic structure. Centuries of celestial observations and identification of patterns, culminating in Brahe's meticulous records, made possible Kepler's theory of planetary motion. Premature theorizing, in the form of religion, alchemy, and astrology, was as likely to impede understanding as it was to advance it. For example, Linnaeus's theory was that he was elucidating the mind of a Creator. Only when a science is mature is hypothesis-testing the best approach, and even then it is not the only approach.

In studies of technology and behavior, descriptive science and a search for patterns are probably most useful today. Patterns are not theory: Physicists constructed cloud chambers to find patterns in particle paths, yet a huge gap separated those patterns from theory. But we may feel that to resemble natural sciences, we must have theory, even when, like McGrath, we manage to avoid controlled hypothesis-driven studies. So we stretch the definition of theory.

For example, in grounded theory, a theory is never right or wrong. It is measured by how well it fits existing data. It may be adjusted given new observations. This seems like descriptive science along with identification of patterns and creation of concepts, as practiced by Linnaeus and Mendeleyev. I think something like it is just what we need. It could be considered pretheoretical, but if we must call it theory to obtain academic respect, OK by me. Social science also has more ambitious theory, which runs the risks encountered by the alchemists and astrologers: acclaimed in their time but poorly regarded later on.

McGrath's theory is not ambitious. He identifies patterns of activity in group projects. It's fine, but for most purposes, the typology and the emphasis that all three functions are continually being addressed are a great prism through which to view much research and practice.

Conclusions

Researchers, designers, and acquirers of new technology: Avoid being swept exclusively into the lower left cell. You can't support activity in every cell, but at least briefly *consider* each one. Might your envisioned application disrupt activities in some cells? For example, could anonymous brainstorming undermine credit for ideas that is important to some participants? Also, recognize that it may be difficult to support activities in some cells: Voting mechanisms for resolving conflicts or "I'm confused" indicators to register member distress have not proven to be as useful as hoped. We may prefer to communicate agreement or uneasiness in less overt ways. For those concerned with assessment, be wary of exhortations to adopt metrics, especially if only performance is to be measured. Examine "proofs of ROI" critically.

Any group activity can be viewed through McGrath's prism. For example, to the traditional conference functions of community maintenance and member support, highly selective conferences such as CHI add a production function that was formerly the role of journals. But are group health and member support enhanced by high rejection rates that benefit the lower left cell?

18

Observing Collaboration: Group-Centered Design

Saul Greenberg
University of Calgary, Calgary, Canada

J. Tang, 1989: "Listing, Drawing, and Gesturing in Design: A Study of the Use of Shared Workspaces by Design Teams"

It is the late 1980s. Along with a other technologists, I am just getting interested in the new discipline of computer-supported cooperative work (CSCW), where my focus is on how geographically distributed groups could work together in real time over a shared visual workspace. In the '80s era, groupware design was mostly by the seat of our pants; what we built was often a consequence of balancing our intuitions about the collaborative process against technical considerations.

John Tang's Ph.D. dissertation (Tang 1989) and his various derivative publications (e.g., Tang 1991) changed my view of groupware design, as it introduced the notion of "group-centered" design.

John, who was interning at Xerox PARC, was interested in technical support for small design groups. Instead of just building technology, he decided to observe, describe, and quantify how small groups actually worked together on conceptual design tasks when interacting over shared visual work surfaces such as a whiteboard or table. His approach was strongly influenced and supported by the user-centered researchers at the Xerox PARC System Sciences Laboratory: Deborah Tatar, Sara Bly, Scott Minneman, Lucy Suchman, and Austin Henderson. PARC had also just created some seminal meeting room systems, and was also investigating how people interact across distance through video.

Observational Studies of Shared Work Surfaces

In 1988, Sara Bly performed an observational study of a pair of collaborators that challenged the intuitive "conventional" view of the communal work surface as a medium for creating and storing a drawing artifact. She saw that the drawing process—the actions, uses, and interactions on the drawing surface—were as important to the effectiveness of the collaboration as the final artifact produced (Bly 1988). She also noticed that allowing designers to share drawing space activities increased their attention and involvement. John extended Bly's findings by studying small design groups, who used large sheets of paper as a shared work surface. Some teams placed the paper on a table, while others tacked it to a whiteboard. He made several important observations.

Orientation Drawings made on the table-mounted paper were oriented in different directions. Although people had greater difficulty drawing and perceiving the images, orientation proved a resource for facilitating the meeting. Because drawings faced a particular person, a context and an audience were established. Marks made by participants that were aligned to an image conveyed support and focus. People working on their own image used orientation as an informal "privacy" boundary until they were ready to call in the group's attention. The group using whiteboard-mounted paper did not exhibit these behaviors.

Proximity When participants were huddled around the table-mounted paper, the sketchpad played a key role in mediating the conversation. This role was lessened in the whiteboard situation where people were seated several feet away.

Simultaneous access Given good proximity, a high percentage (45–68%) of work surface activity around the tabletop involved simultaneous access to the space by more than one person.

John then built a descriptive framework to help organize the study of work surface activity, where every user activity was categorized and quantified according to what action and function it accomplished (Tang 1989; Tang 1991). *Actions* included listing spatially independent alphanumeric notes, drawing graphical objects, and making communicative gestures over the surface. *Functions* included storing information for later recall, expressing ideas as one works over the surface, and mediating interaction through turn-taking and by focusing attention. Although this framework seems overly simplistic compared to what is now known, its purpose at the time was to draw attention to the amount of group interactions *not* supported by the CAD (computer-aided design) and group computer tools of that era. John's classification of small group activities within this framework revealed that the "conventional" view of work surface activity—storing information by listing and drawing—constituted only ~25 percent of all work surface activities. Expressing ideas and mediating interaction comprised the additional ~50 percent and ~25 percent respectively. Gesturing, which is often overlooked as a work surface activity, played a prominent role in all work surface actions (~35 percent of all actions). For example, participants enacted ideas by using gestures to express them, and gestures were used to signal turn-taking and to focus the attention of the group. From these observations, he derived various design criteria that shared work surface tools should support. He stressed the importance of allowing people to gesture to each other over the work surface, and emphasized that the process of creating a drawing is in itself a gesture that must be shown to all participants through continuous, fine-grained feedback. Another key point was that the tool must not only support simultaneous activity, but also encourage it by giving participants a common view of the work surface.

System Building

As these results were being revealed, other groups were building multiuser sketching and drawing systems. I and some students (Ralph Bohnet, Dave Webster, Mark Roseman) immediately latched onto John's design principles. We created a distributed groupware bitmap sketching system called GroupSketch, illustrated in figure 18.1 (Greenberg et al. 1992). Its features directly embodied John's design suggestions: each person had a large labeled cursor whose image reflected gesturing, pointing (for attention) and drawing acts; marks made by a person were immediately visible to all; and people could gesture and draw simultaneously. Later versions included the functionally richer XGroupSketch and the object-oriented GroupDraw systems. What was exciting to us was that these systems "felt right"; people (including artists) could use them immediately and dive into their shared drawing tasks.

Other researchers developing parallel systems were also informed by John's ideas. Commune was a pen-based distributed tabletop system and—like GroupSketch—had multiple cursors and immediate display of all actions, and also allowed simultaneous activity. VideoDraw and VideoWhiteBoard from PARC (Tang and Minneman 1990, 1991), and TeamWorkStation from NTT, Japan (Ishii and Kobyashi 1993), were video-based drawing systems that worked by fusing video images. Figure 18.2 illustrates two of them—how they are built, and how people could actually see each other's arms, body shadows, pens, and drawing marks in the image. What was notable is that these and several other systems—even though based on quite different technologies—had the same fluid feel to them. The common human factors of their design transcended their implementations.

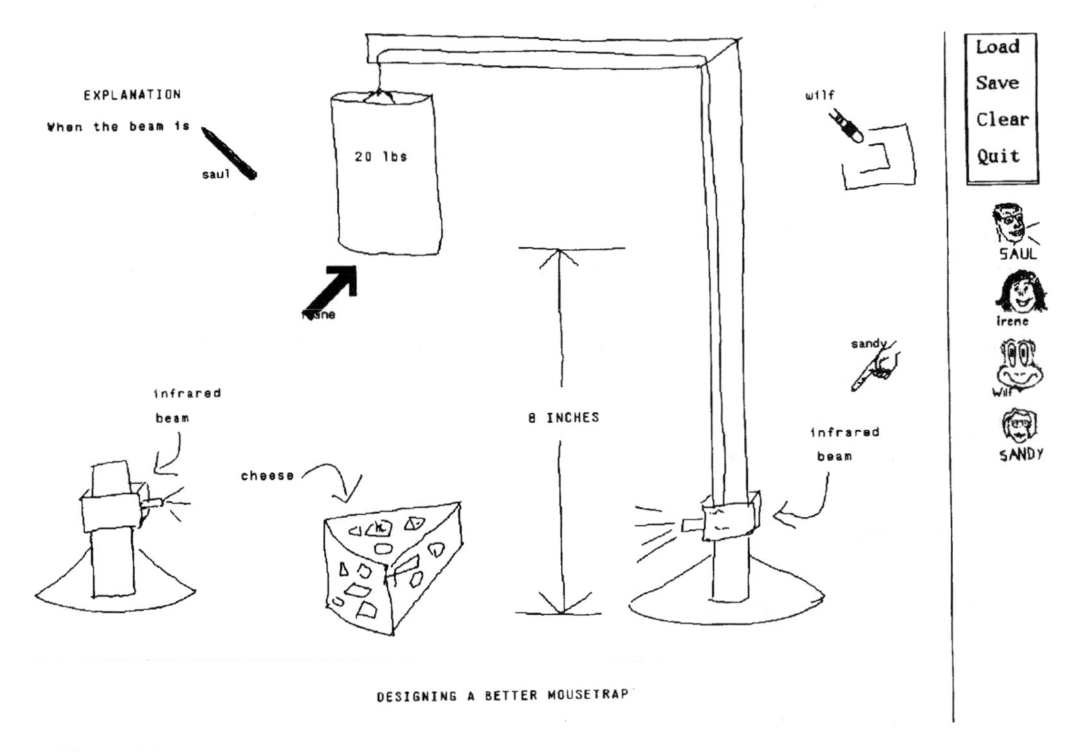

Figure 18.1
GroupSketch (from Greenberg et al. 1992).

Although John's observations and design principles may appear self-evident, many related commercial and research groupware systems of that era (and even of today) have failed to live up to his criteria. Many had no pointers, which meant that users could not gesture around the surface. Neither did participants see each others' actions as they occurred, for actions were not broadcast until a complete graphical stroke was made or a complete text line entered. This meant that people's conversations around their acts of drawing did not make much sense. In contrast to the systems based on John's guidelines, interactions on these systems felt "dead."

Influencing the Future

John's observational work set the tone for much of the shared workspace research in the 1990s. In our lab, we built both distributed and single-display groupware toolkits (e.g., GroupKit, SDGToolkit) that tried to generalize some of his principles,

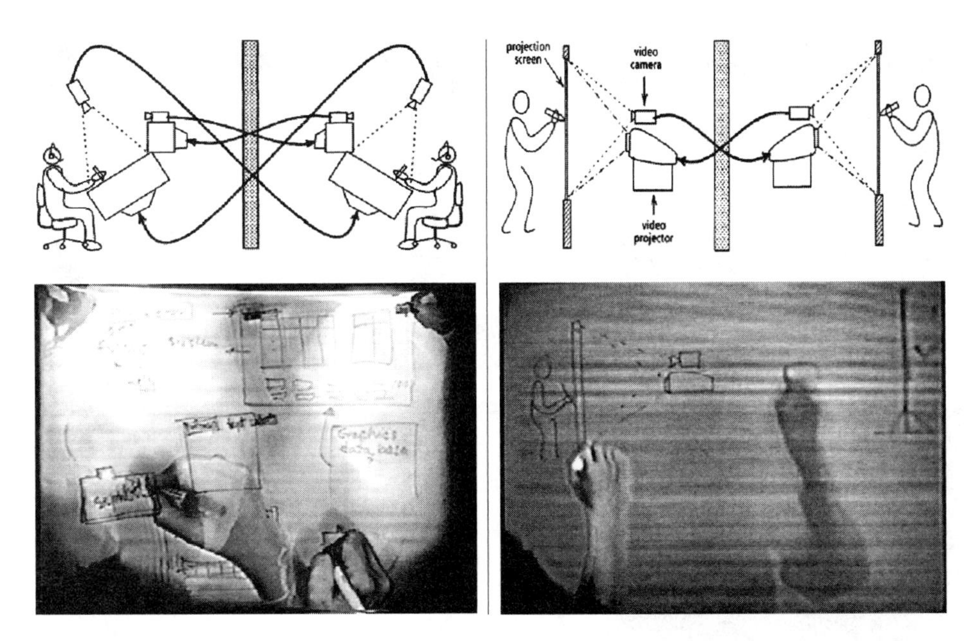

Figure 18.2
The two images on the left show how VideoDraw works (from Tang and Minneman 1990). On the right, the two images show how VideoWhiteboard works (Tang and Minneman 1991). Reprinted with permission from John Tang.

so that programmers had such capabilities as simultaneous actions and multiple cursors "for free." We organized a workshop on real-time drawing, which resulted in a book (Greenberg, Hayne, and Rada 1995). We also started a new research program on *workspace awareness*; we observed the subtleties of how people kept track of what others were doing when working with each other face to face on a drawing, then invented mechanisms that let people re-create this awareness when working over a distance (Gutwin and Greenberg 2002), and finally generalized these as a set of human factors principles articulating the basic mechanical processes that define most collaborative acts over a workspace (Pinelle, Gutwin, and Greenberg 2003).

At the same time, new systems and techniques came out that further leveraged John's work. Several were modeled on the idea of people drawing on opposite sides of a piece of glass, for example, Ishii and Kobyashi's Clearboard (1993), and our own VideoArms (Tang, Neustaedter, and Greenberg 2006). Figure 18.3 shows the latter system, in which we see two groups of multiply colocated people working across two distributed connected surfaces; note that other people's arms are clearly

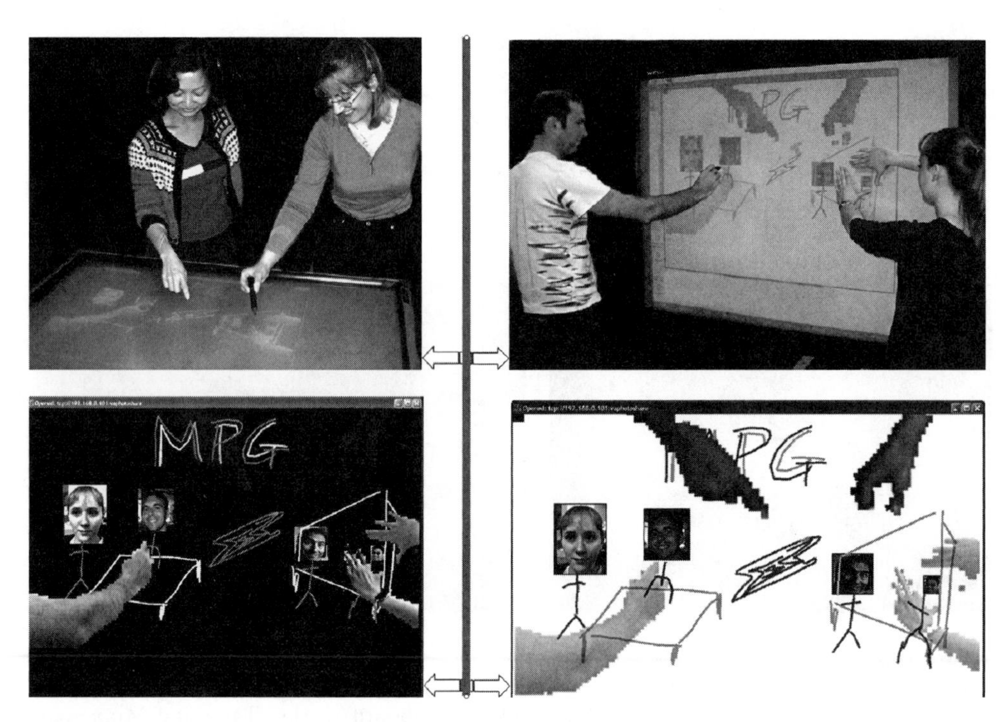

Figure 18.3
VideoArms in action, showing two groups of two people working over two connected displays (top) and a screen grab of each surface (bottom). Local and remote video arms are in all scenes, but local feedback is more transparent.

visible. The groupware community was also busy examining the social psychology literature, which proved to have much fertile information in it that added richness to John's basic observations. More recently, researchers on digital tables for colocated collaborators have also revisited and extended John's work. For example, Sheelagh Carpendale and her group performed further observational studies of how people use the orientation of artifacts on a table as a resource, and how people partition a space into personal and group territories (see, e.g., Kruger et al. 2004).

The Established Paradigm: Observe, Generalize, Design

On reflection, John's work proved important to me, my research group, and the community at large for two reasons. First, it laid the foundations for the basic human factors that play a role in shared visual workspaces, factors that could not only be exploited in system design, but that served as an insight into other human factors that should be considered. Second—and this is more important—it provided an early example of a robust process for groupware development. Beyond the task-oriented observations of single user systems, groupware design must begin with observations of actual working practices. Initial observations will usually expose the major factors that make up not only group task activity, but group processes as well. This suggests ways that factors can be organized and quantified, and also reveals nuances of other factors that could be revisited in later, more detailed studies.

Defining the human factors relevant to collaboration is the key. Design based on these factors should transcend the technology in terms of the collaborative experience it offers the group. As with John's original observations, these factors will have a long "shelf life"; people's collaborative practices today are generally the same as they were seventeen years ago. In contrast, systems and their underlying technologies have arrived, evolved, and been replaced.

19

Infrastructure and Its Effect on the Interface

W. Keith Edwards
Georgia Institute of Technology, Atlanta, Georgia, U.S.A.

S. Greenberg and D. Marwood, 1994: "Real-Time Groupware as a Distributed System: Concurrency Control and Its Effect on the Interface"

With all due respect to Saul Greenberg and David Marwood, one may reasonably forgive an HCI researcher for overlooking a paper when the title contains terms like "concurrency control" and "distributed systems" and "real time." Nevertheless, this paper identifies issues that are central not just to technologists, and not just to people building groupware systems; the issues touched on in this paper are core to the job we do as interaction designers, systems builders, and researchers of the interactions of people and technology.

CSCW'94 marked the first time I presented a paper at the CSCW conference, and my presentation was in the session immediately after Saul and David. So perhaps I was especially open to suggestion because of nerves, but their paper "took" with me, outlining a set of themes that influenced me back in 1994 and are still with me today.

Distributed systems researchers have been designing concurrency control algorithms for years. These are the rules that specify how, when you've got an application that is replicated across many sites, changes to the data get pieced back together into a rational, consistent state. This is low-level stuff, the kind of computer science that scares away not only non–computer scientists, but also a significant number of the people who do claim the mantle of computer scientist for themselves.

Saul and David's point is that this algorithmic minutia, so seemingly removed from the actual user interface, in fact has a deep impact on the sorts of interfaces we can build. Choices like serialization strategy, lock granularity, the use of optimistic versus nonoptimistic protocols, and so on radically affect the user experience of tools that are built on top of this algorithmic infrastructure.

When you think about it, *of course* this is true. Why would anyone suppose otherwise?

Well, the sad truth is that the connection between interaction and infrastructure has been the victim of an almost willful neglect perpetrated by both the HCI and systems communities for years. As Greenberg and Marwood write, "We strongly believe that [technical details of concurrency control] should be user-centered. . . . While this seems obvious, some applications violate this premise simply because *they are designed from a systems-centered viewpoint*" p. 211, (emphasis mine). In other words, the *human-centered* viewpoint is absent when it comes to many of the fundamental technical decisions that determine the interactive experience of the application.

In this light, Greenberg and Marwood's paper isn't so much a discussion of the effects of technical decisions on the interactivity of groupware; rather, it's a call to arms to the HCI community, a call to be involved in those things that are typically just outside our field of view, the things that we cede to those who work further "down the stack" than we do, on the "boring things" (to use Leigh Star's 1999 words) in the computing infrastructure.

This view—that HCI shouldn't be content just to focus on the interface narrowly defined, but can and should touch every aspect of system architecture that affects interactivity—has stuck with me since that presentation in Chapel Hill in 1994.

When I went to Xerox PARC in early 1996, this idea of the impact that infrastructure can have on interactivity kept coming up in the research projects I was working on. Some of these projects built directly on the themes developed by Saul and David in their paper. For example, building on their realization that people *may in fact be perfectly happy* to cope with inconsistencies, I developed an infrastructure to support "inconsistency preserving" applications (Edwards 1997). I unfortunately also gave this paper a title likely to frighten away nontechnologists—mea culpa.

In my work at PARC, these themes surfaced in contexts other than groupware, in domains such as file systems and ubiquitous computing middleware. For example, the Placeless Documents system that my colleagues and I developed (Dourish et al. 2000) can be seen as an attempt to break the hierarchical tyranny of the file system, allowing for on-the-fly creation of organizational structures. Speakeasy (Edwards et al. 2002) is an attempt to design a ubiquitous computing infrastructure that addresses pragmatic concerns about avoiding the hassle of downloading software updates (or the need to replace already purchased equipment) simply to accommodate a new device on the network.

Saul and David point out that "traditional concurrency control methods cannot be applied directly to groupware because system interactions include people as well as computers" (p. 207). Of course, *almost all* software systems include interactions with people as well as computers, and so their arguments apply far more broadly than just groupware. The lack of an HCI voice in these systems is evident. One need look no further than the quagmire that is information security to see that this is true.

Information security is another discipline of computer science that has classically been dominated by a strong systems-theoretical perspective. The research in this area—from new protocols for authentication or secure message passing, to new cryptographic algorithms—has been driven largely by technical concerns (theoretical limits to message security, for instance). Human concerns, when they enter the picture at all, are based on idealized users (the ubiquitous "Alice and Bob") who may have little connection with real-world people, their needs, or understandings (e.g., how well do cryptographic protocols such as zero-knowledge proofs of knowledge fit into social practices, such as the management of self-presentation [Goffman 1959], the "dynamic, dialectic process" of disclosure [Palen and Dourish 2003]).

And yet, just as the underlying concurrency control algorithms affect the user experience, so too do these information security mechanisms. Intentionally or not, these infrastructure notions expose a set of abstractions that *may or may not* match well with human expectations, needs, models, and metaphors. When the abstractions provided by the infrastructure do not match the metaphors which the applications built on them try to support, or the needs of the people who will actually use them, then we see the sorts of usability problems for which information security is infamous.

What is the remedy for the disconnect between low-level infrastructure design and higher-level interaction design? The disconnect exists because neither community sufficiently understands the other's domain, nor do they have good mechanisms for passing requirements up and down the stack to each other. There is the narrowest of pipes connecting those who do "application-layer" work (including interaction designers) and those who do the plumbing; very little information—in the form of design requirements or feedback—passes through this pipe.

I am not suggesting that HCI researchers need to become experts in cryptography, or in distributed systems, or in other topics that have typically been outside our purview. Rather, I am suggesting that we need to develop a new set of metrics that can be adopted by the systems communities to inform their work.

Typically only those requirements that can be described succinctly, and with no ambiguity, survive transmission through the requirements pipe. We tell the plumbers, "if you give us latency of no more than 100ms, the user will perceive the system as being interactive." And off they go, blissfully ignoring other—perhaps even more salient—concerns that are tougher to describe, tougher to build for, tougher to evaluate against. Likewise, when presented with technical concepts in the infrastructure, we application types have few ways to predict the effect they will have on the resulting user experience—until it is too late.

These human requirements are difficult because they can't be boiled down to a single, easy-to-test number; it's not as if there's a single dimension along which we can say that a particular choice is automatically "better" than others. Knowing what to do depends on the application, the needs and understandings of the people who will use it, and their social context. In this sense, knowing what to build at the infrastructure layer is just like all other aspects of interaction design.

To me, the largest question raised by Saul and David's paper is that of how we communicate both up and down the stack: given an infrastructure feature, how can we deduce the user-visible implications of it, and conversely, given a desired interaction, how can we translate that down into system properties? We've been moderately successful so far at covering up ill-suited infrastructure features with interface veneer, but there are limits to how far this can take us. We need to develop practices that allow infrastructure and interaction features to be co-designed. Currently, when this is done at all, it is done ad hoc: while Saul and David do a fine job in their paper, they note that "unfortunately, there is no recipe on how this can be achieved in general" (p. 214).

In 2004 I left PARC to take an academic position. The interdependence of infrastructure and interaction has always been a theme in my research, but it has become its central focus since joining Georgia Tech. My students and I are exploring topics that span the stack. For example, networking research has typically focused on metrics such as bandwidth, latency, and scalability. What if instead we focused on human-centered concerns as the primary motivator? What if other metrics—such as such as installability, understandability, manageability—drove the creation of network protocols and tools? We are also looking at information security: how can we create security technologies that not only support real-world needs, but are understandable by those who use them?

In 1994, Saul and David's paper cogently laid out these issues, using the context of groupware and concurrency control as examples. In the years since the paper was published, the need to artfully balance infrastructure and interaction design has spread far beyond groupware, to any domain where people interact with computing technology—in other words, to any domain touched by HCI.

20

Taking Articulation Work Seriously

Geraldine Fitzpatrick
University of Sussex, Brighton, U.K.

K. Schmidt, and L. Bannon, 1992: "Taking CSCW Seriously: Supporting Articulation Work"

In my annotated bibliography (from my graduate student days when I had the time to keep one), I wrote: "This will be one of the key issues papers in CSCW literature." "This" is Schmidt and Bannon's paper "Taking CSCW Seriously: Supporting Articulation Work" (Schmidt and Bannon 1992).[1] This is also a paper that very much marks the emergence of computer-supported cooperative work (CSCW) as a particular area of research, being the first paper in the first edition of the *Computer Supported Cooperative Work Journal* (JCSCW).

The influence of this paper on my work has been profound. I was new to CSCW (and to all HCI-related fields for that matter, not having had any opportunity to study them as part of my undergraduate computer science degree). I had originally signed up to do a Ph.D. in the area of neural networks but, on the day before applications closed, I came across the term "computer-supported cooperative work" and was so excited about the potential to focus on helping people with how they work that I rewrote my application to be in the field of CSCW, even though I knew nothing about it, nor did anyone in the department. I then had to learn about CSCW from scratch. I started with the first conference proceedings from 1986 and read forward, experiencing firsthand the confusion that Schmidt and Bannon note in how diversely the field was being conceptualized, as evidenced by various terms such as "groups," "teamwork," "groupware," and "business teams."

It was in the context of these more dominant yet diverse conceptualizations that Schmidt and Bannon wanted to set out a different approach by arguing for a conceptualization of CSCW that would focus on "cooperative work," and by laying out a "coherent conceptual framework" with consequent implications for new research directions. This is captured in their definition of CSCW as "*an endeavour to understand the nature and requirements of cooperative work with the objective of designing computer-based technologies for cooperative work environments*" (p. 3), addressing research questions "to *understand* so as to better *support* cooperative work" (p. 5, emphases in the original). In doing so they clearly position CSCW as a multidisciplinary design-oriented field of research rather than a more application-focused field as implied by the term "groupware."

The key concept here is *cooperative work*. Schmidt and Bannon argue that cooperative work is a much more "general and neutral designation [than group or team] of multiple persons working together" that "does not assume or entail specific forms of interaction. (pp. 7, 10). It does, however, entail some *mutual dependence* among the people who need to cooperate and work together. When there is this interdependence there is also an additional layer of work, termed *articulation work* (Strauss 1988), to mediate and manage everyone's activities, for example by allocating tasks, distributing resources, scheduling activities, and so on. Articulation work, in turn, draws attention to the mechanisms that people develop, such as structured forms, scheduling tools, and so on, to help "reduce the complexity and, hence, the overhead cost of articulation work." They variously call these *mechanisms of interaction* or *coordination mechanisms*. Schmidt and Bannon go on in their paper to explore two consequences of taking seriously both interdependence in work and the articulation of this interdependence: how to support the management of workflows and how to support the ongoing active construction of shared understandings through a *common information space*. I leave the details of these discussions for the reader to follow up on.

I experienced my "ah hah" moment about CSCW when I read this paper, and Schmidt and Bannon's definition of it became the hook that defined the area for me—cooperative work as a more encompassing yet specifically implicated unit of analysis, the critical dimension of articulation work, and the iterative multidisciplinary approach of understanding and designing. Before coming across this paper, I had been looking into software process models, workflows and business process reengineering that were all in high fashion in the early 1990s. While Lucy Suchman's seminal work on plans and situated actions (Suchman 1987a) highlighted the reasons why reified models of workflow rarely translated well into practice, it was Bannon and Schmidt's work, specifically the attention they drew to articulation work and its implications for support, that opened up research questions about *how better to understand and support work*.

This led me to investigate further the work of Anslem Strauss, from whom the notion of "articulation work" was drawn, and his newly published "theory of action" (Strauss 1993). His theory provided a coherent, sociologically based framework that not only positioned the notion of articulation work within a much broader set of interactional concepts, but also helped me make sense of many of the diverse concepts and issues emerging from workplace studies being reported in the CSCW literature at the time. This was to become the pivotal text for my own thesis work around the locales framework (Fitzpatrick et al. 1998; Fitzpatrick 2003); it drew heavily on Strauss's work, and it also took seriously Bannon and Schmidt's call to "understand" and "design" by positing the locales framework as a shared abstraction that could support both activities.

The influence of Bannon and Schmidt's paper on the field of CSCW has also been profound. Although the concepts of articulation work, coordination mechanisms, and common information spaces are in a sense just foregrounding different perspectives on the core phenomenon of cooperative work, we can see how each concept has also spawned strands of ongoing research. The authors have taken up their own research call and further developed their ideas of coordination mechanisms (e.g., Schmidt and Simone 1996) and common information spaces (e.g., Bannon and Bødker 1997), in works that are both widely referenced. Strauss's concept of articulation work, largely introduced to CSCW by Schmidt and Bannon, has become a taken-for-granted term and has also become a focus of ongoing research (see, e.g., Grinter 1996). Similarly, "coordination mechanisms" has been drawn on to further explore the role of artifacts in coordination practices (see, e.g., Carstensen and Nielsen 2001) and "common information spaces" has been further developed in various contexts (see, e.g., Bossen 2002). Notions developed from common information space work (e.g., the highly cited paper, Bannon and Kuutti 2002) have also been influential within organizational memory and knowledge management research, highlighting key issues surrounding the work involved in managing and sharing such information spaces.

Interestingly, a lot of the issues raised in this paper are still highly relevant today, especially as we move toward ubiquitous "computer support" that will be more pervasively distributed and embedded in the environment. One of the key issues that CSCW highlights, compared to HCI more generally, is that all work is socially situated (albeit a position that Schmidt and Bannon wanted to strengthen with their emphasis on cooperative work) and that even social situations involve interaction and coordination "work." At the time Schmidt and Bannon wrote their seminal article, offices and white-collar work were the main focus of much CSCW research, and Schmidt and Bannon made a call for researchers to be concerned also with other forms of work, such as manufacturing. Since then the research domains have become even more diverse, with settings such as the home and mixed reality gaming receiving attention, especially as enabled by new mobile and pervasive technologies. Although these settings might not fit Schmidt and Bannon's call for more formally defined notions of work, the need to consider articulation, coordination, and common information spaces still holds, albeit while playing out in different ways. It could be argued that these concepts are even more important in pervasive technology scenarios where we have multiple distributed actors and multiple forms of distributed computation and information that people somehow need to collectively manage, make sense of, and coordinate their interactions with.

It is very timely then to revisit and rethink Schmidt and Bannon's work in relation to pervasive/ubiquitous computing. I would argue that this field is at a very similar stage to that of CSCW in 1992. In ubiquitous computing ("ubicomp"), the work to date has been largely technology led; this has been critical work, necessary for the exploration of what is technically feasible with new and emergent technologies, just as CSCW was initially largely technology led, with groupware developers exploring what was technically feasible with emergent desktop networked computers. Now the question is, how do we go about appropriately designing what is technically feasible into something that is practically acceptable or useful or engaging and that can become part of everyday practices? The concepts laid out in "Taking CSCW Seriously" helped set the agenda for this work in CSCW, and the same concepts can be reworked to help frame an ongoing multidisciplinary research agenda for ubiquitous computing, drawing attention to the roles that ubicomp can play and the work that people will have to do to make ubicomp work. Indeed, a ubicomp environment could alternatively be named a "common information space," with all the same pursuant issues highlighted in the 1992 paper. And Schmidt and Bannon's claim (p. 20) that "the [CSCW] system should make the underlying model accessible to users, and indeed, support users in interpreting the procedure, evaluate its rationale and implications" seems to be all the more important when applied to ubicomp systems that rely on distributed and often automated system interactions on behalf of the user (as a trivial but telling example, think about your experiences in automated bathrooms that try to turn on the taps and flush the toilets for you!).

It will be interesting to see in the years ahead if this will also become one of the key issues papers in ubicomp literature. Even if the paper itself does not make it into ubicomp consciousness, the issues it raises, gaining "taken for granted" status, surely will be key to designing technology that works for people.

Note

1. The genesis of this paper was an earlier Bannon and Schmidt paper, "CSCW: Four Characters in Search of a Context," which was presented at the first European CSCW conference in 1989 (subsequently published in *Studies in Computer Supported Cooperative Work: Theory, Practice and Design*, edited by J. Bowers and S. Benford, 1991). Schmidt and Bannon continued to develop the ideas from this earlier conference paper through discussions with colleagues. Although the resultant JCSCW paper was noted as being "completely re-written with substantively new argumentation and material," it seems only fitting, given its topic of CSCW, that its gestation was highly collaborative.

21

Let's Shack Up: Getting Serious about GIM

David W. McDonald
University of Washington, Seattle, Washington, U.S.A.

L. M. Berlin, R. Jeffries, V. O'Day, A. Paepcke, and C. Wharton, 1993: "Where Did You Put It? Issues in the Design and Use of a Group Memory"

Living with other people is always a challenge. As children we learn to live with a small group of others, our family. That learning takes time as we come to balance our selfish desires with those of our siblings and parents. Often that learning is successful, and when it is, we establish regular patterns, habits, and norms about how space is to be negotiated.

When we choose to share physical space with another person—when we share an apartment with friends, cohabitate with acquaintances, "shack up" with a significant other, or start our own family—our understanding of how to share physical space is challenged anew as we renegotiate how the shared space will be used.

In my case I've lived most of my life with people who are savers; people who like to hold onto stuff. My mother, a community college instructor, taught business and saved textbooks—all kinds of textbooks. You want the third edition of Marwick's *Principles of Accounting*? No problem. Interested in textbooks that cover personal finance from the late 1970s through the early 1990s? No problem, she's got that covered too. And then when I got married—I didn't quite realize it at the time—but I married another saver.

The only real tension in this is that I like to think that I'm a deleter; I just don't like clutter. It has taken me some years of practice, but I'm ruthless with most junk mail and random bits. If it is a catalog, advertisement, solicitation, or anything of that sort, then I consider it for about five seconds, and if I'm not going to use it right then, it is shredded! Quarterly I clean out my office. Once each year I unclutter my parts of our home; I consider the various financial papers, and items in my space—if it is not serving a purpose, it must go!

Negotiating a tension like that between a saver and a deleter is somewhat obvious in shared physical space. I'm not saying that the solution is obvious; but the tangibility of physical objects in a shared space will make the tension clear. When you save physical stuff it starts to accumulate, it piles up. And when you delete or remove physical stuff it is gone. This seemingly simple tension is just one of several consequences of a shared information space—consequences that we have not yet resolved.

In the early 1990s I started my Ph.D. and began working with my advisor Mark Ackerman and another student Brian Starr on the next generation of his organizational memory system Answer Garden 2 (see Ackerman and McDonald 1996). We were doing a version on the World Wide Web (very early Web) and one of my responsibilities was to develop ways to help group members to restructure the information in the system—plant and/or transplant trees and shrubs, for those of you who like to keep up with the analogy.

The paper "Where Did You Put It? Issues in the Design and Use of a Group Memory" had recently been published by Berlin et al. (1993) and was required reading for our research group as we started our design and development. The paper describes the development of a group memory system for their research group. The system was relatively straightforward and included a shared repository with hypertext linking ability and a method to submit items to the repository through email. It had both automatic and user-provided classification that facilitated search and link creation. Users could browse the category scheme to locate items and perform keyword and full text search to locate items.

But the paper also presented an interesting set of side observations. During the development, the research team understood that for their system to support their own needs they would need to settle on a common vocabulary for the data they submitted. The simple task of settling on a controlled vocabulary was not as simple as they had anticipated. As some luck would have it, they videotaped their own design sessions. The analysis of their design sessions revealed some interesting results that highlight key issues for shared information spaces.

First, they found that it was nigh impossible to settle on a universal set of terms to use when organizing their own information. Their admonishment to us is that "It's not enough to agree on a set of categories" (p. 25). This is probably because the nature of a project and its relevant problems shift as a project progresses over time. As well, when conducting research, the terms themselves have not necessarily been created; what do you call something before everyone agrees on a term for the thing? They point out in the paper that even after they had settled on some category terms they faced a recurrent problem of reconciling individual tendencies with the agreed-on group norm. People do not change their personal tendencies even if they happen to agree with the group.

The issue that Berlin et al. raise with categories is interesting given the current interest in *tagging* systems, also known as *folksonomic classification*. Large-scale Web-based systems such as Flickr.com and del.icio.us have popularized user-defined metadata or *tags*. These are strings of text that provide additional meta-data for an object like a picture or another Web page. Tags can be searched and clustered much like any other categorization scheme, except in this case the scheme is created by the distributed efforts of many individuals. Tagging has shown some promising characteristics that could overcome the problems identified by Berlin et al. but tagging is not without its own problems (Golder and Huberman 2006; Guy and Tonkin 2006).

Berlin et al. found that their small group exhibited a wide range of personal information management practices. That is, the way they engaged the problem of storing, organizing, and refinding their information differed—even in their small group! Generalizing just a bit, they identified five dimensions along which individuals differ when working with information.

Purist to proliferator A purist generally believes that each item belongs in its one place, whereas a proliferator believes that items naturally belong in multiple places.

Semanticist to syntacticist A semanticist believes that each item has intrinsic categories that are obvious given inspection of the item itself. A syntacticist considers the context of an item as critical to the way it should be categorized and retrieved.

Scruffy to neatnik A scruffy prefers coarse, fat categories with potentially many items, whereas a neatnik prefers many fine-grained and often hierarchical categories.

Saver to deleter A saver prefers to keep many things, including items that might be tangentially valuable. A deleter wants to limit clutter and keep only essential information.

Purpose-based filing This last dimension characterizes how individuals classify items based on how they anticipate the item will be used at some point in the future.

This one seems a bit more binary than the other dimensions, and it is mentioned here for completeness.

The critical challenge for any shared information system is to account for the wide range of user approaches to saving, organizing, and refinding the information. Berlin and her colleagues had a term for the problem of accommodating all of these different styles: cognitive cohabitation. Clearly, our behavior in a shared information system is somehow a reflection of our individual style (cognitive or otherwise), and getting different styles to live together in an information system is a challenge of cohabitation. The challenges of *cognitive cohabitation* are, perhaps, not too different from the challenges of learning to live together in a shared physical space—but they lack all of the social cues and certainly many of the physical cues.

The Berlin et al. piece influenced our group's thinking about how shared information systems work and how people "cognitively cohabitate" in everyday life. As we designed the system that would eventually become Answer Garden 2 we were careful to consider how to support different views of the same information space, how to support different styles of contribution, and how to support gradually diverging models of interaction with the system. For example, users could initially share the same view of an information repository, but as one or another made changes, another person could be shown those changes and decide if he or she wanted to keep them or not. We didn't specify what to do as views continued to diverge, but allowing the views to diverge was an interesting contribution to the development of shared repositories.

The subtle influence of this piece continued through some of my thesis work and my development of the Expertise Recommender (McDonald and Ackerman 2000; McDonald 2001, 2003). In particular, our notions of how the social milieu reflects and shapes expectations of individuals' expertise can be viewed as a social manifestation of cognitive cohabitation.

Yet, still, the Berlin et al. paper has perhaps been underappreciated by researchers who study and build shared information systems. The dimensions that the paper outlines form a veritable cornucopia of research possibilities. The challenge of understanding how groups organize information could have a profound impact on the design of file systems and shared information stores. Even researchers in human information behavior have not directly addressed these dimensions; instead they mostly opt for a scientific rationalist view of information needs, including searching and retrieval behaviors.

During the last few years we have seen the development of a new area known as PIM (personal information management). Approaches to PIM can be organized along two general lines: improved search and improved structure. One approach to PIM is largely based on search and retrieval techniques. Motivated by the success of Google and other "network influence"–based algorithms, the basic stance of researchers promoting this approach is that one can solve personal information management problems with better search. The jury is still out on this. In fact, some recent results suggest that people are quite attached to the information-organizing structures that they create for themselves.

The second approach is to develop tools to improve the structuring of the information. Researchers taking this approach recognize that the predominant strategy for structuring information is based on the hierarchical file systems supported by modern operating systems. This approach recognizes the need to support other organizational schemes, but it is often hamstrung by the existing technical constraints of the current operating system (Dourish et al. 2000).

From my perspective both approaches overlook something important. As someone who considers groups and their information-sharing practices a fundamental problem for systems, I find the principle drawback to both approaches to be that they focus largely on individuals. Sure, it is good to help individuals with their solo information problems. But for me, some of the most valuable work we accomplish is accomplished only through collaboration. That is, the way I see it, a fundamental characteristic of our work and social lives is the exchange and sharing of something important to us—information sharing.

This implies that the real challenge for researchers, designers, and developers is to support a diverse range of behaviors when groups cognitively cohabitate—when they shack up in a shared information space. The Berlin et al. paper was not just about a specific group or organizational memory system; indeed it remains one of the earliest articulations of challenges for GIM (group information management; Erickson 2006) as distinct from the current framing of PIM. This is not specific to work systems but rather pervades our day-to-day interactions with information. This may be a source of the problems with tagging systems (folksonomies) described earlier.

What can we do to resolve these problems? Certainly, a better understanding of the dimensions described by Berlin et al. would be a good start. In particular, we should maintain a focus on the everyday information practices of groups currently using shared information spaces. File shares and shared Web spaces are widely available but often seem to be frustrating for groups. It is also instructive to see how critical group-reflection on collective practices can provide important insights. Finally, self-reflection can provide some important distinctions between the group's information practices and our own.

Applying that same self-reflection I ask myself how can I resolve the challenge of being a deleter who happens to live with savers? Really, this is not as bad as it sounds. I understand why they are savers. I recognize that I'm a product of my environment—over the years I've learned when to say something about it and when to just let it go. As well, since I'm a product of my environment, I recognize that I too have saver tendencies. Perhaps I'm just masquerading as a deleter, and my email reveals how bad I am at the masquerade.

22

A CSCW Sampler

Leysia Palen
University of Colorado, Boulder, Colorado, U.S.A.
University of Aarhus, Denmark

E. Francik, S. E. Rudman, D. Cooper, and S. Levine, 1991: "Putting Innovation to Work: Adoption Strategies for Multimedia Communication Systems"

Before the advent of the World Wide Web in 1993, which propelled computing as a social phenomenon into popular consciousness, the world of information technology had been experiencing a slower but ongoing shift in focus from single-user to multiple-user, networked applications. A 1991 article by Ellen Francik, Susan Ehrlich Rudman, Donna Cooper, and Stephen Levine of Wang Laboratories—"Putting Innovation to Work: Adoption Strategies for Multimedia Communication Systems"—was among the first such studies to describe, in a comprehensive fashion, the deployment of a real-world groupware system at a level of insight and discourse that offered practical information about the nature of adoption problems and strategies for how they might be overcome. The article examines the introduction of the Wang Freestyle system into office places and discusses its design and intended uses as well as the problems encountered in its deployment.

Freestyle, released at COMDEX 1988, was a sophisticated multimedia messaging system that ran on networked PCs. The system was built on a central design that allowed any kind of digital document to be annotated using stylus-and-tablet-supported freehand writing along with synchronized voice annotations. Annotated documents could be stored on a desktop that allowed for personalized information filing and organization, relying on what Nielsen (1989) called the "desktop metaphor to the third degree": file icons were simply miniature versions of the real documents themselves, and could be freely moved about on the desktop interface and even "stapled" together. Annotated documents could be emailed to other Freestyle users, who could then replay the voice annotations synchronized with reanimated written annotations. Documents could also be faxed or printed for workers or work groups who did not have the system and for use in downstream paper-based work processes. Similarly, paper-based documents could be scanned into the system to allow for subsequent digital manipulation.

As one of the first articles I read during my graduate training a little more than two years after it was published, this paper provided an early "aha" moment because it crystallized many lessons I struggled to understand from what seemed like more removed accounts of groupware use and failure. Here was an exciting, email-like but sophisticated and well-tested groupware system that had trouble being adopted in the workplace. Why was this so? "Putting Innovation to Work," in contrast with other papers for me at the time, provided an accessible account of its adoption problems, linking organizational and institutional obstacles with affordances and demands of system design. After struggling with an academic move from cognitive studies to more socially defined studies of technology use, I found that this paper helped me appreciate some of the core sociotechnical mechanisms at work in a real-world groupware deployment.

For example, the paper explains how low-level workers—not managers—might be the ones who needed the more sophisticated (and therefore more expensive systems) to help them do their work. Pointing to the critical relationship between work practice and technology adoption, the authors found that stylus use and annotation creation added a new element to some types of work practice that was often hard for workers to adapt to, but was highly conducive to and supportive of other types of work, including design and engineering. A similar finding—that different kinds of workers and work groups need different ways of organizing information—was one reason for Freestyle's highly flexible desktop. In a last example, the paper points out that informal or "unstructured" peer-to-peer communication, which Freestyle supported, was hard to "see" in daily business life and therefore appreciate as important—meaning that the benefits of Freestyle were in turn not clearly visible to the business enterprise.

As a summary of such analyses, the authors presciently noted (p. 62) that

> each CSCW product develops its own architectural [i.e. design] strengths and weaknesses as designers make trade-offs. These design decisions have organizational effects.

This seemingly simple observation about the relationship between design and environment is nevertheless one that is not always recognized, and it is an example of the analytical integration of perspectives this article offers. Rather than treat the challenge of adoption as a problem rooted purely in system design, or alternatively as a problem rooted only in matters of organizational "culture" where the "system" is black-boxed analytically, this analysis of Freestyle's problems included an appreciation for how feature design could influence behavior, as well as how organizational constraints might mean that people use the system differently than designers expected or perhaps resist it altogether.

This point stayed with me and became a central one in my dissertation research, where I considered the differences in how groupware calendar systems were used in two global high-tech companies. In one case, the default privacy settings were such that the "world" of the network could see the detailed contents of individual calendars. In the other, the default privacy settings allowed people to see only the free and busy times in calendars. In both cases, well over three-quarters of users maintained the default settings, leading to very different uses of the system not just individually and interpersonally, but organizationally as well—an effect not likely predicted by the original developers of what were first systems with small audiences (Palen 1999).

"Putting Innovation to Work" also serves as a historical landmark. How the authors described their role in the design and deployment of the system reflected a larger change that was occurring within the human–computer interaction community at that time (Grudin 2005). The authors explained how human factors specialists, as they identified themselves, must take into account larger matters of organizational structure and behavior (p. 59):

> the human factors team advocated design changes to encourage adoption, while at the same time provided organizational consulting.

Their need to understand organizational issues signaled a time of real change, of a shift, to borrow from Bannon, from "human factors to human actors":

> Understanding people as "actors" in situations, with a set of skills and shared practices based on work experience with others, requires us to seek new ways of understanding the relationship between people, technology, work requirements, and organizational constraints in work settings. (Bannon 1992, p. 25)

The Francik et al. paper manages in a short amount of space to pointedly highlight the issues raised by Bannon, making them, to a young student of CSCW, quite real. The very idea of "design" was expanding: it was clear that this award-winning system required just as careful "deployment design" as "interaction design" if it had a chance of being used in the real world.

I consider the Francik et al. paper to be a kind of CSCW "sampler" because it covers many of the critical issues that the field has identified and studied. It references the big issues of critical mass, power structures, and emphasizes work practice over work process. Although the world of computing continues to change—costs have diminished, users have more experience, and computing is increasingly ubiquitous—some basic core lessons from this paper remain: design of groupware systems needs to reflect and support both individual and group work, a lesson I carried into my dissertation work on calendar systems. The most important communication to support often consists in the informal acts that make cooperative activity actually work. Work occurs across different kinds of media, and across different kinds of groups in any given organization, which may be differentially supported by a single system, which in turn needs to accommodate these differences. And, two points that dictate a very different kind of deployment strategy from what is often first sought: power-users of information and communication technology (ICT) are often the clerical staff, not management; and group interaction is not best anticipated by organizational charts.

In spite of these contributions, and though it also appeared later in the Baecker et al. 1995 HCI reader, "Putting Innovation to Work" has drawn less attention than other CSCW papers on system deployment. For example, an important and well-loved piece, Wanda Orlikowski's "Learning from Notes," appeared one year later, but received far more notice, even though some of its contributions are similar.[1] For example, Orlikowski explains that successful acquisition means

> ensuring that prospective users have an appropriate understanding of the technology, that is, that their technological frames reflect a perception of the technology as a collective rather than a personal tool. (Orlikowski 1992, p. 368)

Francik et al. similarly discovered that the customer "tendency [was] to focus on individuals' use of the system" (p. 56) and that less attention was paid to group communication:

> The system's appeal for individuals could not justify the purchases needed for critical mass. . . .
>
> Unlike single-user applications, CSCW systems must meet the needs not just of many separate individuals but of entire groups. (1991, pp. 56, 62)

Orlikowski's paper is outstanding. But the prescient findings from "Putting Innovation to Work" also make it worthy, I feel, to be situated among a set of groupware adoption papers that are important markers of CSCW's intellectual history.

Ellen Francik, Susan Ehrlich Rudman,[2] and their Wang colleagues, in this paper and elsewhere, offered valuable insight during the early days of multiuser application design and deployment. Regrettably, one of those voices is now silent. Dr. Rudman, before her untimely passing in 2003, developed a significant body of work on online communication systems, including papers on scheduling and calendaring systems that influenced my thinking and again demonstrated the link between design and organizational use (Ehrlich 1987a, b). She continued her innovative work on communications systems at US WEST's Advanced Technologies Lab, marrying her insight with real, practical design and deployment. It is that ability and analytical skill that is reflected in "Putting Innovation to Work." Though the paper addresses matters of technology use in a work environment, it continues to offer to students of collaborative computing today clear and accessible identification of some of the "big problems" that are encountered in any significant deployment of a collaboration-support system.[3]

Notes

1. At the time of this writing, the "Learning from Notes" paper had over 550 citations according to Google Scholar (http://scholar.google.com/; searched 12 May 2006), whereas "Putting Innovation to Work" had about 50—an order of magnitude of difference.

2. Susan Ehrlich Rudman also published under the names Susan Ehrlich and Carrie Rudman.

3. This manuscript was prepared while the author was on sabbatical from the University of Colorado and employed by the Center for Interactive Spaces at the University of Aarhus (Denmark).

23

Video, Toys, and Beyond Being There

Brian K. Smith
The Pennsylvania State University, University Park, Pennsylvania, U.S.A.

J. Hollan and S. Stornetta, 1992: "Beyond Being There"

My mother was diagnosed with leukemia in February 2005 and was immediately admitted to a California hospital to undergo chemotherapy. She was obviously concerned about her illness, but she was more disappointed that she could not be in Pennsylvania to meet my first daughter, Samantha, who had been born two days after her diagnosis. In the best case, she would have been in the waiting room to see her first grandchild just after her birth. Since her health made travel impossible, she had to wait a few hours for me to get to a computer and upload digital photographs to my Web site. Not a bad substitute, but nothing can compare to "being there" for a grandmother.

We shifted from photographs to video conferencing once my daughter moved into her new home. My mother couldn't be in Pennsylvania to hold her granddaughter, but she could spend a year watching her learn to hold her head up, sit on her own, and crawl over to the camera to give kisses. It wasn't "being there," but it was the best we could do.

Somewhere during the year of video conferencing, I was reminded of a paper by Jim Hollan and Scott Stornetta (1992) entitled "Beyond Being There." I first read the paper in a graduate human–computer interaction course taught by Louis Gomez, not long after its initial publication. It seemed like a warning to researchers developing computer-mediated communication (CMC) at the time. They described developers' intentions to create systems that could provide rich interactions similar to face-to-face (F2F) conversation, a gold standard they referred to as "being there." The "beyond" in the title of their paper challenged the HCI community to develop CMC tools that people prefer to use *even* when given the option of communicating face-to-face.

My mother was perfectly happy to watch her granddaughter's growth on a fifteen-inch screen during her chemotherapy, but she certainly didn't resort to her computer when they finally met in person. Video was a good surrogate for face-to-face interaction, but "being there" allowed Grammy to hug, kiss, and play with her baby. Even smelling dirty diapers seemed like a treat during their occasional face-to-face meetings.

Hollan and Stornetta provided an analogy for thinking about telecommunications tools that involved comparing crutches and shoes. A person who injures a leg often uses crutches to assist mobility, but he will stop using them once he returns to full health. However, humans wear shoes regularly, because they facilitate mobility better than does running around barefoot. CMC tools like video conferencing were described as crutches for communication, rather than shoes, as they provide temporary value until physical contact can be established. No grandmother would ever consider video conferencing when she could be sitting face-to-face with her loved ones.

Beyond Being There Revisited

"Beyond Being There" eventually challenged researchers to design communication tools that contribute added value to face-to-face interactions. This challenge essentially revisits ideas previously articulated by Vannevar Bush (1945), Douglas Engelbart (1962), J. C. R. Licklider (1960), Marshall McLuhan (1994), Ted Nelson (1974), and other proponents of computation as a means to augment human performance. Like those researchers, Hollan and Stornetta were interested in designing tools to *extend* human communication capacities rather than to *replace* face-to-face interactions.

More specifically, Hollan and Stornetta argued that the ways computational media support asynchronous, anonymous, and automatically archived communications could provide interactions superior to F2F. They provided a number of examples that are taken for granted now, sixteen years after the paper's publication. They describe "ephemeral interest groups": these are what we currently see in newsgroups, Weblogs (blogs), and Wikis. Their "meeting others" example are today's home pages on the Web and sites like Myspace and Facebook where individuals share personal information in communal settings. Their ideas concerning automatically archiving activities have been realized in projects like Classroom 2000 (Abowd 1999) and MyLifeBits (Gemmell et al. 2002).

There are many examples of CMC tools designed for distributed communication that also enhance face-to-face interactions. For instance, I was in a face-to-face meeting at a major computer company a few years ago. As various people took turns giving presentations at the front of the room, everyone else sat typing behind their laptops, commenting on what was being said over instant messaging (IM). Although we were all face-to-face, IM provided ways for us to have productive metaconversations about the ongoing discussions.

Similarly, I've been using 37signals LLC's Basecamp[1] application in my research and teaching for over a year. Basecamp is essentially a Web-based project management system that allows people to share files, generate to-do lists and milestones, and post messages. My research group creates and stores all of our content and discussions asynchronously. Since these are automatically archived, the tool is invaluable during face-to-face meetings when we need to retrieve documents, update milestones and to-do lists, and coordinate future goals based on past progress.

To use Hollan and Stornetta's analogy, IM and Basecamp are more like shoes than crutches (at least in my daily routines). Despite the focus on communications, the paper's main argument—enhancing versus mimicking human performance—can be applied to many areas of computational design. For instance, search engines aren't communication tools per se, but I often see students "googling" terms as I introduce them in my classroom teaching. Google and other search engines actually allow me to conduct better student-centered teaching, as I can throw out broad concepts and know that students will research them and share their findings during the class period.

The challenge posed to designers in "Beyond Being There" is to develop systems that are in some sense more revolutionary than evolutionary in their ability to enhance human performance or needs. Those needs can take many forms, including communication, productivity, and learning. My students and I have tried to live up to Hollan and Stornetta's challenge over the years by designing opportunities for face-to-face learning that emerge as a result of the presence of computational tools. For instance, we've developed systems that act as conversational props in medical interviews (Smith et al. 2007). Our visualizations synchronize physiological data with patient photographs of their behaviors: the resulting visuals allow nutritionists and other medical practitioners to see relationships between behavior and health and to better prescribe treatments and alternative routines during face-to-face consultations.

Terms like "emotional design" and "experience design" have recently become part of the HCI vocabulary (e.g., McCarthy and Wright 2004; Norman 2003). Researchers in these areas argue that we do more than *use* computation: We *live* with it. Those lived experiences have rational/intellectual components, but there are also emotional/sensual aspects of working with technology. "Beyond Being There" captured the rational/intellectual side by calling for the design of machinery that people would want to use at all times. However, emotional/sensual side effects of computation may lead people to use certain systems more than others, perhaps to the point of beyond being there that Hollan and Stornetta's described.

In studies of our health visualizations, we were surprised to see some patients describing their difficulties coping with illness. These were often emotional discussions tied to the data they had collected and explained in front of computer monitors. Hollan and Stornetta did not mention that computer systems are often used in unanticipated ways. Opportunistic uses of computation may lead people to find utility that is beyond being there, regardless of a designer's intentions. We designed our software to elicit rational/intellectual discussions between patients and physicians, but the unexpected emotional discourse around the software is perhaps more important for both parties.

Video provided a way for my mother to "be there" with my daughter. It was effective, but she relied on a different form of computation when she was face-to-face with her granddaughter. That device was developed by Leapfrog, a toy called Learning Friend Lily (figure 23.1). Lily sings songs about numbers, colors, and objects on her clothing when her torso and feet are squeezed. The song lyrics ("Hi, I'm Lily, and you can count on me") and melodies are simple enough for kids to remember and memorable (or perhaps, annoying) enough to stick in parents' heads.

I imagine that Learning Friend Lily's designers believed that young children would be the primary users of the toy, but my daughter's love for the doll spilled over to the rest of my family. Lily came with us when we traveled to see my mother at her home or in the hospital, and we all sang and danced to the counting songs with my daughter. Lily was much more than a simple computer toy: she provided common ground for my mother and daughter to sing and play together. More so, I saw my mother disappear when she was with Lily: she became a grandmother as she squeezed and sang along with Lily.

At one point during my mother's final weeks of life, a nurse came out of her room and told us to prepare for the worst. My mother was babbling and referring to herself as another person, a typical sign that the end was near. A family friend went to the bed to listen to my mother who was quietly singing, "Hi, I'm Lily, and you can count on me . . ." She lasted two more weeks singing that song, presumably thinking of her granddaughter every time she did.

Figure 23.1
The best medicine for a sick grandmother was playing with her granddaughter and their favorite toy, Leapfrog's Learning Friend Lily.

Video conferencing allowed my mother and daughter to simulate "being there," but Lily played a central role in their face-to-face interactions. I was—and remain—surprised by the impact a doll had on my mother simply because it was an object that my daughter grew to love. When it came time to view my mother's body, I put a Lily doll with her and started it up. Upon hearing the signature tune, my daughter started dancing and singing along (as best as a one-year-old can). I'm sure my mother smiled and laughed from above seeing her baby dancing in a funeral home (I know I did).

Computers play an important role in the human experience, and I suspect Hollan and Stornetta would discuss the emotional dimensions of technology if they were to rewrite "Beyond Being There" today. All sorts of gadgets surrounded my mother, but none were as meaningful as her video camera and my daughter's Lily doll in her final year. Video let her be there with her granddaughter; Lily allowed them to go beyond being there when face-to-face. Whether being there or beyond, I revisit Hollan and Stornetta's paper when designing new projects to remind myself that one goal of computational design should be to enhance human experiences, both intellectual and emotional.[2]

Notes

1. See http://www.basecamphq.com/.

2. Thanks to Louis Gomez for introducing me to "Beyond Being There" in his HCI course, to Samantha for showing me a new way to appreciate computation, and to my mother for inspiring me to go beyond for thirty years and more.

V

Reflective Practitioners

One challenge of interaction design is the speed with which things change. Technology advances, media evolve, and work practices adapt—the rates of change can often be measured in months or years rather than decades. A core competency in interaction design is understanding how to approach new technologies or media and how to use known media in new ways. The essays in this section are by reflective practitioners and are about work by reflective practitioners. They examine how designers have approached designing technologies for voice, graphics, animation, video, and information spaces. They consider problems ranging from how to design something before the technology exists to how to come to grips with an unfamiliar design terrain.

The first two essays provide contrasting answers to these questions. Chris Schmandt's essay describes the development of the "Wizard of Oz" technique by John Gould and his colleagues, and reminds us of the immense amount of work that went on "behind the curtain" during their study of a simulated listening typewriter. In contrast, in "Seeing the Hole in Space," Steve Harrison describes the early interactive artwork by Kit Galloway and Sherri Rabinowitz that opened a real-time video connection between sidewalks in New York and Los Angeles, and reflects on the role of art in advancing our ideas about technology and its possibilities. Next, we move into the realm of visual design. Scott Jenson discusses Edward Tufte's "1 + 1 = 3" visual design principle and, inspired by a mishap in an elevator, considers its general applicability to interaction design. In the next essay Jodi Forlizzi describes the intersection of computation and typography fostered by Muriel Cooper, and the subsequent development of kinetic typography. From visual design we move into territory more familiar to mainstream HCI, with Steve Whittaker's reexamination of Allison Kidd's "The Marks Are on the Knowledge Worker," and Paul Aoki's discussion of "Voice Loops" by Watts and colleagues. The section concludes with Paul Resnick's "Decomposing a Design Space," in which he reminds us that, in addition to his foundational work on Fisheye Views, George Furnas's paper made a further contribution in its use of a design space as an analytical framework.

24

A Simulated Listening Typewriter: John Gould Plays Wizard of Oz

Chris Schmandt
MIT Media Lab, Cambridge, Massachusetts, U.S.A.

J. Gould, J. Conti, and T. Hovanyecz, 1983: "Composing Letters with a Simulated Listening Typewriter"

In the early 1980s I had the fortune to design and build some of the first speech-based conversational human interfaces, in projects such as "Put That There" and "Phone Slave." My "fortune," in part, was access to $70,000 speech recognition equipment; that price provided near real-time recognition of five words spoken together, out of a vocabulary of 120 words.

Although many industrial and academic researchers at this time were developing speech recognizers, which would of course become cheaper and better, the high cost of early hardware kept speech systems at the periphery of HCI research. Although quite enthusiastic about speech input, I believed it was essentially error-prone, necessitating appropriate interfaces applied to domains where the benefit of hands-free operation outweighs limited recognizer accuracy. With my computer science education I could decode the digital signal processing (DSP) math in the speech algorithm publications, but I nonetheless felt somewhat of an outlier in the HCI community, where few were exploring actual speech interfaces. Then I met John Gould.

Evaluating a Device Before It Exists

By the late 1970s speech recognition was just starting to migrate from research to product; that $70,000 recognizer I used in 1980 was the top of the line. Products were computationally limited, although specialized digital signal processors appeared around 1980 and soon improved performance. Indeed, the glamour at the time was in algorithm development, be it DSP techniques, methods of characterizing speech, or efficient language modeling for very large-vocabularies. Speech recognition was improving and becoming more available, but, especially with hindsight, the rate of progress was exaggerated.

Yet, if one adopted a speaking style conducive to recognition, it was a thrill to control a computer with one's own voice. What excitement for a young HCI researcher! I was certain that appropriate user interfaces would allow error-prone recognition to be useful to certain communities in some situations. John Gould wanted to prove it.

John worked at IBM's Watson research center, which was also the home of IBM's flagship large-vocabulary continuous speech recognition project, under Fred Jelinek. Researchers were building dictation-style systems that would be able to create text documents from speech, without a keyboard. This was a large (twenty-year) and ambitious project; and, as with all speech recognition work, it faced several tradeoffs. First, the greater the number of words to recognize, the harder the recognition task, as more and more words begin to sound similar as vocabulary size grows. Second, we slur words together in "connected speech," but it is much easier computationally to recognize "discrete speech," in which the talker pauses, unnaturally, between each word.

John's research, summarized in a dense but succinct paper (Gould, Conti, and Hovanyecz 1983), tried to answer questions such as:

Would people enjoy using recognition for dictation?

Would such a system be speedy and efficient?

Could naive users dictate high-quality documents?

What are the usability tradeoffs between vocabulary size and speaking style (connected vs. discrete)?

As editing commands may be confused with input text, are there differences between composing drafts and "first time final" documents?

How would these results change once potential users gained experience with the technology?

It was impossible to evaluate actual recognizers; they were not yet robust enough. So John developed what later became known as the "Wizard of Oz" technique, in which a hidden human manipulates a computer interface under evaluation, without knowledge of the subjects. Specifically, a subject spoke into a microphone in front of a computer monitor, and a skilled typist in another room listened in and typed the text. An algorithm intervened before text was displayed to enforce the characteristics of different classes of simulated recognizers. The typed words were filtered against lexicons of 1000, 5000, or unlimited vocabulary; a word out of vocabulary was replaced with "••."[1] When a discrete speech recognizer was being simulated, the subject's audio was muted for a few seconds every time the typist started entering a word.

The paper describes two similar experiments; in each, subjects were asked to compose letters making requests, such as a job or grant application, using various simulated recognizer configurations, and different composing methods (draft or first-time-final). Subjects used all the different configurations, which were compared using within-subject metrics for speed, length of the letter and its "effectiveness," and subjects' self-expressed preferences. In the first experiment, subjects also composed letters by hand, to establish a baseline. Effectiveness was partially based on rank ordering by English teachers judging whether a reader might grant the request. These subjects, who were inexperienced with dictation, participated for two days each.

Dictation in itself is not new, and in fact contemporary (in 1983) users of dictation were most likely the early adopters and most perceptive critics of a computerized replacement. In the second experiment, subjects were experienced IBM executives who routinely dictated to tape or directly to secretaries taking shorthand. These experienced users also composed baseline letters using both conventional dictation equipment and a secretary taking shorthand during their day-long participation.

Concise tables and graphs in the paper summarize the voluminous data. It is striking (and, I think, testimony to John's thoroughness) that subjects participated for long durations; this lends credence to the results. Many results were consistent with hypotheses, simply quantifying the expected (e.g., larger vocabulary is better, and connected speech is the preferred input modality). It is noteworthy that the masquerading of human as computer system—the Wizard-of-Oz approach—seemed entirely convincing to the subjects. This is described repeatedly, in discussing both naive and experienced subjects, thereby supporting the validity of "simulation" for evaluating interfaces preceding full hardware or software development. Today, this technique is common, but imagine how refreshingly novel it was twenty-three years ago!

This experiment also reveals the importance of between-subject variability. Especially in the first (naive users) experiment, variability of composition time was much greater between subjects than between conditions. And this is an important variable; the judges' ratings were correlated with composition time. For the experienced dictators, between-subject variability of composition time was half that of naive subjects, and the judges found their compositions to all be of similar quality.

Interestingly, the naive users found the small vocabulary size condition more frustrating than that of discrete speech input. I found this surprising, as I have always had trouble speaking in isolated words, except when responding to discourse in which the system takes the initiative. This may, however, have been an artifact of the experiment. With discrete input, subjects received immediate feedback as to whether their input was within vocabulary and recognized. With connected speech the error might not be noticed until several words had been spoken, and editing commands were quite limited. Furthermore, the experienced dictators found discrete input less desirable than connected for each vocabulary size tested.

The naive users of the first experiment would rapidly become expert users if they adopted recognition once it became available. Although many results for the practiced dictators were consistent with those of the naive subjects, there were some telling differences.

Although the experienced subjects worked well with the better recognition conditions, their remarks were not nearly as "enthusiastic" and pointed out more weaknesses of the simulated recognizer configurations. They were more bothered by both limited vocabularies and discrete input. Although they enjoyed seeing their results as they spoke and not having to worry about word spelling,[2] they consistently found the recognition conditions to be annoyingly slower than the dictation to which they were accustomed. In other words, inevitable limitations of the technology are a significant limitation to its utility, after some initial period in which computer-assisted dictation is more highly rated.

The implications to research in recognition algorithms were several. First, vocabulary size is critical. Second, the integration of editing with text input must be addressed. Finally, although the listening typewriter is an attractive invention, its perceived performance will be critical to acceptance.

The Legacy of This Paper

What does nearly twenty-five years of hindsight reveal about this paper? Most striking is the success of its "simulation" or Wizard-of-Oz methodology, a technique John Gould had already been developing in previous studies. It is now a well-established and accepted method of evaluating emerging technology, although, unfortunately, today many studies draw conclusions after much less exposure time to subjects.

Equally important are issues in human factors of speech recognition systems, for dictation and more general use. Predicted problems with small vocabulary size and discrete input delayed the deployment of dictation products, and not surprisingly early discrete speech products were not very successful. But now, when large-vocabulary connected-speech dictation systems perform remarkably well at consumer prices, they still have not been hugely successful. Part of the reason is not technological at all, but rather social. Today's equivalents to the midlevel IBM managers who were using dictation in 1983 now type their own memos and email. Computers became essential for so many tasks that kids learn to "keyboard" in elementary school; it is hard to imagine a college graduate who cannot type!

Although John's experiments utilized an experienced typist, that was the one condition which was not evaluated against the recognition scenarios, presumably because typing was not then a widespread skill. But the shortcomings of recognition as compared to dictation are also aptly compared with word processing, which provides the same advantages (e.g., document visible during production, spell-checking) the experts appreciated. In short, perhaps the business world needs this invention less today. Alternatively, it is the poorly educated who might benefit the most from dictation as a means to access the online information world; automatic dictation may shine as a literacy tool (Shankar 2005).

But John's work unequivocally shows the value of determining, by human factors analyses, for whom and how an emerging technology may best be appreciated. In fact, we all use recognition on an almost routine basis over the telephone now, where it compares more favorably to a telephone keypad than it might to a computer keyboard. In any case, this work helped convince me that research into speech interfaces was a worthwhile career, but care must be taken to craft such interfaces for users who could benefit in direct ways. In particular, this led to years of work into telephone-based conversational agents (Marx and Schmandt 1996) and mobile speech interfaces, such as real-time spoken driving directions (Schmandt and Davis 1989).

Notes

1. A minor nit here: in reality recognizers are equally likely to simply replace an out-of-vocabulary word with some other word from the active vocabulary. This makes it harder for the user to realize when a mistake has been made.

2. One presumes that those who often dictated had no experience with word processors with built-in spell-checking, or that the latter was not a readily available feature in 1983.

25

Seeing the Hole in Space

Steve Harrison
Virginia Tech, Blacksburg, Virginia, U.S.A.

K. Galloway and S. Rabinowitz, 1980: *Hole in Space* (video)

This is a story about how one little-known work of art changed the way I think about video-mediated communication. In turn, it has shaped the fundamental insights that have formed much of my CSCW work and gone on to spawn research by many others. It was called *Hole in Space*. The extant, scanty documentation can be found at http://www.ecafe.com/getty/HIS/. I'm going to talk about what it was and how it affected me, and finally give some thought to its specific and general implications for current and future research and researchers. There are lessons for researchers in many parts of the story—even in how I came to know about it. But I am getting ahead of myself.

The Media Space

Coming to Xerox PARC in 1985, I was one of the instigators of the Media Space project. The Media Space was the first research project on electronically created shared work spaces. Open, always-on video, shared computing environments, and reconfigurable audio environments created connected office spaces at a distance. Although it would later spread, when we first encountered *Hole in Space* in 1986, the Media Space existed entirely in the System Concepts Laboratory at PARC, which was split physically between Palo Alto, California, and Portland, Oregon.

The fact that three of the creators, Bob Stults, Ranjit Makkuni, and I, were all architects had implications at three levels. The first is that we were all concerned with the creation of place from space; the second is that we saw people as legitimate creators of their own places; the third is that we were accustomed to working in large shared drafting rooms and wanted to use that as the model for collaborative workspaces. We saw it variously as supporting a distributed group, as supporting collaboration, and as a design environment. Furthermore, we saw these characteristics as connected; collaboration—"the social practices of design" as we referred to it—should be enabled by the spatial characteristics of a drafting room (Stults 1986; Bly, Harrison, and Irwin 1993; Harrison et al. 1997). But the drafting room model was not the only way that the Media Space and its various progeny were used: we were pleased that some people would use it to create continuous office sharing, while others would use it to roam the virtualized hallways and common areas, and yet others would just use it to look out a window in another office. In all of these uses, we saw Media Space as being about space and place.

How I Came to Learn about *Hole in Space*

A friend of mine, also an architect, called one day to say that I should talk to a couple of tenants living in an apartment owned by his mother in Santa Monica (near Los Angeles). This did not sound very promising, but he was a friend. He explained that the tenants—Kit Galloway and Sherrie Rabinowitz—were artists, working in what they called "aesthetic research in telecommunications." What could that mean?

I was wary that my friend's recommendation resulted in part because his mother was concerned that they were not getting commissions for their art work and thus might become deadbeats; PARC looked pretty flush in the mid-1980s. Immediately after my first phone call to Galloway and Rabinowitz, they called back with plans to fly up to Palo Alto to meet with us about how we could work together. This was both gratifying and worrisome.

Although such technologies are now commonplace features of computers, in 1986 video-mediated connection was not considered part of computing or networking research. It was certainly outside of office systems research and therefore was almost too radical for most people to comprehend. Computing workspaces supported "tasks" not space that could be social, task-oriented, ambient, or any number of other truly spatial characteristics. Nonetheless, a couple of people had "gotten it"; a researcher from NTT in Japan came to visit and was excited by the shared drawing components and the seamlessness created by thinking in terms of space and not application. That researcher was Hiroshi Ishii who went on to Media Lab fame. Bill Buxton from University of Toronto also came through and would argue a few years later that Cambridge EuroPARC should have a media space as part of its initial infrastructure. However, most people were seeing it as absolutely blue sky, and we were frankly not sure that we knew how to work with anyone outside of our lab, to say nothing of working with artists.

But Sherrie and Kit came up, and presented us with a documentary video about *Hole in Space*.

The Work of Art

The *Hole in Space* website, alas, does not have that video—black-and-white, possibly shot on a Sony PortaPak recorder. However, both forms of existing documentation show a remarkable project; over the course of three evenings in November 1980, a hole was opened in space between the sidewalks at Lincoln Center in New York and those in Century City in Los Angeles. This was accomplished by projecting full-size images of the passersby at both sites in black-and-white in store-front windows, using rear-projection display of the video, and manually echo-cancelled full-duplex audio. There were no user instructions, no local feedback monitor, no explanatory didactics, just the image of a place three time zones away.

Crowds gathered quickly once the artwork was turned on. People would stop, realize that they were hearing what was probably the sound from the remote location and ask the people they were seeing—total strangers—where they were. People at each end realized that it must be somewhere far away because of the difference in sky color and the way people were dressed. The people had nothing in common except they happened to be in the same real-virtual location at the same time. Yet they took the time to find out where they now "were." They asked if they were being seen. They asked why they were "there."

Existential inquiry gave way to spontaneous games like charades. People behaved in ways they would not with strangers on the same physical sidewalk: they lingered instead of moving on; they were engaged with one another across the link and, in turn, with those next to them on the sidewalk. Because of the video mediation, these sidewalks and these people were creating an event and a fleeting community.

As creators of the Media Space, we resonated with what we saw in this project. It expanded our understanding of the great potential we were playing with. In the corporate context of our work, we focused on the quotidian aspects of the Media Space and justified the aesthetic ones in terms of pragmatic ends—keeping our split laboratory together. What we realized from *Hole in Space* was that we might be able to truly alter our sense of community. In fact, "community" was very powerful *juju* in our Laboratory. The Systems Concepts Laboratory had a long tradition of close togetherness, of actively maintaining the social fabric of the group. This had become a de facto part of the research with half of the research staff located in Portland. The Media Space already had elements of lab community, but *Hole in Space* showed that media space might be a way to engage and constitute community differently. It was truly art in that it made us see our familiar world with new eyes.

Yow! What a possibility.

I know Sherrie and Kit were disappointed that we did not have a project in mind nor did we see them as consultants. It was a very odd position to be in—while justifying very expensive computers was quite easy for researchers at PARC at the time, justifying the purchase of any sort of video or audio equipment, to say nothing of hiring video artists as consultants, required enormous amounts of argumentation and took months. But here were artists who had worked with live coast-to-coast broadcast-quality video feeds that had cost hundreds of thousands of dollars to set up. They must have wondered why we didn't just write them a big check on the spot. But because of facts of PARC culture and because it took us too long to understand their contribution, this was not on the table.

The Contributions

In the moment, Sherrie and Kit showed us the possibility of radical reseeing. But over the years since then, I have come to see other radical messages inherent in their work. We had been focusing on space and place in mediated connection. Beyond new forms of community, they showed us that *events* were also an essential element of mediated communications. However, because they were performance artists, creating events was such deep background that they never talked about the "eventness" of what they were doing, only the nature of the particular events. By the time I coauthored "Re-Place-ing Space" (Harrison and Dourish 1996), this had become obvious to me. I noted that mediated connection is composed and explainable in terms of people, events, and places, but that placeness and spaceness overshadowed eventness then.

The Medium Is the Message

Artists work with media. It is obvious that Kit and Sherrie used telecommunications systems as the medium of their art, and that's why they called it "aesthetic research in telecommunication." I came to realize over the years that telecommunication was only one part of their medium. If you look at other projects on the website, you will notice that most of the artwork is about social connection that attempts to break down alienation through mediated connection. Thus, their other medium was *human relations*.

Human relations as an art medium? Since they were working with human relations, they were open to showing and seeing the effect of telecommunications absent the rhetorical and actual aspects of spatiality. "Hole in Space" was a cute title and it did describe the "physics" of the situation in quasi–science fiction terms, but it was the social realm in which they operated most effectively.

They also took a very direct stance to their subjects and their media. That is, they did not base their work on irony. This made them not very hip. Thus many in the art world found it difficult to take this work seriously. Yet there was irony present at a different level; it was the irony of the separation that creates connection. It was, at least, a reflection about relationship engendered by strangeness.

Pioneering Efforts, Commodified Results

There is another kind of irony in their work as well. Sherrie and Kit became quite attached to the idea of cafés as community centers. These cafés located in different L.A. neighborhoods were linked together using fax, chat, and slow-speed video. The last project listed on the website is Electronic Café International. It took the model of the electronic café and tried to extend it to the entire world. It abstracted the social qualities of creative people encountering one another as part of communities attached to particular locations.

What they did not foresee was the Internet. The Internet did not need the grounding of particular locations. Encounters could happen almost without any context or excuse in cyberspace. Worse, they did not see how arty café culture would become co-opted and commodified by chain coffee houses selling hip Euro-style ambiance and connected by wireless service providers out to make a buck. Ideas, inspiration, human connection, community were not the central reasons to hang anymore. The irony is that Kit and Sherrie are known in the art world for these electronic cafés and not the body of their work, including *Hole in Space* (Wilson 2002).

But we must acknowledge the insight they had. And we should be very careful not to be dismissive when someone says that we should look at the research being conducted by artists who are tenants of the mother of some random acquaintance.

26

Edward Tufte's 1 + 1 = 3

Scott Jenson
Google, Mountain View, California, U.S.A.

E. R. Tufte, 1990: *Envisioning Information*

Visual activation of negative areas of white space in these exhibits illustrates the *endlessly contextual and interactive nature of visual elements*. This idea is captured in a fundamental principle of information design: 1 + 1 = 3 or more. In the simplest case, when we draw two black lines, a third visual activity results, a bright white path between the lines. . . . *Most of the time, that surplus visual activity is non-information, noise, and clutter.*
—Edward R. Tufte, *Envisioning Information*, p. 61

The above quote comes from chapter 3, "Layering and Separation," of *Envisioning Information*. Though only a modest part of Tufte's broader work, this chapter has had a profound impact on my work as an interaction designer. On the surface, the chapter is about how layering and separation can calm the visual clutter that comes from 1 + 1 = 3. There is, however, a very clear corollary to interaction design.

Let's review the basic idea. A single line is just a line. However, by adding a second parallel line, something special happens: a third "object" is created. This object is the white space, or negative space, between the two lines. (See figure 26.1.) The effect can be seen in graph paper, musical staffs, and displays that use boxes to enclose sections. The desire to separate and delineate information is well intended, but the heavy-handed and simplistic use of lines and boxes has an unintended effect: the cure creates its own side effects. Tufte closes the chapter by redesigning a visual guide for a flight handbook, calming down the effects of 1 + 1 = 3 and producing a significantly calmer and clearer presentation.

Applying 1 + 1 = 3 to Interaction Design

I've always enjoyed Tufte's works on multiple levels: their clear thinking, the impeccable craftsmanship, and sheer, "here, let me show you" executional brilliance.

Figure 26.1
Tufte's lines.

Figure 26.2
Original elevator buttons.

However, the direct transference into actual interaction design came to me while I was in an elevator. Just as the doors began to close, I could see a woman with a large suitcase running toward me. Sympathetically, I reached down to push the "door open" button. To my horror, I pushed the "door close" button by mistake and the doors slid silently shut. As she could clearly see me reaching over to push a button, it looked to her like and I had intentionally closed the doors. I was mortified.

Standing there in the now empty elevator, I couldn't help but thinking I had been set up. This wasn't simply "pilot error"; there was something very wrong. I took out my camera and took a picture of these buttons (shown in figure 26.2). As I reflected on the experience, it became clear that as I had reached down to push the "open" button, I had been confronted with not one but two buttons: the open and the close button. I had to choose, in a split second, which to push. There was a momentary panic as my brain tried to decode arrow direction and expected outcome and, as most errors have it, I choose the wrong one.

I realized at that point that I was staring at the interaction design equivalent of Tufte's 1 + 1 = 3. If there had just been a single open button, my choice would have been clear. But as there were two buttons, a third "object" had been created: the cognitive load required to visually parse, understand, and then choose the correct button. This extra load is the unseen, untallied cost of feature creep.

Where Tufte discussed visual clutter, we interaction designers have cognitive clutter. His solution of layering and separation also works for us. The intent is to separate the data from the framework that surrounds the presentation of the data. In earlier chapters, he calls this "data ink," the actual data that we need to interpret, and "chart junk," the labels, grids, and overall framework for presenting the data. It may seem counterintuitive to interaction designers, but Tufte celebrates complexity. However, this is only within the data, not the chart junk. He ruthlessly removes excessive presentation detail that is not central to the data itself. That is the crucial insight: what excessive "presentation details" of our user interfaces are making decisions more complex?

There are two design sins that these elevator buttons have committed. The first is sloppy presentation. The buttons are identical in size, shape, and color. But, more important, the icons are nearly identical. There are just two elements, a triangle and a line, that make up the design of the open and close icons. A very clever reductionist approach, it nevertheless presents two icons that need to be deconstructed in order to ascertain which one is open and which is close. Bottom line: they are buttons that "make you think."

The second sin assumes that the need for both of these buttons is self-evident: an "open" button requires, even demands a corresponding "close." This seems so clear, so obvious, that in pointing it out to many people, they think I'm completely overreacting. However, this is the beauty of this design problem. It is the perfect example of Tufte's 1 + 1 = 3. Not only is the presentation creating clutter, but the very existence of the second button does so as well. We need to understand this cost, not because we must remove the second button, but because we must be sure the cost is worth it.

Fixing Sin 1: Reduce the Clutter

In order to redesign the buttons, we must first understand their context of use. I'm simplifying a bit but the open button is usually a spur of the moment, one-shot use. It is used by novices in an infrequent act of helping others.

The close button is much different: it is meant for people who are in a hurry. They will use this button frequently, possibly pushing it multiple times in a single trip. It is used by expert users who perhaps drink a little too much coffee.

This allows us to address the cognitive clutter problem much more clearly. The open button is a more "panic use" button. It needs to very clearly labeled, possibly

Figure 26.3
Redesigned buttons (with red and green borders, respectively).

even much larger than the close button. It has to be very obvious and easy to understand. The close button can be made harder to find. This isn't a concern, as it will be used repeatedly by a more seasoned user: they'll quickly get over any initial targeting problems. Figure 26.3 shows a potential redesign of these buttons.

There are many possibilities, of course; I'm taking a fairly conservative approach. In this example, the open button is larger in physical size and the icon conveys the situation, opening the doors to let in a person. The close button is smaller and shows an icon of closed doors. They don't have the extreme graphical simplicity of the earlier icons, but that is because they are trying to do something else: to be easier to decode in a hurry. One last touch: as a redundant encoding, the buttons have a red and green border, respectively, to further reinforce the stop/go nature of these buttons.

There are many quibbles you can make about these buttons: neither colors nor icons may internationalize well, for example. This could indeed be true. The broader point is the process: 1 + 1 = 3 warns us to be wary of presentation confusion. Recognizing that these buttons were nearly identical was the first step, as it framed the problem better: we had cognitive clutter. By reflecting on what is actually required, when, and by whom, we can create a choice task that is easier for the target user, creating a much calmer environment for the user in which to make decisions.

Fixing Sin 2: Remove the Choice Altogether

The ultimate solution to reducing the clutter is to just remove the second choice completely. Instead of having two buttons, just go to a single button to open the door. This design is shown in figure 26.4.

In this design we have gone back to just "1." There is no more "1 + 1" with this solution. While indeed this clearly solves the cognitive clutter problem completely,

Figure 26.4
Single button design.

it usually also raises screams of protests, typically from programmers and product managers. For them, it is anathema to remove any functionality.

This is the tension that is at the core of most design problems: the ostensibly obvious value of the close button contrasted with unseen and hard to quantify cost of its extra cognitive clutter. Which is more important, the functionality of "+1" or the cost of the "=3"?

The goal here isn't to prove that the button must be removed, but to point out that we have a real choice. I've presented this design problem in many talks and I always get a very strong reaction: the second button just must be there. What amazes me is how unquestioned the desire is to have this second button. Even if they admit that removing the close button reduces the clutter significantly, it is still, in their eyes, not worth the removal of the functionality. The user just needs to "figure it out." I believe this is a core decision-making pattern for many people, as having a complete list of features is easier to understand (and defend) than the more complex task of understanding which features are actually needed and how they are used.

In this case it isn't as simple as having an open and a close button. The issue is to understand *why* this extra close button is needed. It isn't just the opposite of open; its use is far different. The open button is used to fix a problem, to stop a situation in a quick and urgent matter. The close button is quite different: it is primarily meant to hurry things along. The door will close no matter what; this button just closes it a bit faster. In fact, it really isn't a close button at all, but, a "hurry" button. This is very different indeed.

If it only closes the door two seconds faster, can we really argue that this is feature absolutely essential? In that case, it doesn't seem bad to remove it. However, what if pressing the button really does speed up the door's closing significantly, what then? Doesn't that just beg the question, "Why does the door stay open so long in the first place?" Isn't it the case that by having such a nice and easy-to-use open button, we could actually decrease the wait time on the elevator doors a bit so that there isn't even need for the close button?

There is no perfect solution to this problem, nor should there be. The point of this essay is to show that design problems, much like Tufte's 1 + 1 = 3, can be full of presentation clutter that confuses and complicates interaction. Many people first react to this by denying the significance of the clutter. Their second reaction is that the perceived cost of removing the feature is a far greater than that of removing the clutter. This all stems from a lack of insight. A little exploration can often unmask the various "close" buttons in our work as the pretentious little "hurry" buttons that they truly are. Just recognizing that 1 + 1 = 3 effects are possible is a powerful motivator to explore problems in more detail and pinpoint the underlying issues that are at the heart of designing an appropriate solution.

27

Typographic Space: A Fusion of Design and Technology

Jodi Forlizzi
Carnegie Mellon University, Pittsburgh, Pennsylvania, U.S.A.

D. Small, S. Ishizaki, and M. Cooper, 1994: "Typographic Space"

The culture of graphic design has long been known for its obsession with typographic form. As an undergraduate design student at Philadelphia College of Art in the 1980s, I had the opportunity to study and meet some contemporary typographers and even to undertake my own letterform design. Such began a decade of working with type that included setting lead characters and slugs into compositions, pressing plastic press type onto boards to create communications, and using a photo typesetting machine to create, manipulate, and generate strips of text that were "pasted up" into design compositions.

Desktop computers and printers such as the Apple II and the Apple Laser Writer revolutionized design work, as computer technology was first introduced to the discipline of graphic design. By 1985, Aldus Corporation released PageMaker for the Mac (which many graphic designers nicknamed "PainMaker"), enabling text and photographs to be designed in a unified composition and printed from a laser printer (printing time for an average page containing text and graphics hovered between forty-five minutes and an hour). Graphic designers struggled to design the simplest of static pages within the limits of those early systems.

Yet at the same time, even more revolutionary experimentation with computation and typography was beginning to take place. At the Massachusetts Institute of Technology, a woman named Muriel Cooper was embracing the role that new technology could play in manipulating typographic form. Trained as a designer, Cooper had run her own design firm for many years, had been an art director for MIT Press, and joined the MIT faculty in 1977, teaching a class called "Messages and Means" that looked at graphic design in relation to technology. By 1988, she had formed the Visible Language Workshop, a lab that investigated issues related to technology and graphic design long before the majority of traditional graphic designers had even begun to engage with technology.

Along with graduate students Suguru Ishizaki and David Small, Cooper began to explore how time and interactivity could serve as design variables in typographic design. An early system, called Typographic Space,[1] applied typographic variables used in two-dimensional graphic design to the design of time-based, three-dimensional information graphics. Type could be manipulated dynamically along the x, y, and z axes, and type could be used to create three-dimensional spatial compositions that provided clues about the structure of the information space.

Sadly, Cooper died of a heart attack suddenly in 1994, the same year that the first published paper about Typographic Space appeared in the CHI Conference Companion Proceedings. Cooper's work was carried on by her graduate students Small, Ishizaki, and Yin Yin Wong.

The paper described the Typographic Space system, which allowed the designer/programmer to lay out text in a very large three-dimensional space, and to apply a basic set of typographic attributes (for example, color, size, and style such as italic or bolding) to the layout. Once composed, a reader could move through the three-dimensional typographic space using just a mouse and keyboard, changing viewpoint and viewing distance.

This radical approach—offering the reader a nonstable viewpoint and a means for viewing typographic information in three dimensions—revealed several design issues, which were discussed in the second half of the paper. The first issue the authors discussed was that of distortion, caused by perspective and the arbitrary movement of a viewpoint. In extreme cases, text could be illegible, or even appear as a line or disappear entirely. The second issue was related to type size. When the reader "travels" through the layout, the size of typographic elements changes, rendering type size to be a less than effective visual cue. The third issue was that of sense of space, or perception of nearness to a typographic element. A reader could have trouble differentiating elements that are close by and those that are large but at a further distance. Finally, when adding motion and interactivity as design variables, speed of movement and view angle had to be carefully controlled to ensure that layouts were maximally legible.

The Typographic Space system opened up many new possibilities for designers to create expressive typographic compositions. With the addition of motion as a design variable, a new research domain emerged within interaction design and human–computer interaction.

In 1996, Ishizaki joined the design faculty at Carnegie Mellon University after receiving his Ph.D. from MIT, and work on what is now known as kinetic typography continued to expand and grow.[2]

In the two years that followed, my colleague Shannon Ford and I worked with Ishizaki as graduate research assistants at Carnegie Mellon University, creating hundreds of systematic studies of letters, words, phrases, sentences, and short dialogues, in order to understand the potential of this new communicative medium (Ford, Forlizzi, and Ishizaki 1997). The process was labor-intensive, taking hours to implement subtle effects, and revealing (to us, at least) a drastic need for tools to support more quickly designing kinetic typography. Using Macromedia Director, we changed the color, size, and position of type throughout a composition. The addition of time as a design element further enriched the communicative potential of typography and enabled developments in both design methods and tools for designers working in the fields of interaction design and human–computer interaction.

One of our influences in the research was a set of psychological studies of perception and reading that helped us to understand the communicative potential of kinetic typography. One fruitful presentation method, known as Rapid Serial Visual Presentation (RSVP) (Potter 1984), displays text one word at a time in a fixed position on the screen. Perception studies have shown that because scanning eye movements are unnecessary when using RSVP, this text can be read more rapidly than static text. The RSVP technique proved to be advantageous for designers because it allowed words to be treated independently and minimally, often using one design variable such as bolding. Designers saw RSVP as a means for trading time for space, potentially allowing large bodies of text to be shown at readable sizes on small displays. Using just a few design variables, such as bolding and italics, along with the RSVP presentation method, resulted in the effective communication of the emotional intent of a message (figure 27.1).

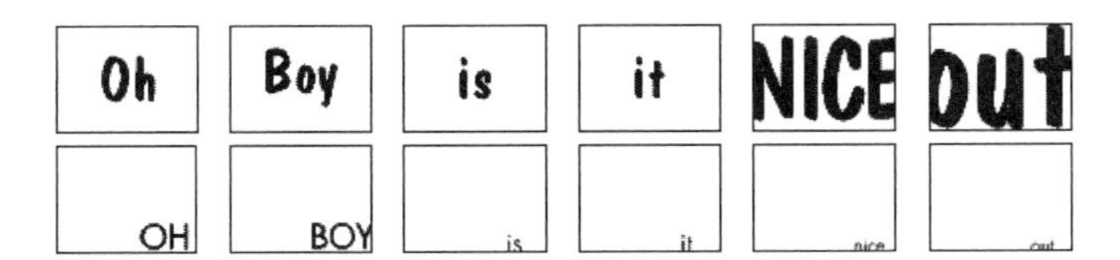

Figure 27.1
RSVP is used to convey emotional content in a story.

Figure 27.2
Two characters from the Monty Python "argument clinic" sketch.

We learned that aspects of pitch, loudness, and tempo can also be effectively conveyed. For example, large upward or downward motions can convey rising or falling pitch. Speed of delivery and tempo are temporal effects, and we found these could be expressed by manipulating timing, duration, and pacing.

We also discovered that analogous motion, mimicking human and lifelike action, was a compelling means of conveying emotive content. For example, we used small vibrations to illustrate trembling, which conveyed emotions such as anticipation, excitement, or anger. Slow rhythmic motions reminiscent of calm breathing appeared to induce feelings of empathy.

We also found kinetic typography to be successful in portraying characters and dialogue (figure 27.2). Design variables were used to establish identification and reidentification of a character over time. Recognition was handled through distinct, persistent, and identifiable visual, spatial, and other properties. A second important technique related to character creation is attachment. The use of spatial location on the screen is one way to establish attachment.

Although this corpus of examples was important, kinetic type designers were not without compelling examples that could be used to inspire new compositions. Saul Bass and his colleagues had been exploring the use of moving type for years. One of the first uses of kinetic typography was in film—specifically, Saul Bass's opening credit sequence for Hitchcock's *North by Northwest* (Bass 1959) and later *Psycho* (Bass 1960). Bass, also trained as a graphic designer, designed with the goal of having the opening credits set the stage for the film by establishing a mood and conveying some of the clues of the story along with conveying the information of the credits. Use of kinetic typography is now commonplace in television, where the ability to convey emotive content and direct the user's attention aligns with the goals of advertising. Bass's award-winning designs revealed the power of kinetic typography and its potential benefit for other areas of digital communication.

From Saul Bass's credits to Muriel Cooper's vision, from the commonplace use of kinetic type today to the tools that have been created in response to the designer's need for speed, a research domain has been created that successfully blends traditional graphic design with human–computer interaction. The history of kinetic typography is valuable for what it has helped us discover, as well as the questions it leaves unanswered.

Notes

1. The typographic Space video can be found online at http://www.ibiblio.org/openvideo/video/chi/chi94_03_m4.mp4. Retrieved December 2006.

2. A showcase of kinetic typography examples can be found at http://www.kinetictypography.org. Retrieved December 2006.

28

Making Sense of Sense Making

Steve Whittaker
University of Sheffield, Sheffield, U.K.

A. Kidd, 1994: "The Marks Are on the Knowledge Worker"

This is a quirky, stimulating, original, and wide-ranging paper. It challenges critical assumptions about the functions of computers; the nature of information and work (there are three types: knowledge, communication, and clerical); the utility of PDAs (their small displays limit them to being memory prostheses); and about the fit between work type and system. The presentation is eclectic, mixing philosophy, Gibsonian psychology, and ethnographic user data to generate some provocative design and organizational implications. To cite just one: "Don't encourage organizations to think that storing information is an alternative to being informed by it."

The paper makes two important claims about the use of computers, which I will review—with the benefit of twelve years' hindsight. But before starting, I need to make a clarification. In one way the paper is anachronistic because it predates the Web, blindsiding some of its claims. However, this shouldn't detract from Kidd's main arguments, because public data (like the Web) isn't the paper's central focus. It is concerned with personal use of information, where the two claims it makes are profound and still highly relevant.

(1) Memory prosthesis Computers are mainly used for (and are good at) passive storage of information; but this type of information is not particularly useful (certainly not to the knowledge workers who are Kidd's central interest).

(2) Sense making Computers aren't very good at the important process of making sense of the information we encounter, and a radical new "perceptual" approach is needed to tackle this, relying on large displays and spatial layout. Current techniques based on folders or future AI techniques will not solve this sense-making problem.

These were important claims because in 1994 the uncontested view was that storing lots of long-term information was a Good Thing. Hot research topics at that time presupposed the need to create large archives for organizational memory, meetings data, and personal information. And, though not stopping that approach dead in its tracks, Kidd at least made researchers pause to consider their central premise. At that time, too, there was little HCI interest in sense making—an area previously dominated by AI—so that Kidd's work created a new focus inspired by human-centric concerns rather than AI technologies. On a more personal note, it caused me to reorient my research to focus more on what people did when encountering and working with information and less on how they organized information in the long term.

Computers as (Useless) Memory Prostheses

Kidd's claim (based on observation of knowledge workers) is that there is little value to passively stored information, because information is useful only during the act of informing. Once understood and integrated into the user's mental structures, it has little value and is seldom accessed.

If this is true, it's an important and radical claim, because current research is directing massive efforts at helping users to construct huge collections of personal data, for example, in Microsoft's influential Memex initiative (Gemmell, Bell, and Lueder 2006). Reductions in the cost of storage make it possible to "keep everything," and users are amassing large collections of personal digital information including photos, music, as well as documents. New tools (e.g., Google Desktop and Microsoft Desktop Search) aim to help access this data—inspired by research prototypes such as Stuff I've Seen (Dumais et al. 2003).

Although we can dismiss as rhetoric Kidd's assertions that digital collections are fundamentally useless (after all, we do peruse old digital photos and access old tax returns), it's clear that we need to know more about exactly *when* and *why* long-term information is accessed. And Kidd's argument is more subtle than a blanket rejection of digital memory. She claims that the *process* of constructing a digital memory store is costly and error prone, which in turn compromises the utility of the stored information. Errors creep in because the main tools we have for organizing digital memories are folders. Folders force *classification*—a cognitively difficult task—requiring users to predict the future contexts of retrieval. Such prediction is hard. There may be fundamental shifts in the ways that users construe certain information (as work or interests change), rendering old folder labels useless. Folders also *hide information*; once an email message or document is filed, I may never think to look for it again, because it is "out of sight and out of mind." Finally, "premature filing" can occur—where users' anxiety to keep their workspace clear for future information processing leads current information to be filed in inappropriate places. These claims about the problematic nature of categorization have now been well demonstrated (Boardman and Sasse 2004; Whittaker and Hirschberg 2001). And though some have touted desktop search as the antidote to folders, there are strong reasons to believe that organization and access problems will not disappear with greater use of search (Whittaker, Bellotti, and Gwizdka in press).

The Lack of Support for Sense Making

Kidd's arguments aren't restricted to attacking digital memory; in fact her real focus is on managing new information, a process she calls *sense making*. Changes in the digital landscape relating to increased connectivity mean that we are inundated by large amounts of information. But much of this information is of unclear value. According to Kidd, we need more support for *making sense* of it. And strikingly, dedicated support for sense making hasn't changed much in the last thirty years. Computers still provide "the desktop" along with ways for people to file information into folders, and email has its inbox with similar folders.

Kidd is absolutely correct that we lack good tools for processing new information. Email is the main conduit for new work information, and it's currently a disaster. Our inboxes bulge with huge amounts of ill-structured, outdated, and irrelevant information. But this may not be a problem of sense making. Contrary to Kidd, users aren't complaining that they can't *make sense* of this information; rather they're concerned that they can't *manage tasks* involving this information. So, how is sense making different from task management? Sense making implies a cognitive act of imposing understanding on information, creating new relations between formerly unconnected information. Task management instead demands a more lightweight form of organization, requiring information to be available and invoked at the appropriate time (Whittaker, Bellotti, and Gwizdka in press).

Leaving open for the moment whether the key issue is one of sense making or task management, let us return to Kidd's more detailed claims about processing new information.

(1) Perceptual and spatial processes are crucial Contrary to the current classification-oriented approach, Kidd states that key processes in understanding new information are visual, spatial, and context sensitive. Her study looks at how users make sense of physical documents—finding that they rely on "pre-linguistic, perceptual, and visual" processes to mediate understanding. For example, users organize paper documents into piles in space to understand complex connections between them. The physical workspace becomes an external representation that retains and mediates users' understanding. It also holds context, allowing them to defer judgments about where a specific piece of information belongs, which results in better judgments being made.

(2) AI won't help The above characterization motivates another of Kidd's assertions. Processing complex information is a specifically human activity that cannot be helped by machine surrogates or artificial intelligence.

How true are these assertions? Studies show how users organize paper documents spatially into desktop "piles" to avoid premature classification and to keep working information more easily available (Whittaker and Hirschberg 2001). Email, too, is an excellent case of perceptual processing; studies reveal that users routinely keep over 1,400 messages in the inbox (Whittaker, Bellotti, and Gwizdka in press). They do this to exploit visual processes: users know they will return to the inbox to process new messages, and then they will *see* and be *reminded* about these outstanding messages. Just as Kidd says, the inbox functions as an attentional space that serves to hold context, being used to collate and organize information about ongoing tasks. And retaining messages in the inbox allows a user to defer judgments about their value until their utility is clear. But the same studies also reveal the limitations of perceptual processes. Spatial strategies rely on visually scanning to "see" connections and be reminded about outstanding information. But scanning does not scale well for vast amounts of heterogeneous information (and let's face it, 1,400 messages is a large amount of information). As a result, important messages and documents get overlooked as spatial collections become unwieldy.

And although the "AI won't save us" claim may apply to the complex synthetic and subjective area of sense making, AI techniques do seem to be highly promising for task management. For example, spam filtering is a successful AI technique that prevents irrelevant information from entering the users' workspace. Other new AI methods may help users identify important messages, collate related information, or re-create the context of a current task (Whittaker, Bellotti, and Gwizdka in press).

Although there are obvious issues concerning user trust in automatic processes, these AI techniques may soon support important information-processing problems.

So where does this leave us? It's clear that Kidd's observations still represent a major challenge to HCI. Even though they haven't emerged in quite the way she characterized them, key issues still surround her two claims.

Memory prosthesis Although it's a useful straw man, the strong hypothesis (digital memories are useless) is clearly wrong; but we definitely need more studies to determine how, when, and why digital memories are useful. We know that people want to keep music and photos as mementos, but what are the uses of work-oriented memorabilia? We also need to understand how the landscape will be changed by new tools such as search. Let's state these issues as follows:

- What are the uses of digital memories? (An empirical question.)
- Once we know the answer to this, we can ask other questions that have technical ramifications. How can we help people create useful archives? How effective are current tools for accessing archives? In particular, is search sufficient?

Support for sense making Again, there's a crucial issue here, but not exactly the one that Kidd identified. Like Kidd says, people have major problems in processing working information, although it seems that the key problem is task management rather than sense making. (This isn't to say that sense making is unimportant, it's just that it's not as critical as task management.) The second crucial conclusion supports Kidd—that managing working information involves perceptual processes of reminding and organization. The outstanding questions then are:

- What processes are involved in handling working information? (Again an empirical question.)
- How can we better support these processes? Will Kidd's perceptual techniques involving large displays help? At the same time, we shouldn't neglect other philosophically different approaches. Can AI-based techniques of filtering and collation help with task management?

To conclude, Kidd's arguments remain highly relevant today. We are now in a digital era when we are inundated by increasing amounts of information, but where we can also "keep everything." In this context it is even more vital to address Kidd's main questions of how we *process new information* as well as what is the *value of stored information.*

29

Does Voice Coordination Have to Be "Rocket Science"?

Paul M. Aoki
Intel Research, Berkeley, California, U.S.A.

J. C. Watts, D. D. Woods, J. M. Corban, E. S. Patterson, R. L. Keer, and L. C. Hicks, 1996: "Voice Loops as Cooperative Aids in Space Shuttle Mission Control"

Imagine sitting down at a desk for an eight-hour shift, slipping a headset onto one ear, and finding four separate conversations going on at once. How would you approach such an environment? What practices would evolve to enable people to make sense of this while working and making highly technical decisions for hours on end?

As it happens, these are not hypothetical questions—in particular, they relate to the Voice Loops system in use in NASA's "Mission Control" at Johnson Space Center, described in a fascinating paper in the CSCW 1996 proceedings (Watts et al. 1996). Further, they highlight the kind of issues that the "Voice Loops" paper continues to raise for HCI in general. Access to voice communication is spreading rapidly, particularly through the worldwide adoption of mobile telephony—in 2006, the GSM Association reported its two billionth subscription, with 82 percent of the second billion coming from emerging economies. Yet for most users, the actual *experience* of voice communication has changed very little since the nineteenth-century invention of the telephone: a simple, additive, monaural voice circuit. This model is fine for conversation between two people, but as anybody who has ever participated in an audio conference can attest, it hardly lends itself to use in group conversation. In practice, it's quite difficult to understand anything if multiple people speak at once, which slows down talk drastically. In spite of its highly specialized setting, the "Voice Loops" paper gives hints of a way forward for the rest of us, one that is still largely unexplored.

Overview

The paper has two general areas of interest. First, it is one of a few papers in the HCI and CSCW literature that illustrate how complex command and control environments work. Second, it discusses how multiple multiparty voice communication flows arise in such an environment, and how users successfully manage these flows for hours on end.

The Role of Voice Loops in Mission Control

If one simply wants some "local color" about the management of space missions, it might be better to read one of the several firsthand accounts written by former NASA flight controllers. The "Voice Loops" paper focuses on the webs of highly concurrent communication that arise, and the resultant monitoring of many activities and conversations at once. From the abstract:

> We describe how voice loops support the coordination of activities and cognitive processes in event-driven domains like space shuttle mission control . . . how the loops help flight controllers synchronize their activities and integrate information, and how they facilitate directed communication and support the negotiation of interruptions. (Watts et al. 1996, p. 48)

In particular, the paper describes the physical and organizational layout of Mission Control and how Voice Loops is overlaid on this layout. Briefly: the main "front" room contains the flight director, who has overall responsibility for the mission, and a supporting team of specialized flight controllers, who sit at computer telemetry consoles and are responsible for their respective subsystems. In separate "back" rooms, teams of subsystem specialists support their respective flight controllers. This hierarchy is mirrored in Voice Loops, with the flight director talking to the flight controllers over a flight director loop and flight controllers talking to their respective support teams on dedicated front-to-back support loops. Communication within ad hoc groups of flight controllers is supported by a conferencing loop. Finally, a special loop is used for communication with the spacecraft. Hence, individuals monitor four separate loops. Separation into multiple loops provides a structure for information to be aggregated as it flows "upward" and monitored by concerned parties at all levels.

The seminal work of Heath and Luff (1992) on the London Underground Line Control Rooms brings across some of the nature of this coordination "in the small," and the work of Hughes and colleagues (e.g., Harper and Hughes 1992) on air traffic control centers gives a somewhat better feel for the technical work of control rooms. However, the "Voice Loops" paper gives a good sense for the pervasive, critical role that voice communication plays in the coordination of the multiple, interlocking teams.

Managing Attention in Voice Loops

While most of the paper describes the organizational aspects relating to Voice Loops, an extremely important section at the end discusses how individuals interact with the system. As previously noted, controllers routinely monitor four loops—up to four separate, simultaneous conversations—at once, and they do this for eight-to-twelve-hour shifts. The paper explains how people can manage many simultaneous conversations given a few interface primitives for managing them:

> we suggest factors like attentional cues, implicit protocols, and the structure and features of the loops, which might govern the success of voice loops in the mission control domain. (Watts et al. 1996, p. 48)

The authors allude to psychology papers on the subject of human attention, then plunge into a discussion of factors that allow the flight controllers to manage the "cacophony" of multiparty talk. Some are protocols specific to the Mission Control environment, such as specialized ways of speaking ("response on demand" and "coded language") and patterns of loop use ("which loops are monitored" and "functionally separate loops"); such protocols and patterns reduce overall traffic on the loops but do not explain how multiple loops are navigated. However, the authors do also talk about cues and tools: the "internal cues" and "external cues" that prime and trigger listeners' attention, and the abilities to use "different volume levels" and to "tailor the set of loops" to separate and prioritize loops when allocating attention. Through these cues and tools, the system provides means for augmenting human capabilities for selective attention.

Impact

I've claimed that Voice Loops, as an illustration of how a system can augment human selective attention abilities, suggests a way forward for the design of voice coordination systems. But given that the paper itself talks about "experienced practitioners in space shuttle mission control," is it clear that these kinds of cues and tools can be applied in other environments?

Consider other multiparty voice applications. Audio conferencing for focused communication tasks has received a great deal of attention in the networking and multimedia literature, and media spaces as open environments for awareness (Stults 1986) have been much more prominent in the HCI literature. (For example, to place the "Voice Loops" paper in a historical context, consider that CSCW 1996 also saw the first report of the Thunderwire audio space [Hindus et al. 1996], a simple audio-only communication space from Interval Research that descended from the Xerox PARC and EuroPARC line of research on media spaces.) In nearly all of this research, the "solution" to the awkwardness of synchronous multiparty interaction has been to increase media quality—higher audio bit-rates to improve immediacy, spatialized audio to ease speaker separation, greater video fidelity to capture non-verbal cues. But such solutions come at the cost of bulky and immersive equipment—cameras, multiple microphones, stereo headsets, and so on.

When developing a research agenda in mobile, multiparty audio communication, I thought back to the "Voice Loops" paper. Because NASA inherited many cultural and institutional aspects from the U.S. military, Voice Loops naturally shares common ideas with military command and control environments such as the Naval Tactical Data System (NTDS; see Boslaugh 1999), in use since the 1960s. I had experience using NTDS as a Navy officer and knew that environments like that of Voice Loops have been in use for many years by a much wider range of people than seasoned, highly educated NASA flight controllers. Having seen ordinary sailors—most without postsecondary education or relevant previous work experience—work in these environments for hours at a time, it seemed plausible that one could extend media spaces to enable highly spontaneous, concurrent, multiparty social interaction (the kind seen in sociable dinner table conversation) through mobile audio, without the fancy headsets and cameras. Drawing on some design fieldwork of lightweight mobile audio communication (Woodruff and Aoki 2004), I and colleagues prototyped a system for multiparty voice conferencing that recognized "who is talking to whom" based on an analysis of participants' turn-taking behavior as determined through audio processing and machine learning (Aoki et al. 2003); when the system recognized a change in conversational configuration, it adjusted the volume levels for each participant so that the people in "their" conversation were louder and others were quieter.

The "cacophony" of multiple conversations is something that we manage in social environments all the time. One might think that we must make remote communication more and more like face-to-face communication for this to be practical for ordinary users. The paradigm suggested by the "Voice Loops" paper—that human selective attention can be augmented through careful design and interface primitives—suggests an alternative for increasing our ability to hold spontaneous, multiparty conversation remotely. It suggests that we should aim to build tools to augment and enhance attention—tools that need not fully replicate human perception and understanding, but (as in the example above) might simply recognize human behaviors sufficiently well to enable mundane conversational practices.

30

Decomposing a Design Space

Paul Resnick
University of Michigan, Ann Arbor, Michigan, U.S.A.

G. W. Furnas, 1986: "Generalized Fisheye Views"

These days, I often ask Ph.D. students to select a few published papers as models of what they aspire to write—it forces them to move beyond looking for a topic that seems interesting and on to thinking about what a research contribution looks like. When I was in grad school, Furnas' paper on fisheye views is one I would have selected. It served as a model to which I aspired, not so much for its content (which has become justifiably famous) but for its approach to decomposing a design space into a set of independent choice dimensions.

The paper begins with two observations. The first is that our output devices, and our eyes, at any one time can only provide a window onto a small piece of larger information structures such as menu systems, organization charts, calendars, maps, and computer programs. The second is that, for any current focus of attention (a particular line of code, a particular appointment, a particular street), it can be helpful to

> show places nearby in great detail while still showing the whole world—simply by showing the remote regions in successively less detail. An instructive caricature of this appears in the "New Yorker's View of the United States," a poster by Steinberg and now much imitated for other cities. In the poster, midtown Manhattan is shown street by street. To the west, New Jersey is a patch of color on the other side of a blue-grey ribbon labeled "Hudson." The rest of the country is reduced to a few principal landmarks (Chicago, the Rocky Mountains, California, etc.) disappearing in the distance. (Furnas 1986, p. 16)

These observations inspired the design of a class of display algorithms that automatically select what contextual information to display around any focus of attention. The selection decision can be characterized simply as a scoring function and a threshold, where each item's score is based on a combination of the item's overall importance and its distance from the current focus of attention. Thus, items farther from the focus are displayed only if they are of great *a priori* importance. The paper provides example applications to tree data structures, to program code, and to an appointment calendar.

For example, consider a tree data structure. One could define the *a priori* importance based on the level in the tree—the paper's example assigns a score of 0 to the root, –1 for the children of the root, –2 for their children, and so on. One could define the distance metric, relative to a focal item, as the minimum path length to the item. Thus, the overall degree of interest (the sum of the *a priori* importance and the distance) would be highest along the path from the root to the focal item. A first cousin would have lower overall interest, and a second cousin still lower.

The figure I found most compelling from the paper is a fisheye view applied to the text of a computer program (figure 30.1). It treats the program as a tree data structure based on enclosing blocks (the lines inside a "for" loop or "if" statement are children of the line beginning the loop or statement). In the diagram, the current focus is on line 39. The lines right around 39 are included, but a more distant line is included only if it's of greater "importance," meaning closer to the root of the tree. Amazingly, the scoring function is tuned so that just the right stuff is shown to let a programmer know the useful context for the statement on line 39.

```
   1 #define DIG 40
   2 #include <stdio.h>
...4 main()
   5 {
   6         int c, i, x[DIG/4], t[DIG/4], k = DIG/4, noprint = 0;
...8         while((c=getchar()) != EOF){
   9                 if(c >= '0' && c <= '9'){
..16                 } else {
  17                         switch(c){
  18                                 case '+':
..27                                 case '-':
..38                                 case 'e':
>>39                                         for(i=0;i<k;i++) t[i] = x[i];
  40                                         break;
  41                                 case 'q':
..43                                 default:
..46                         }
  47                         if(!noprint){
..57                         }
  58                 }
  59                 noprint = 0;
  60         }
  61 }
```

Figure 30.1
A fisheye view of the C program. Line numbers are in the left margin. "Ellipses" indicates omitted lines. (Figure 4 from the original paper.)

The paper had a huge impact in the field of information visualization. Google Scholar documents more than a thousand citations, from the ACM CHI, UIST, CSCW, Hypertext, and InfoVis conferences, among others, and a wide variety of journals. The general class of visualizations came to be known as *focus+context visualizations*.

Many subsequent techniques used visual distortion rather than just selection of which information to include or omit. For example, items that are of greater interest are magnified, and less interesting items are smaller or abbreviated in some way. Indeed, the analogy of "fisheye view" probably applies better to these distortion-based visualizations than to the examples included in the original paper, where lower interest items are hidden.

Still, many of these techniques cite the original paper as an inspiration. One of its important legacies is its articulation of the idea of focus and context, which thus pointed the way for useful further exploration by others. If that were the paper's only contribution, however, I would not be writing about it twenty years later, since I never worked directly in the field of information visualization.

The paper made a further contribution, however, by decomposing the design space in terms of three dimensions: an importance metric, a distance metric, and a threshold function for whether something should be displayed. A design space framework of this sort can serve three purposes.

First, it can serve as a unifying framework for understanding a range of designs that at first seem only vaguely related, and the dimensions of the design space can be used to classify, compare, and contrast alternative designs. Furnas wrote his own retrospective on the paper (Furnas 2006), emphasizing and extending the reach of the unifying framework. In that paper, he shows how many additional interactive displays of information rely at heart on something that can be characterized in terms of an interest metric, computed from a combination of *a priori* importance and distance from a focus. In the example above, the *a priori* importance is the distance from the root of the tree, and the overall interest is the sum of the *a priori* importance and distance from the focus. However, the interest metric need not be simply compared to a threshold to decide what to show—instead, it can be used to determine how much time, space, or resolution to give to items, thus accommodating distortion views and multiscale interfaces.

Second, a design space framework can be used to generate novel designs, by combining choices on the design dimensions in the framework. Many purported design space frameworks fail when used in this way, but the framework in the paper passes this test as well. For any given information structure, a slight variation in the *a priori* importance metric, distance metric, or threshold function can lead to a quite different interface. For example, for a tree data structure, the paper offers three plausibly useful diagrams of tree displays that would be generated by different cutoff thresholds. Changing the *a priori* interest or the distance metric, even while holding the threshold constant, would similarly yield different subsets of the tree to display.

A third potential use of a design space framework is to identify the fit of certain regions of the design space to certain tasks or usage scenarios. For example, it might be that while writing a new program, the best fisheye view of the code involves a distance metric that weights more heavily line number distance, while for code inspection or debugging it would be best to use a distance metric that weights more heavily the path length in the tree structure of program blocks. The paper's only shortcoming is its failure to pursue this possibility—it does not make any claims about the fit of choices on particular design dimensions to different usage scenarios.

When I was in grad school, my work was on audio interfaces for touch-tone phones, which would make me a poor candidate to be inspired by a paper on visualization techniques. But the elegant decomposition of a design space as a way to understand a range of designs and to generate new ones was a model that I aspired to replicate in the realm of audio interfaces.

Having such a model can be a little discouraging, though. A year or two into my work, I once lamented to someone who knew Furnas that I had been unable to match the elegant simplicity of that paper, though I longed to do so. I received some reassurance when I was told that the paper was actually the culmination of several years and several related projects. It is, after all, titled "Generalized Fisheye Views," and it was published several years after he began investigation of many different particular fisheye views.

Eventually, working with Robert Virzi, I did characterize the design space of audio menus in terms of two dimensions. One dimension was how users select: absolute numeric (e.g., "press 3 for . . .") or positional (e.g., "press 1 at any time to select the current item"). The other dimension was how users advance between menu items: auto-advance with timeouts, an explicit skip-to-next key, or both. We conducted lab experiments and made arguments about types of users and applications for which different points in the design space were best suited. A similar design space characterized audio forms in terms of four independent dimensions. Unfortunately for my career, touch-tone interactions with audio turned out to be of far less long-term interest to researchers than visual information display. Our capstone paper on audio menus and forms (Resnick and Virzi 1995) has, well, let's just say a lot less than a thousand citations on Google Scholar.

A paper can be seminal because it draws attention to a new approach or content area and thus inspires exploration by others. Or, a paper can be seminal because it unifies a body of work while capturing the differences using simple parameters. The amazing thing about George Furnas's paper, "Generalized Fisheye Views," is that it did both. Many years later, it is a model of design space analysis that I continue to aspire to. We all should.

VI

There's More to Design

A common image of the designer is that of a solitary thinker struggling with a design problem, working through multiple iterations of a tricky problem. This, however, is a rare case. Design is necessarily embedded in broader contexts—organizations, histories, and cultures—that designers ignore at their peril. The essays in this section illustrate this broader view of design and include reflections on history, cultural criticisms, and organizational analysis. Each essay considers methods that—in the pragmatics of everyday life—take into account the wider context that the designer must consider.

The section begins with Terry Winograd, whose reflection on Henry Dreyfuss's *Designing for People* reminds us that many of the methods we now consider so central to HCI—prototyping, iterative design, to name just a few—were developed previously in other contexts. The essay by Jonas Löwgren reflects on Wroblewski's work on the issue of whether design is more of a science or a craft. The essays by Lynn Cherny and Michael Muller both examine power relations in design, but from different perspectives. Cherny, drawing on Diana Forsythe's work on "studying up," takes the perspective of the designer as an underdog in the context of complex organizational power structures. In contrast, Muller, drawing on Arthur Krupat's book *Ethnocriticism*, examines the role of designers as potentially dominant players in design practice, and considers their responsibilities to the users who will have to live with the result. The last two essays by Gilbert Cockton and Susan Dray each revisit a broad, comprehensive, design methodology that had its roots in the early days of HCI. Cockton examines the beginnings of contextual inquiry, with his essay on Whiteside, Bennett, and Holtzblatt's "Usability Engineering," and argues for its continued relevance, provocatively noting that by the standards of 1980, too much of today's work could be considered incompetent. Finally, Dray, invoking the days when mainframes hummed and user interface techniques included reverse video and the use of the tab key for accelerated screen navigation, reminds us that the methodology far surpassed the technology in sophistication as she revisits Mumford and Weir's sociotechnical systems approach to design.

31

Discovering America

Terry Winograd
Stanford University, Stanford, California, U.S.A.

H. Dreyfuss, 1955: *Designing for People*

My grandfather would sometimes say, when I shared my newest brilliant insight, "Oh, so you discovered America!" This was his kind, sarcastic way of letting me know that my great discovery was already conventional wisdom.

He came to mind recently when, in creating the new "d.school" interdisciplinary design program at Stanford (see Kelley and VanPatter 2005), I first encountered Henry Dreyfuss's classic book on industrial design, *Designing for People*. On the cover was a quote that captures the essence of human-centered (or user-centered) design:

> We bear in mind that the object being worked on is going to be ridden in, sat upon, looked at, talked into, activated, operated, or in some other way used by people individually or en masse. When the point of contact between the product and the people becomes a point of friction, then the industrial designer has failed. On the other hand, if people are made safer, more comfortable, more eager to purchase, more efficient—or just plain happier—by contact with the product, then the designer has succeeded. (Dreyfuss 1955)

As I read more, I found that Dreyfuss had eloquently laid out many aspects of design that have since been rediscovered and reinterpreted in HCI. From a half-century's hindsight, I saw the roots of principles that we now espouse, along with ideas we should revisit in light of today's technologies. After all these years, *Designing for People* is a timely and charmingly readable lesson in what it means to do design right.

Dreyfuss was one of the pioneering product designers who brought modern design to everyday objects on a mass scale. Beginning in the 1920s, he engaged in a wide variety of projects, from the classic Westclox "Big Ben" alarm clock, to John Deere's farm equipment, to the complete industrial design of the 20th Century Limited—known as the "world's greatest train"—including the cars, locomotives, and passenger experience. In his long productive association with the Bell system, he designed the telephones that Americans used for many decades, including the classic "500-series" dial phone, the Princess, the Trimline, and the modernist aluminum-and-glass telephone booth that dotted our countryside until the ascendance of the cell phone.

Designing for People is an engaging account of how product design emerged in America. Through simple language and personal stories, it conveys the deep essence of design thinking. As I read through the book, I mentally checked off the sections of my course (and the textbooks) on HCI design, reflecting on how my own thinking has evolved and can develop further.

The Role of the Designer

HCI has been shaped by an ongoing tension between designers and programmers. As interface design moved from the domain of programmers to that of a new generation of interaction designers (Winograd 1997), there has been a persistent struggle over whose concerns should drive the process. Dreyfuss worked with mechanical engineers and fought their tendency to treat design as a cosmetic to be applied after the "real work" was done. Early in his career, he turned down a commission from Macy's:

> A fundamental premise was involved in my refusal—one from which I have never retreated. An honest job of design should flow from the inside out, not from the outside in. . . . Some manufacturers were reluctant to accept this point of view. They considered the industrial designer merely a decorator, to be called in when the product was finished. . . . In time manufacturers learned that good industrial design is a silent salesman, an unwritten advertisement, an unspoken radio or television commercial, contributing not merely increased efficiency and a more pleasing appearance to their products, but also assurance and confidence. (1955, p. 18)

HCI has developed a wide range of methods to produce efficiency, and we draw on graphic and industrial design to provide pleasing appearance. But what contributes "assurance and confidence?" In creating the d.school, we focused on students learning the essence of "design thinking." This is not a specific technique or skill, but an approach to the people and design problems, one that was so well articulated by Dreyfuss.

Affordances

Although he didn't have the theoretical analysis of Gibson's ecological psychology (Gibson 1979), Dreyfuss emphasized the visibility of affordances:

We consciously avoid hidden controls or concealed handles on everything we do. If a door or a panel is supposed to open, we try through design to show how it opens. If something is to be lifted or operated by a handle, we try to integrate the lifting device into the design, but never conceal it. At the expense of forfeiting originality . . . we try to make things obvious to operate. (1955, p. 71)

In describing his experience as a stage scenery designer, Dreyfuss even uses Norman's (1988) favorite example of affordances, the doorknob, in pointing out that function needs to be treated in conjunction with appearance. The creative challenge is how to achieve visibility without forfeiting originality. The book shows plentiful designs by Dreyfuss in which he was able to achieve both.

Human Factors

The book devotes an entire chapter to "Joe and Josephine," the personification of human needs and capacities:

If this book can have a hero and a heroine, they are a couple we call Joe and Josephine. . . . They occupy places of honor on the walls of our New York and California offices. . . . They remind us that everything we design is used by people and that people come in many sizes and have varying physical attributes. . . . Our job is to make Joe and Josephine compatible with their environment. (1955, p. 26)

As a pioneer of ergonomics, much of Dreyfuss's focus was on human physical measurements and capacities, as presented in *The Measure of Man* (Dreyfuss 1960). This led to "human factors" research, which in turn was the origin of HCI. The new challenge we face today is to keep visible reminders of the subtler and less easily depictable social and cultural differences that determine the compatibility of people with products and interfaces as they become global in their reach.

Contextual Design

Dreyfuss deeply understood that design grow's from empathy with the people who buy and use his clients' products. He was relentless in entering the field and experiencing from the perspective of the "users" (though he didn't use that term):

I have washed clothes, cooked, driven a tractor, run a Diesel locomotive, spread manure, vacuumed rugs, and ridden in an armored tank. I have operated a sewing machine, a telephone switchboard, a corn picker, a lift truck, a turret lathe, and a linotype machine. . . . I wore a hearing aid for a day and almost went deaf. (1955, p. 64)

For every design, the starting point is human experience. The skill he developed in his design staff was knowing how to see and to listen. I recently cotaught a course in which empathy with the user was the key focus, and we explored methods from cameras and probes to experience prototypes and bodystorming. No matter how many times we repeat the mantra "know your user," there is always more that can be done, and Dreyfuss well understood this.

Interface Metaphors

The adoption of the "desktop metaphor" reflected a sensibility that Dreyfuss called "survival form":

> Almost without exception, our designs include an ingredient we call survival form. We deliberately incorporate into the product some remembered detail that will recall to the users a similar article put to a similar use. People will more readily accept something new, we feel, if they recognize something out of the past. (1955, p. 59)

But he also recognized the need to move beyond survival form. Predicting the airline seats of the future, he said:

> We appear to be in a transitional period. Such earth-bound symbols as upholstered seats and carpets and little window curtains have given this pioneer generation of air travelers a security that as needed. Now that they have that security, passengers may anticipate interiors designed along functional lines. (1955, p. 133)

Dreyfuss worked at a time when electricity and engines were becoming common in America, and the designer was motivating and smoothing the transition so that these potentially intimidating technologies—motors, irons, refrigerators, telephones—could become accepted and even taken for granted. Today we are doing the equivalent for computing technologies, and a key question is how to give our users the security to let go of the "window curtains" in their interfaces.

Iterative Prototyping

Dreyfuss's methods rested on a cycle of sketching, prototyping, and learning from feedback.

> We enter into close co-operation with the engineers. . . . Our common denominators are the same—Joe and Josephine. We go over countless rough sketches. . . . Three-dimensional clay, plaster, wood, or plastic models are developed . . . as soon as possible we get a form into clay and actually do our designing in this pliable material. The final model—a working one, if possible—is presented to the entire client group. (1955, p. 46)

He pioneered "experience prototyping" in projects ranging from trains and ocean liners to a futuristic interactive workspace designed for the Chiefs of Staff in World War II:

A highly practical form of research is possible when mock-ups of our designs are built. When we worked on the designs of the interiors of six liners for American Export, we rented an old stable . . . and built eight staterooms. . . . The rooms were completely furnished and made livable in every detail, but were entirely different in size and type. We invited guinea-pig travelers who packed luggage as if they were going on an ocean voyage. (1955, p. 69)

Although there has been much discussion of user experience in HCI, the move to explicit experience prototyping (rather than artifact-centered prototyping) has tremendous future potential. It has been part of participatory design (Ehn and Kyng 1991), and more recent developments (Buchenau and Suri 2000) provide an exciting new avenue of exploration in our design courses.

Emotional Design

As an industrial designer, Dreyfuss saw the emotional appeal of products in terms of sales:

Sales appeal is an elusive, psychological value. It is the subtle, silent selling the product must do, over and above its eye appeal. The product must express quality through the unity of design, through texture, through simplicity and forthrightness . . . an amalgam of how a product feels to the touch, how it operates, and the association of pleasant ideas it conjures up in the purchaser's mind. (1955, p. 182)

He campaigned for clean, functional design in a world that was just emerging from the decorative excesses of Victorian tastes. At the same time, he opposed the trendy use of "streamlining" for everything from toasters to pencil sharpeners, while appreciating the aesthetic drive behind it:

The designer was in the right stable but on the wrong horse. . . . out of the era of so-called streamlining, the designer learned a great deal about clean, graceful, unencumbered design. Call it cleanlining instead of streamlining, and you have an ideal that the designer today still tries to achieve. (1955, p. 77)

These ideas are still highly relevant today, raising such questions as: Have notable examples such as the Google interface and the iPod brought "cleanlining" to interaction design? Is the proliferation of virtual three-dimensional object interfaces the current version of "everything streamlined"?

Calm Technology

Dreyfuss saw design as meeting more than merely practical needs. He had a higher goal of bringing serenity to the life of the people who used his products, presaging Weiser and Brown's (1996) later appeal to "calm technology":

A person can aspire to live and work in an environment of meditative calm. . . . I have the temerity to suggest that, by reducing objects to simple, unobtrusive forms, by relieving them of absurd and excessive decoration, by using appropriate colors and textures, and by avoiding obtrusive noises, we contribute to the serenity of those who use them. This is what we try to do. (Dreyfuss 1955, p. 240)

As we have progressed from "interface programming" to interaction design, we keep rediscovering territories of Dreyfuss's America. His focus on human factors created an intellectual strand still visible in the name of our major HCI conference. His model for industrial design was taken up as the core of the product design field, and is alive today in the major firms, such as IDEO, which cross over between traditional product design and interaction. His intellectual influence has become pervasive, as people from the various provinces of the design world have brought the spirit of design to human–computer interaction (Winograd 1996).

The HCI world has come a long way in its thinking about design, and there is still a long way to go. In creating our interdisciplinary design courses at the d.school we have found Dreyfuss an inspiration to keep a focus on the essence of design thinking—on empathizing deeply with the user, on relentless iterative prototyping, and on the power of design to affect people's lives. For Dreyfuss, the quest of the designer was to bring serenity to the Joes and Josephines of the world. In today's world of massively increased technological sophistication and complexity, we should aim for no less.

32

Interaction Design Considered as a Craft

Jonas Löwgren
Malmö University, Malmö, Sweden

D. Wroblewski, 1991: "The Construction of Human–Computer Interfaces Considered as a Craft"

In 1991, David A. Wroblewski, of the MCC Human Interface Laboratory in Austin, Texas, published a book chapter entitled "The Construction of Human–Computer Interfaces Considered as a Craft" (Wroblewski 1991). The work has not been heavily cited since then (ten citations in Google Scholar, June 2006), and I consider it something of a forgotten gem.

I read Wroblewski's work a couple of years after its publication, and when I revisit it now thirteen years later, the expressive margin notes convey my excitement about the ideas. What is even more striking in retrospect is how strongly Wroblewski's ideas have resonated in my own career as what we might today call an interaction designer in academia. In what follows, I will go through Wroblewski's main points and discuss their significance not only to me but to the interaction design discipline as a whole. But first, a few words on the personal history that has led up to my current perspective on interaction design.

I completed a Ph.D. in computer-science flavored HCI in 1991 and then worked for a year in a user-centered design consultancy. I found that the HCI ideals and techniques I'd learned in academia were more or less irrelevant to professional work at the time, which led me to return to university and form a research group to study software development practice and ways of making it more use-oriented. One of our most important results was that the parallel growth of problem framings and proposed solutions should not be seen as a shortcoming to be addressed with more structured methods, but rather as a core property of the practice. This was the starting point for an ongoing orientation toward the design disciplines and the field of design theory, which included studying Wroblewski's paper.

In 1995 I felt ready to "come out" in the academic community with the idea that software development can be seen as a design discipline (Löwgren 1995). Since then, I have spent my time helping to build a new teaching and research institution for interaction design, teaching future interaction designers, practicing interaction design as a way to develop knowledge (primarily in the fields of cross-media products and interactive visualizations), and reflecting on the practice in order to develop contributions to the field of interaction design theory and methodology.

It should be pointed out that when I use the term "interaction design," I refer to a design discipline concerned with the digital materials most closely related to product design and architecture in terms of its practices and intellectual foundations. Characteristics of interaction design include the parallel exploration of problem framings and solution possibilities; a focus on transforming use situations; and the synthesis of instrumental, aesthetical, and ethical perspectives. Thus the foundations of interaction design are different from those of HCI (Löwgren 2002), even though the two fields share a focus on use situations and ways of transforming them.

But it is high time to return to Wroblewski's work. He starts from the assumption that what he calls the construction of human–computer interfaces can be seen as a craft, in the traditional sense of the word, and then draws out a range of implications from this perspective exercise. At the end of the paper (p. 17), he summarizes his main insights in seven key points:

1. A craft is any process that attempts to create a functional artifact without separating design from manufacture.
2. Significant by-products of the craft process are new tools and materials as well as the intended artifact. The distinction between tools and materials begins to dissolve when viewed this way.
3. Creating software is sometimes, but not always, a craft. The degree of variability in practice is due to the availability of a reliable specification.
4. Creating a human–computer interface is usually, and perhaps always, a craft, because of the investigative nature of each design.

The first four points mainly address the validity of his perspective experiment, by identifying the similarities between interaction design and other craft-based disciplines. It is particularly interesting for our purposes to note that software—and to some extent also hardware—by necessity dissolves the distinction between tool and material, as is suggested in Wroblewski's discussion of blacksmiths: "As you might expect, this categorical breakdown [of tools vs. materials] is complete in situations where the craftsman's trade involves working the very materials from which his tools are made" (1991, p. 4).

In the contemporary world of digital artifacts, Wroblewski's observation is relevant far beyond the secluded camps of professional designers and engineers; a new craft culture is rapidly emerging among hobbyists and skilled amateurs who are appropriating, hacking, and subverting the digital tools/materials through open source software, mashups, shareware, plugins, game mods, machinima, and new media arts. This development means that interaction design is in fact moving toward an even more traditional craft culture where not only tools and materials blend, but also design and use.

5. Productive HCI research can take the form of facile tools and responsive materials, articulate craftsmanship, or craft-methodology.
6. We can begin to codify operational design knowledge by searching for and articulating design economies at work within individual interfaces.

Wroblewski's points 5 and 6 sketch the implications for research of considering interaction design a craft. We can note that fifteen years have not in fact led to significant advances in "facile tools and responsive materials." When it comes to articulate craftsmanship and codifying operational design knowledge, however, we find that some promising directions are starting to emerge. Wroblewski discusses the discrepancy between HCI research and practical craft knowledge: "The traditional answer has been to investigate and describe the physical and logical processes at work within the work materials, or the psychological processes that guide human performance in the appreciation or use of the craft product. Unfortunately, much information generated this way is not used in practice because it is not posed in a form useful to making decisions in the context of crafting actual products" (1991, p. 13). He moves on to outline an alternative: "Another role we could play is that of the *articulate craftsman*. In this role, the researcher reports the forces that shape crafted artifacts as a result of undertaking the craft activities, in a form meaningful to the practice context, though not necessarily useful in traditional analytic or quantitative techniques."

Recent years have seen several attempts to codify operational design knowledge. For instance, the notion of *patterns* as a way to capture best-practice and inspirational design knowledge has attracted significant interest in interaction design (for an overview, see http://www.visi.com/~snowfall/InteractionPatterns.html/). Patterns aim primarily to support the generative side of design by extending the designer's repertoire (Schön 1987); a complementary approach is to articulate *experiential qualities* (Löwgren 2006) to support design assessment (Nelson and Stolterman 2003). Furthermore, Krippendorff (2006) identifies *accounts of solution space explorations* as a means for validation in a design research context. Finally, it should be mentioned Malmö University and other design schools routinely ask students for *design process accounts*, highlighting key decisions and their grounds, directly building on Wroblewski's notion of the articulate craftsman. Similarly, the idea of craft methodology is increasingly making its influence felt as interaction design continues to draw on existing work in design studies, including seminal concepts such as Schön's (1987) notion of the *reflective practitioner*.

7. Two approaches to teaching HCI as a craft are apprenticeship and exposure to paradigmatic examples.

Wroblewski's final point concerns teaching, or, more generally, ways of facilitating people's building of knowledge. Partly owing to Wroblewski's influential emphasis on apprenticeship and exposure to paradigmatic examples, Malmö University has implemented a studio-based learning model similar to standard pedagogical practices in traditional design schools, where learning is based on studio work guided by a "master" designer. Typical studio projects involve an introduction to the design field and its key issues, background research (including the study of paradigmatic examples), explorative design work and assessment, and collective critique sessions. What sets interaction design slightly apart in pedagogical terms is its multidisciplinary nature, which necessitates more focus on group work than in traditional design schools.

Wroblewski concludes his summary of the seven key points by pointing out the uniqueness of each design discipline, which resides in their respective materialities:

> The future of software practice and HCI construction belongs to those who take their craft most seriously and least respect the bounds of tradition, be they craft or science. I have argued that it is instructive to study other craft and design professions, but we must also be mindful of the limits of such analogies. Fundamentally, the materials shape the craft. Computer programs are unlike any other material, and the form of craftsmanship in software will surely be unique. (1991, p. 17)

Interaction design, or "craftsmanship in software" as Wroblewski puts it, is unique in the sense that the digital materials we shape are temporal as much as they are spatial. That is, the experience of using a digital artifact is shaped not only by its two- or three-dimensional form, but equally by its behavior over time.

As I have explored the directions suggested by Wroblewski fifteen years ago, I have found that the temporal/spatial nature of the material implies a number of specific issues. First, there is the question of an *aesthetic* of interaction design. Aesthetic concepts from graphic design and product design do not capture the feeling of use over time—how the interactive behavior of the digital artifact is experienced. Second, the practical work of interaction design demands new *sketching techniques* that are as fluent as the pencil-and-paper sketching of form but that capture temporal qualities in richer ways. Finally, and related to Wroblewski's points 5 and 6, we are only beginning to understand the ways in which an articulate craftsman can communicate in professional and academic settings.

In retrospect, it is striking how much intellectual debt the research issues I today find important in interaction design owe to Wroblewski's prescient craft perspective.

33

Designing "Up" in the Software Industry

Lynn Cherny
Autodesk, Inc., Waltham, Massachusetts, U.S.A.

D. Forsythe, 1995: "Ethics and Politics of Studying 'Up' in Technoscience"

As I finished graduate school, Diana Forsythe introduced me to the concept of "studying up," a situation in which the ethnographer studies a community or institution of people with higher status and power over her. Diana's field at the time was in medical informatics; she worked among and wrote about the builders of expert systems that incorporate medical expertise. She found that collaboration between social scientists and artificial intelligence (AI) researchers was challenging because of their very different understanding of users and data. Her contributions to system design were not taken seriously; she believed this was the result of her position as a social scientist rather than technical contributor on the project.

Diana presented "Ethics and Politics of Studying 'Up' in Technoscience" in 1995 to an audience of fellow anthropologists (and me) at their annual meeting. She described challenges faced by ethnographers working in technical settings, which I paraphrase:

Complex roles We are studying similarly educated people with interests that overlap with ours (e.g., software). The roles of participant, observer, critic, employee, and colleague are blurred and difficult to separate.

Power differential Informants and colleagues are not powerless, but have power over us financially and in terms of access to field sites and resources. If they contest what we say about them or their work, they can have a significant impact on our job and career.

Minority status Although not called out explicitly, it's implicit in all her work that the social scientist working in the field is a minority among a majority of engineers and scientists.

"Your job is easier" The data that we collect and consider important for design are considered dismissible in various ways, including: "It takes no expertise (anyone can do ethnography)" and "It's all just anecdotal." (See also Forsythe 1998.)

I was at the time a participant-observer among a young technical community in an online chat system, a constructed virtual world known as a "MUD" (or "multiuser dungeon"). My informants were potential future colleagues or employers after my graduation, and all were reading and arguing with my papers as I produced them. My ethical and methodological concerns are summarized in the postscript of my book (Cherny 1999). Over the next few years, I did work with some of them at different companies, suffering lingering doubts over our historical reader-writer relationship.

During this period, in midnight introspection I concluded that I didn't want to continue in research but instead wanted to move into interface design. I wanted to focus on creating visible change in products, rather than obliquely influencing social systems and research methods as a social scientist studying forms of online community.

As I transitioned, the issues Diana sensitized me to didn't vanish; they mutated. I've now worked as a designer or usability engineer at Excite.com, TiVo, Adobe, The MathWorks, and Autodesk. I am a colleague of engineers who build systems, as Diana was; but I am still a minority, designing from a social science perspective, with a very different understanding of what it means to collect data and create "good design."

The Job of the User-Centered Designer

User-centered design (UCD) is understood within the HCI community as a philosophy and process that involves iteration of design based on user feedback at multiple work stages. Job titles often associated with this practice include "usability engineer" and "interaction designer." In my experience, the concept of user-centered design is an HCI-internal concept, rarely spoken of by outsiders in business or development organizations. Development methods such as "agile" are better known among the software community. Nevertheless, there are lots of jobs for UCD professionals. Yahoo posted open positions 875 times on the Bay Area SigCHI job bank in the period from spring 2003 to spring 2006; Google, the closest runner-up, posted 585 (Cherny 2006).

In such listings, the UCD professional is required to collect user data (e.g., perform site visits, deploy surveys); transform this data into design concepts at various levels (workflow diagrams, low and high fidelity mockups, style guides); evaluate design and iterate (via usability testing and heuristic evaluation, then revising and re-presenting the new designs to the team); deliver detailed specifications conveying confidence in the designs documented therein; update specifications based on development input and testing results; review implementations to check that they have been built to spec; file UI bugs and track resolution; and, meanwhile, start collecting data to feed the next release cycle.

Obviously, this is a lot of work. And yet there is more to it. A recent scan of job postings netted phrases suggesting a secondary job function that hasn't yet become obsolete, the role of the UCD "evangelist": "Are you a person who enjoys creating and evangelizing feature design and UI architecture and who has strong, proven customer affinity and user empathy?" The UCD professional still has to argue for the validity of her position and methods, while doing the job itself at the same time. She is asked to be an agent of change, which suggests there is something recognized to be "wrong" with the current work processes by at least the hiring manager. Though not officially studying her organization and colleagues as would an ethnographer of technology creation, the designer must still bring a critical outsider's eye to her role in order to understand and improve on these flaws in the processes. I have experienced this myself. At one company that has had a sizable UI team for the last six years, I was informed by my manager that I could be "a great ambassador for the UI team." We were indeed still fighting a war, I discovered. The mantra "pick your battles" is common in design organizations, suggesting ongoing negotiations over disputed territory—decision making about the product—that may at any point erupt into conflict and potential loss of professional capital.

A third distinct function in many advertized UCD jobs is project management. The UCD professional must, while evangelizing, also "manage the design process, drive decisions, create schedules, and track issues"; she "must have strong project and people management skills and be able to function as project leader as well as individual contributor." Note that this is the role of project manager of the status quo—or enough of the status quo to be producing results from diverse individuals in harmony with existing schedules, admitting only negligible possibility of radical change to the process at the same time.

UCD professionals are usually employed by executives who do not have an HCI background (the glass ceiling above us remains an industry fact; see Shneiderman et al. 2002); they often have poor understanding of what we do and how we do it, and of the challenges we face daily. These executives are supporters insofar as they have secured a certain head count for us, but we remain critically outnumbered, minorities like Diana in her role as ethnographer. A colleague told me he was looking elsewhere because his current company "wasn't ready" to implement UCD, despite having hired him as a gesture in the right direction; one sole person isn't capable of changing an entire organization's methods, as many of us have learned the hard way.

Supportive executives may at times offer support within circumscribed limits. Evangelism might be required for cultural change, but the resulting conflict is often not welcome. "Champions" must be vocal, question tacit assumptions, expose criteria for decision making at the most basic levels, instantiate design concepts (often other people's ideas) before implementation in order to facilitate inspection and evaluation. This is not a comfortable process for many team participants. Higher status individuals often respond poorly to critique of their ideas by people they don't recognize as possessing skill or authority. (One consulting client told me that he would "believe" my usability testing data, but not my proposed expert review of their corporate design work, despite the greater cost of a test with twelve subjects.)

Hiring and performance reviews uncover status disparities by revealing outrageous or unrealistic expectations about our work or, frequently our personalities—while many engineers appear to operate free of psychosocial evaluation. At one company, one of my design candidates was criticized as "boring" and "hard to interrupt" by an engineering manager, these attributes apparently more important than her potential contributions to design quality. A usability manager told me that her staff were required to "get along with everyone" and that this was a critical competency. Salaries and shipping bonuses reflect a disparity in perceived contribution; UCD staff are often paid less than engineers despite their workload and the stress under which they operate. Their work is assumed to be nontechnical, when they are not writing code; and nontechnical work is seen as less valuable than technical work in most software organizations.

Data and Design Are "Easy"

Diana frequently encountered an assumption that qualitative field data were "anecdotal" and "easy" to collect, because the ethnographer, the actual instrument of analysis, made the work invisible to observers. I've encountered the same attitudes, both regarding data collection and design.

Minority status and conflicting roles for the designer often result in design failures when decisions are being made by a team at the whiteboard. Design discussions may lead to less than ideal compromises for the sake of project advancement when the sole designer in the room is also required to bring issues to timely closure, given her project management role. Don't assume that the team bows to her expertise in any way during these discussions; I've rarely seen design direction accepted without debate, and on some teams the most trivial of details (radio buttons or checkbox?) causes the most severe bickering. Design looks simple and sometimes random to outsiders and so the substance of it is sometimes assumed to be trivial as well; and big picture workflow issues or capability decisions are often assumed to be outside our domain or skill set, unlike, say, icons.

Business reliance on second-hand market research data often leads to conflict for the UCD professional armed with an alternate or deeper understanding of research methods. A product management director once provided feedback to my manager that I was allowed "to listen, not talk" at product team meetings, after an incident in which I questioned the product plan rationale based on data I had previously presented from user research. Market research data is often not shared or exposed to examination, unlike UCD data which is integrated into the design process.

Usability testing, often made as visible as possible to the development team, is routinely questioned as to its validity. I find this particularly discouraging since such testing is regarded within the HCI community as a good way to ease "usability" into many companies. Observers may dismiss the qualitative data with complaints about too few subjects, recruitment of the "wrong" or "stupid" users or users who didn't read the required documentation, flaws in the prototype or tasks, and so on. During observation of the first usability test ever done on a version 8 product, one developer asked me, "Don't we already know all of this?" I was paralyzed for a minute, reflecting on our relative frames of reference for what was going on here; who "we" were to him, what we might "know," what "this" meant to him, and how to explain what I was seeing and why it might be different from what he saw but was nevertheless—and perhaps *because* of that difference—potentially valuable.

I thought of Diana.

Implications for Design

As UCD professionals, we are hired and evaluated by metrics that reflect how enlightened the organization is to the value we bring and the challenges we face. In my experience, many of these organizations are less sophisticated than we expect at this point in HCI's evolution. Our ability to be innovative designers and to effect change in products and processes are challenged by the simultaneous requirement that we be "team players" and project managers. Design looks "easy" when it's done by a trained professional. Our qualitative data appear dismissible to engineering colleagues. Like Diana among AI researchers, we are outnumbered, and many executives are not yet truly supportive of our contributions as nontechnical team members in software development.

We may be required implicitly to be critics of our organizations in our role as evangelists; but I believe it's time explicitly to critique corporate design politics and our occasional complicit acceptance of our lack of influence. If we expose the differences in power and status that limit the practice of effective UCD, we might improve our position, and the position of our junior colleagues and students in the future.

34

Revisiting an Ethnocritical Approach to HCI: Verbal Privilege and Translation

Michael J. Muller
IBM Research, Cambridge, Massachusetts, U.S.A.

A. Krupat, 1992: *Ethnocriticism: Ethnography, History, Literature*

When I first read Arthur Krupat's book, *Ethnocriticism: Ethnography, History, Literature*, I was looking for serious, constructively critical interpretations of Native American cultural works. I had become frustrated by the seemingly narrow range of choices that were conventionally available. I wanted more. I wanted some sense of what the Native stories were and are, before they had been domesticated into forms that were easy for the dominant culture to assimilate. And I wanted some help in understanding what I was reading, exactly because I was a member of that dominant culture, and I wanted to educate myself to know more than that culture could teach me.

Krupat's work did indeed provide me with ways of thinking about Native American cultural works. But, somewhat unexpectedly, his work also provided me with new ways of thinking about the difficult issues in ethics, politics, and epistemology that HCI workers face when they work with users who have less organizational power than they themselves. To borrow a phrase from Barbara Kingsolver (1989), Krupat's work helped me to see myself and other HCI workers in "a new perspective on a power structure in which they were lodged like gravel in a tire." I found that his analysis of an analogous situation provided both an alarmingly precise description of our problems and a number of heuristic approaches for solutions to those problems. I will explain.

Krupat described the situation of the ethnohistorians during the period immediately after World War II, when the U.S. government was evaluating the claims of hundreds of Native Nations to sovereign nation status. For each nation, tribe, or band of Native Americans, the granting of sovereign nation status led to important advantages in their struggle for cultural survival within a majority culture that operated by different values, different concepts of what constitutes knowledge, different ways of preserving knowledge, different rules of evidence, and above all different ways of making and justifying decisions. A Native Nation that achieved sovereign nation status was allowed to conduct its own limited self-government, to manage land that it controlled, and to preserve its own values through education and community resources.

Yet the irony was that decisions about sovereign nation status were determined by rules specified by the U.S. Congress in establishing the Indian Claims Commission, whose working principles were written within the value system and cultural assumptions of the European colonists. Enter the ethnohistorians, who were anthropologists charged with the responsibility to translate from each Native Nation's language, culture, history, and claims into the language and evidentiary rules that were required by the first-world members of the U.S. Congress. Each ethnohistorian was thus at the cusp of two cultures, and had to face two bodies of knowledge, two ways of thinking about those knowledges, and two sets of rules for legitimating or delegitimating claims based on those knowledges.

The Native Nations had very little power when facing the U.S. government, and thus their survival depended on presenting their histories and making their claims in terms that the majority culture would find persuasive. Although an ethnohistorian might understand and sympathize with the Native view in a particular case, he or she was required to ignore any knowledge that did not fit into the rules of evidence and argumentation that Congress had specified for the Commission. Ethnohistorians faced a series of challenges, in ethics (how to mediate between two nations of vastly unequal powers), politics (how to argue for the Native Nations while remaining within the limits set by the Act), and epistemology (what did they know? how did they know it? what were they allowed to know?).

But what is the relevance to HCI? I have claimed (Muller 1997) that, when an industrial HCI worker analyzes the work practices of users, the situation can be eerily similar to that of the ethnohistorians—especially if the users have less organizational power than the HCI worker and the team that he or she represents. Like the ethnohistorian, the HCI worker must translate between the worlds of the less powerful (the users) and the more powerful (the development team, or the executives who assigned the project to the development team). Like the ethnohistorian, the HCI worker has access to the users' concepts of knowledge, the users' ways of using that knowledge, the users' rules of evidence, and the users' strategies for making and carrying out decisions. Like the ethnohistorian, the HCI worker must provide a version of the work of the users that fits into the rules of evidence and argumentation that are used by a more powerful constituency—software engineers or executives. Like the ethnohistorian, the HCI worker faces significant problems of ethics, politics, and epistemology.

Many of my own work dilemmas in product organizations now made much more sense to me. When I woke up in the middle of the night, sweating and guilt-ridden about a report or recommendation I had made, I could begin to see my work *not* simply in terms of analysis and engineering, but rather as a series of political acts, made within a political structure, and strongly shaped by conflicting loyalties within that structure—loyalties to the users, to my project teammates, to my own organization, and to our client organization. How was I to mediate between the nearly powerless users and the very powerful executives who had commissioned our work? How could I represent the complexity and subtlety of the users' work practices, when my own teammates and their executives wanted simple answers that were often based on erroneous and sometimes dismissive assumptions about the users?

Fortunately, Krupat (1992) went beyond problem analysis to propose a set of principles through which people in his position—in a position similar to that of the ethnohistorian—could come to understand a culture that was not their own; could learn to criticize the basis of their own power; could analyze how their perspective was unintentionally influenced by that power; and could explore ways of communicating effectively and respectfully across those dimensions of difference and power. Krupat wrote of three major principles:

- *Multiculturalism* in education, including a tolerance for ambiguity, a commitment to dialogue, and an active questioning of the assumptions of any culturally rooted perspective.
- *Polyvocal polity* in relationships, including an embracing of different views, a commitment to negotiated interactions and conclusions, and a *democratic epistemology* (my phrase) in which any characterization of a person or group should be stated in ways that allow the person or group to verify or validate the characterization.
- *Heterogeneity as a norm* in ethics, in which judgments and decisions are based in and reflect the interests of all the concerned parties, whose perspective are assumed to have equal validity (if not equal weight).

These concepts resonated for me with the participatory design methods that I had been reading about (Bjerknes, Ehn, and Kyng 1987; Schuler and Namioka 1993) and developing (Muller 1992, 2003; Muller et al. 1995), and provided me with a richer theoretical approach than the then-dominant, purely political rationales to participatory design. I modified Krupat's approaches to cultural critique, and, drawing on a large body of work in HCI and cultural studies, developed a series of questions or "ethnocritical heuristics" to help me think through the diverse and troubling choices I faced as an HCI worker (Muller 1997). These questions focused on the following general areas:

- *The analyst's location* with respect to the boundaries or hybrid regions between users and other stakeholders (e.g., within one group, or at the boundaries between groups).
- *Translation as a core process in HCI* (see also Muller 1999), in which the HCI worker translates the user's domain into terms understandable by the software professionals, and the HCI designer back-translates the system or product concepts into terms understandable by the users.
- *Verbal privilege as a core problem in HCI*, in which the HCI worker is required to speak with the other members of the team *on behalf of* or *in place of* the users (see also Roof and Wiegman 1995).

These concepts have continued to inform my approaches since then. I don't claim that these concepts have saved me from all mistakes in areas of ethics, politics, and epistemology, but I think that Krupat's influences on my work have reduced the number and impact of those mistakes.

35

Some Experience! Some Evolution!

Gilbert Cockton
University of Sunderland, Sunderland, U.K.

J. Whiteside, J. Bennett, and K. Holtzblatt, 1988: "Usability Engineering: Our Experience and Evolution"

John from IBM, and John and Karen from DEC (Digital Equipment Corporation), liked to share, and in 1988 they shared the experience and evolution of their usability engineering in the first ever HCI handbook (Whiteside, Bennett, and Holtzblatt 1988). They wrote as facilitators looking for collaborators in a new endeavor. They advised usability practitioners to discover results personally by adopting, adapting, and extending their methods. They knew that their work was provisional and evolving, and that cookbook-style method advocacy and authenticity could not mix. Usability specialists had to actively shape their own work, and not just copy from others.

This chapter introduced *contextual inquiry* to the HCI world. It excited my colleague at the Scottish HCI Centre, Brian Sharratt. He explained their shift from testing in the laboratory against preset targets to inquiring in the field, in the context of use. For the next eighteen years my knowledge of this chapter was based on these initial conversations with Brian and an occasional skim of the chapter in libraries, publisher's stands, or of colleagues' copies.

Only now have I finally read the chapter from beginning to end, and it is *more* fresh and relevant today than in 1988. When Brian ran through the points of their argument it all made sense to me. I was a school teacher before starting my HCI Ph.D. in 1983 and my education degree had covered the sociology of education, which emphasized the community context of schools. Context-independent HCI made no more sense than context-independent education. The philosophical background was familiar too. My initial history major had included the history of political thought, and my education degree added more philosophy. However, I was skeptical about how many HCI readers would (want to) grasp the authors' messages. My initial use of social perspectives in my Ph.D. work had been labeled as "purple prose" and I expected the authors to suffer the same fate within an HCI community that remained dominated by the program set out by Card, Moran, and Newell (1983). Human information processing and cognitive optimization were the order of the day, much as drill and rote learning had been the bedrock of education in a previous century. Thus I read far more cognitive psychology as an HCI Ph.D. student than I had as an education undergraduate! But, as a school teacher, social perspectives from my degree had proved far more effective in the classroom than cognitive ones.

I followed Karen and collaborators' work as it evolved within and beyond DEC (Wixon, Holtzblatt, and Knox 1990; Beyer and Holzblatt 1996). One of my Ph.D. students, Steven Clarke, was excited by the 1993 CACM paper, and based much of his Ph.D. (Clarke 1997) on the 1996 book.

I've always felt that I understood everything in the chapter, even though I'd never properly read it. Discussions with Karen at Morgan Kauffman receptions at CHIs since 1998 reinforced this misunderstanding, as we focused on issues concerning contextual inquiry and interpretation of field data within the handbook chapter.

My enduring memory of the authors' argument was that laboratory testing doesn't work and that field methods are essential. Reading the chapter properly for the first time, I can see that this is an oversimplification. The chapter is in three parts. The first covers their experience with usability engineering over several years at DEC and IBM. This *unevolved* experience actually remains close to the state of the art. It is clear that their approach to laboratory testing *did* work, but that with field methods *they could do even better*, creating improvements of 300 percent rather than 30 percent. Part 2 is a short introduction to phenomenological approaches. As I'd used these in my undergraduate dissertation on commonsense knowledge and humanities curricula, I'd just skimmed these pages, but even there I'd missed so much. Part 3 is the first-ever coverage of contextual inquiry, DEC technical reports apart. This is largely what I remember about the chapter, that is, the *evolution* of usability engineering into contextual design.

Part 1 is excellent. John and Mashyna (1997) had argued that *downstream utility* should be the main evaluation criterion for evaluation methods. Practices at IBM and DEC had relevant measures for this in place at least a decade before there was any extensive HCI research focus on downstream utility (which is only now reaching any critical mass; see, e.g., Stage and Hornbæk 2006). User testing in the 1980s at IBM and Digital was focused on "what will count as success" with a clarity and repeatability that failed to inform 1990s research dilemmas on the true nature of usability problems (Lavery, Cockton, and Atkinson 1997). The usability process was then firmly located in a well-managed commercial engineering design process. It thus did not suffer from current difficulties in making usability relevant to development processes that come closer to simple "making" or "building" than "design for a purpose" (Cockton 2006). IBM and DEC's processes had explicit goals and shared understandings of "how satisfactory completion will be judged." There is a painful gap between the maturity of these usability processes and the development chaos in some current research studies of downstream utility.

Usability at IBM and DEC was a well-managed process, with sensible and flexible joint target setting. Usability specialists acted as facilitators, empowering designers through coaching to set project-specific usability targets, and avoiding the naive researcher's obsession with universal definitions of "usability." Lists of possible usability attributes are presented in part 1, with a clear warning that these are neither universal nor mandatory. The phenomenological and existential perspectives in this chapter require responsible independent action from usability specialists. Although parts 2 and 3 of the chapter focused on context, part 1 clearly took a contextual approach to defining and measuring usability: "we find that we tailor the construction of actual usability specifications to fit the needs of each individual situation" (p. 798). This process is illustrated via the iterative development of DEC's EVE text editor.

You have to read the rest yourself. However, I would regard approaches in part 1 as the minimal competences for specialists *and* organizations employing usability approaches. Sadly, their standards of empirical evaluation, causal analysis, design change recommendations, and process management are rarely met in published HCI research. Compared with DEC's and IBM's standards from the 1980s, too much HCI research today could be regarded as incompetent.

Why has this wisdom been buried for so long? Quite simply, because myself and others were drawn to the *evolution* part of this chapter (and its further evolution) and not the *experience*. However, their experience remains state of the art as far as laboratory-based testing within an engineering process is concerned. An important part of HCI history must be recovered here.

The *evolution* part is better known, because it introduced contextual inquiry to a wider world, but just as psychologically focused HCI remained dominant and drove social perspectives into a largely separate CSCW community from 1986 onward, so ethnography came to dominate research discourses on context. Holzblatt and colleagues' pragmatic development of contextual design was eclipsed by ethnography's arrival, with Karen giving a long overdue HCI conference keynote in 1999 at INTERACT in Edinburgh. HCI research in the 1990s thus failed to absorb the *experience* of Whiteside, Bennett, and Holtzblatt, as well as the evolution of contextual design. The *evolved* approaches in their chapter were taken up by few HCI researchers and usability practitioners. The main influence was to extend the best usability practice to include field methods, but the excellent engineering design in their experience has been largely ignored. HCI research missed out on developing a balance of approaches from design, engineering, psychology, and social science, and thus failed to integrate the authors' *evolution* with their *experience*.

In HCI research publications, social approaches have remained largely academic and detached from real engineering and design practice, especially commercial practice. The potential of grounding engineering design in social approaches has thus been largely missed. Instead, *interaction design* within its largely unpublished commercial design contexts has taken the best of HCI and claimed it for itself, transforming it into a general "design thinking" approach (Brown 2005) that now underpins innovation and competitive advantage across a range of industries.

This chapter remains essential reading. The equivalent chapter in the second edition of the handbook was written by colleagues of Whiteside, Bennett, and Holtzblatt (Wixon and Wilson 1997), and focused much more on experience rather than evolution. Contextual inquiry/design became one of several "other approaches and methods" in the newer chapter. It was no longer an approach that delivered far more than laboratory testing by addressing inherent limitations of mainstream usability approaches (which once again are covered with a breadth, depth, and credibility of understanding by Wixon and Wilson that is sadly rare in current usability writing).

Although the original chapter is now hard to access, it is a key historical turning point in HCI, not from the laboratory to the field as many may believe, but from the laboratory *alone* to the laboratory *and* the field. Also, the term *user experience* is ubiquitous in the chapter, fifteen years before the first SIGCHI cosponsored DUX conference. As with *design thinking, user experience* is now largely a product of design communities who have taken HCI ideas and actually done something with them. At least this chapter shows where it all began as R&D staff at IBM and DEC moved HCI beyond Taylor's stopwatch to Heidegger's detached phenomenology. Their experience with usability engineering was not enough, and they drove themselves through an evolution into something deeper, broader, and more authentic.

The question now is whether HCI can currently generate the breadth and depth of authenticity and innovation that were present at IBM and DEC in the 1980s.

HCI can start by reappropriating what interaction and service design communities have borrowed from us and refined in leading-edge practice across many domains. Returned to after eighteen years, Whiteside, Bennett, and Holtzblatt's chapter raises issues of whether HCI research can be effectively (and authentically) separated from leading-edge practice. I have no doubt that this chapter is one of the most substantial contributions ever, in both breadth and depth, to HCI research and practice. I hope that others will now read it and benefit from its magnificence.

36

Mumford Revisited

Susan M. Dray
Dray & Associates, Inc., Minneapolis, Minnesota, U.S.A.

E. Mumford and M. Weir, 1979: *Computer Systems in Work Design—The ETHICS Method*

Transformational inspiration is a wondrous and rare thing, yet this is exactly what Enid Mumford and Mary Weir achieved with their book, *Computer Systems in Work Design—The ETHICS Method* (Mumford and Weir 1979). This book was published in the days when computers were just beginning to move from the back office to the front office. At that time, the field of human–computer interaction (HCI) had not yet emerged as a separate subdiscipline from human factors. I was a newly minted Ph.D., working in a group that was just transitioning from the traditional human factors paradigm where we worked with design of physical controls ("knobs and dials"). Coming at such a pivotal time, this book inspired me and many others to broaden our thinking. It encouraged us to focus not only on designing computer systems for individuals, but also on the fit with organizations and organizational systems. It presaged the emergence of the participatory design, computer-supported cooperative work, and macroergonomics communities. In addition, Mumford and Weir's emphasis on the importance of the organizational environment required actually spending time in the field *with* representatives of all of the stakeholders in an organization. Thus their methods were precursors of the more field-based and contextual ways of collecting user data that have become so central to HCI and user-centered design (UCD) today.

To appreciate just how radical this book and the sociotechnical systems (STS) approach which it demonstrated and advocated really were, it is important to understand the technical environment of the time, as well as the then-standard practices for system design and implementation.

Office Technology in the Late 1970s

It is all too easy to forget the upheaval and stress that accompanied the introduction of computers into the office environment in the 1970s. Users were encountering these devices for the first time, without the basic computer background that is taken for granted in office workers today, and they often met them with anxiety. These users were far more diverse and far less technically inclined than the technical people who had developed the computers for data-crunching in the first place, and who were now responsible for rolling out the new office technology. These new "end users" faced vast changes in their jobs and in their lives. Their fears were exacerbated by the top-down way that technology was typically implemented.

The technology itself was intimidating. The first computers in offices were dumb terminals connected to mainframes, using command line interfaces or hierarchical menus. These terminals, which had so-called green screens, were monochrome CRTs with either green or amber or, later, white characters. Design was hampered by technical constraints and by lack of attention to usability. Lacking color, the only ways of highlighting were to use **bold face**, underlining, blinking, or reverse video characters. Sometimes, developers combined these to make text both **bold and underlined**, or worse, added blinking to that! In addition, in early word-processing menus, TEXT WAS PRESENTED IN ALL CAPITAL LETTERS. The result was a visually chaotic environment. Without pointing devices, people moved the cursor around with the tab key, and hit "enter" to make a selection. But even worse, the underlying mainframe technology was rigidly hierarchical, immutable, and extremely unforgiving of user mistakes. Imagine the headaches (literally) that this caused for users, of course made all the worse by the fact that many were none too thrilled to be working on these machines in the first place.

Although the technology in those days was far less sophisticated than it is today, even so it was vastly more sophisticated and complex than what most users, most of whom were clerical staff, had encountered up to that time. For them, the shift to mainframe word processing was fraught with challenge. For older secretaries, there was a loss of status as they struggled to master this new form of technology and lost much of what had been satisfying to them in their jobs. One secretary I worked with early in my career broke into tears while trying to explain how much she missed the status she had previously enjoyed because she was the fastest typist and could use her political savvy to get meetings scheduled with anyone in the company. With her "new computer," she was "just one of the typing pool again—and no longer the fastest at that because of these new-fangled computers!"

Organizational Contexts of System Implementation

Typically, word-processing implementations were managed by information technology (IT) departments. As is often true today, they were filled with people who understood and even loved computer technology. They were often the very technophiles who were responsible for companies' adopting word processing in the first place. Typically, they did not understand the users' context, fears, or concerns. In addition, even if they had understood the needs of users, their ability to fit the technology to them was limited, given the nature of the mainframe and the challenges that the technology itself posed. Making changes was costly and time-consuming, so it was easier to try to change humans (by training them) than to try to change the technology. Designing to improve the fit between users and technology, or even considering that fit might have anything to do with performance, was not "on their radar" at all.

Enter Sociotechnical Systems

It was in this context that *Computer Systems in Work Design—The ETHICS Method* was published. Enid Mumford was a longtime visionary and pioneer. Early in her career, as an action researcher, she did industrial relations research that included talking with coal miners (while they were working the coal face itself) and studying stevedores on the Liverpool docks. At Manchester Business School, as the first woman with a full professorship in a U.K. business school, she began doing research on the "human side" of computing long before it was fashionable. She was the first person to apply "sociotechnical systems" (STS) thinking to the design and implementation of computers in offices. She remained active in the field until her death in April 2006.

Perhaps it was because Mumford originally approached computers from an organizational perspective that she realized the significance of the organizational dynamics to the failure or success of the computer implementations that were becoming so widespread by the late 1970s. The term "usability" wasn't in the lexicon yet and wouldn't be in wide usage for at least another decade, but the issues which she made her priorities—the fit between the individual, the organization, and the technology—are clearly key elements in HCI today. As she pointed out:

> For many years past, engineering systems have been designed with little attention paid to the job-satisfaction needs of the worker operating the production process. These systems were introduced with the implicit assumption that the human being would and must adapt to the demands of the technology. (Mumford and Weir 1979, p. 8)

In addition:

> Because the human part of the system is either not included in the design process, or not considered until a very late stage, the human consequences of these decisions may not be recognized until the system is implemented. This can lead to the technical system influencing the human system in a way which was never envisaged by the systems designers. (Ibid., p. 9)

She clearly saw the problems that resulted from this lack of human involvement in system design.

The ETHICS method (Effective Technical and Human Implementation of Computer Systems) was defined as "a set of principles which assists the systematic and integrated design of both the technical *and* human parts of any system so that both technical efficiency *and* job satisfaction are increased" (ibid., p. 10). Mumford and Weir argued that this would naturally lead to many benefits to both organizations and individuals, most notably job satisfaction and a higher "quality of working life." Mumford's previous work in industrial relations gave her a broad understanding of the elements of job satisfaction from both an academic and a practical perspective, and, indeed, the first section of the book gives a review of the various schools of thought on the elements of job satisfaction. Her definition of job satisfaction was "the achievement of a good fit between job needs and expectations and job experience" (ibid., p. 15). She further broke this down into several categories of "fit," ranging from psychological fit to efficiency fit, task structure fit, and ethical fit.

This framework structures both measurement of current circumstances as well as job and technology (re)design efforts. The ETHICS method includes the following steps:

- *Diagnosis* of long-term organizational needs to assess current and future "fit."
- Sociotechnical systems (STS) *design* to match potential technical and social advantages in order to maximize both.
- Systems *monitoring* to track the process of implementation to correct issues as they arise.
- Post-change *evaluation* of the design and design approach in order to make future efforts more effective.

Not only does this book give readers an introduction to the ETHICS method, but it also provides three case studies in the form of "exercises." This makes it extremely useful for students and practitioners alike. I remember that I personally found this to be one of the most valuable parts of the book since it helped cement the core learning by guiding the reader through the process of applying the methods to three very different cases. Although the technology in these cases may seem dated, the exercise of applying the knowledge may still be valuable for readers. Indeed, the unfamiliarity of the technology itself may force the learner to focus on the situation described, rather than falling back on preconceived ideas of the world.

It is safe to say that Mumford is the "foremother" of much of the participatory design and computer-supported cooperative work that has been done over the past two decades. The ETHICS method was an early attempt to focus in a structured way on the importance of including and understanding the needs of humans in the design process. As such, it played a major role in shaping the fields of organizational design, management, information systems, and HCI, among others. It was not only interdisciplinary and participative, but also eminently practical. Her pragmatic inclusion of workers (now referred to as "users") on interdisciplinary teams helped to make her approach effective. In addition, her work was the basis for the development of many of the field research methods that are now common in HCI. Her interdisciplinary philosophy encouraged and supported the extension of her ideas and their application to ever-widening areas, including the areas she was focusing on at the time of her death, namely the problems of cyber-crime and drugs.

Enid Mumford gave a plenary address at CHI86. Unfortunately, the CHI community was not ready to hear her message. I remember my embarrassment at the number of people who walked out on her session. I only hope that we, as a community, can finally see the relevance of her work and her message as we develop and implement new technology. Only by understanding the technology, the user, and the user's context can we design technology that truly "works" for people and for the organizations in which they work.

VII

Tacking and Jibbing

How do we grow as researchers, designers, or practitioners? At times we encounter a new idea and we don't quite know what to do with it. What we eventually make of a new idea can have a profound impact on who we are and what we think. The essays in this section all have to do with, in one way or another, how particular pieces of work have changed people. In some cases the work changes how they see things and approach problems, in others it influences their direction of personal and professional growth, and in still other cases it provides fodder for shifting the views of colleagues. Research makes a difference in many ways, but in our opinion this—the altering of individual trajectories—is one of the most profound.

Although it is a bit difficult to take Judy Olson's claim to be a "slow learner" seriously, her account of Wanda Orlikowski's "Learning from Notes" is a fascinating description of a researcher versed in quantitative methods encountering qualitative research, and her resulting musings and gradual shift in approach. The next essay picks up this theme, with Elizabeth Churchill's discussion of King Beach's paper, "Becoming a Bartender" and her exploration of the tensions between a lab-based cognitive modeling perspective and a more situated perspective that tries to take into account the social, cultural, and material factors. Next we have Allison Woodruff's account of Mateas et al.'s early paper on computing in the home, which aptly demonstrates that even a short, "nonarchival" paper can have a lasting impact. The next two essays take up works from beyond the borders of HCI, Wendy Mackay discussing the impact of James Lovelock's book about the Gaia hypothesis on her view of HCI, and John Thomas recounting how *Peopleware*, a practitioner-oriented book by Tom DeMarco and Timothy Lister, shaped his approach to managing HCI groups. Next, William Newman asks why it is that HCI research so rarely offers answers to specific design questions, and takes us on his quest—beginning with Walter Vincenti's *What Engineers Know and How They Know It*—to find out. The section concludes with Michel Beaudouin-Lafon's reflections on Peter Wegner's "Why Interaction Is More Powerful Than Algorithms," a paper that, one senses, he delights in sharing with his harder-core computer science colleagues.

37

Learning from "Learning from Notes"

Judith S. Olson
University of Michigan, Ann Arbor, Michigan, U.S.A.

W. J. Orlikowski, 1992: "Learning from Notes: Organizational Issues in Groupware Implementation"

I am a slow learner. I, like many of us, take a while to assimilate new ways of thinking. Thus I was a slow learner with Orlikowski's 1992 CSCW paper, "Learning from Notes: Organizational Issues in Groupware Implementation." And, in the end she didn't persuade me wholly to take her side (see later comments about her philosophy). But I was significantly influenced by this paper in that it changed what I focused on in research and how I approached the issues.

In "Learning from Notes," Orlikowski reports on an in-depth analysis of one consulting office's adoption of Lotus Notes. Orlikowski, as an ethnographer, views this situation through the lens of structuration theory, which focuses not on the individual but the social order in which individuals are situated—the cultural norms, the reward structure, the distribution of power, and so on (Giddens 1986). Interestingly, neither the phrase "structuration theory" nor Giddens appears in the paper. With a keen ear, Orlikowski heard about a number of incidents where people expressed their frustration both with the rapid roll-out of the technology and their limited understanding of what Notes could do for their work. As a consequence, Notes was considered a failure—not because it wasn't used, but because people were not using the power of Notes. Instead of taking Notes as a "breakthrough technology," as the CIO had hoped, people merely used it to support the activities that had already been part of their work. Instead of sharing information, such as client backgrounds, proposal drafts, and the like, in shared folders, they used it as an email platform, sending attachments around as they had with their previous email system.

Several aspects of their culture proved to be barriers to full adoption as well. Since there was strong pressure to work on client projects and accumulate "billable hours," people were reluctant to take extra time, their own personal time, to learn Notes and appreciate its functionality. Furthermore, even if they did know how to use it, they were reluctant to share their best material because the path to promotion was individual achievement. Although the whole organization would be better off by everyone sharing their expertise, the individuality-focused reward structure fought against that. Why would their stars share their best work and make others more competitive?

These findings are often cited as things one has to do to ensure a smooth adoption:

Train people not just how to use the system, but how to incorporate it into their work (although they will adapt the technology a bit differently than the developers might have envisioned).

Design the incentive systems to encourage people to learn the systems (in this case, they should have opened an account to which to charge the learning time) and to make the purported goal attractive (in this case, they should have altered the reward structure to support the goal of sharing).

It might gall Orlikowski to have prescription arise from her work; as a good ethnomethodologist, she does not believe in generalizations, but holds rather that everything is highly specific. And yet, I react to her work through my own lens and adapt it to what I know and believe. The irony here is that I am doing what structuration theory would say I'd do. I'm taking her artifact and altering to fit my needs. My attitude about her philosophy was, "If you can't generalize, then what's the point?"

As an HCI researcher, I was looking for design or implementation prescriptions. "If you have the right functionality and the right design, and roll it out with the right social conscience, they will come." So the philosophy of not making generalizations inherent in ethnography did not fit my beliefs. But her method—being intensely engaged in an organization, doing lots of interviews, and then pointing out trends—was intriguing. I didn't know whether I could do it, but I did recognize that it was the only way to answer questions that I had not been able to address before.

I'm a lab person, a detail person, a quantitative measurement person. I was trained in experimental psychology, the predecessor to cognitive science, and at the time of Orlikowski's paper, I had been doing that for twenty-two years as a professor. Some old saw about old dogs and new tricks came to mind. I had studied expertise, memory organization, mental models, mnemonics, Cognitive modeling, then collaboration technology and small group dynamics—all in the lab. Even when I got out of the lab (twice) and videotaped software design meetings at two organizations, I looked at the details. We transcribed these meetings and coded them for who was talking, how long, what were they talking about, when were they talking about content as opposed to orchestrating themselves (Olson, Olson, and Carter 1992). We were counting things. We were drawing pictures of the state-transitions in the meetings and the growth of ideas and argumentation. I was happy.

Although fascinated by the insights in the Orlikowski paper, I, a scientist, was somewhat troubled with the method. She did ninety-one interviews in one office in over five months. Admittedly that's more than talking to a few people and getting their opinions. But, recalling that the scientific method requires replicable data collection and analysis, I was doubtful about whether this was genuine science. Even the paper itself says that "These findings need to be interpreted cautiously as they only reflect the adoption and early use experiences of a sample of the individuals within a specific office in what is a larger implementation . . ." (p. 363). And she continues, "it is possible with time, greater use, and appropriate circumstances, these early experiences will change." And yet hundreds of people cite this work. They believed. Why was that? Could I do the same thing?

What made this work believable?

First, the paper is very readable, and judiciously did not mention the body of philosophy which she espoused. This was not a paper to convince people to believe in structuration theory or the inability to generalize. It was a field study with very interesting results.

Second, readers could relate to the findings and see parallels in their own experience with the adoption of new technologies. Once the results were pointed out, people said, "Of course." In my own experience in the field (which later became field studies), I informally asked people about their adoption of various technologies. In one case, I was asking about the adoption of Notes. One high-level person said casually while walking down the hall, "I think I missed a meeting. I know how to operate it but I don't know why I want to." This resonates with the findings in the Orlikowski paper.

Third, the paper is filled with a number of quotes in everyday English, from real people, clustered to make a single point per group. Instead of one pithy quote, which a journalist would call a "sound bite," Orlikowski used twelve quotes to make one point, three long quotes to make another, and so on. Use of material like this is much like the use of Personas in HCI—it highlights the reality of the situation, that these were real people with real concerns expressed their own ways (Pruitt and Grudin 2003).

I was still troubled by the issue of replicability. But in my subsequent self-guided training to do this kind of work, I sat in on two important experiences. One was a session with Giddy Jordan and Lucy Suchman at Xerox PARC analyzing five minutes of videotape (for countless hours), and the other was a seminar on field studies at UC Irvine where one researcher challenged another researcher about whether she had done her analysis right. The idea is that after being immersed in the rich data corpus, you begin to extract patterns, conclusions. Soon thereafter, one has to have the discipline to take those new hypotheses and go back to the data to try to find counterexamples. Only by a thorough search, and here with a second analyst helping with that part of the work, can one be confident that the conclusions are sound. But in reporting the results, one always puts the disclaimer that this is what you saw in this situation and that results in other circumstances may differ. One hopes that with a number of cases, then, the real generalizations emerge.

What makes the work interesting?

Ethnographers look at life through the lens of culture, power, trust, and norms, things so implicit as to be hidden from normal consideration. Therefore, most things that are noticed in ethnography are interesting. Sometimes a phenomenon noticed in one arena (e.g., Alpha, the company in which the original paper's observations were made) is seen in another. My hearing "I must have missed a meeting," quoted above, serves as this kind of example.

In other cases, you observe something that is unexpected given your own experience. For example, on the way to a meeting at a large automobile company I saw one engineer walk into another's cubicle to find out that he was not there. He then wrote on the personal paper calendar open on his desk. This surprised me; I would neither leave my paper calendar open on my unlocked desk nor wish others to write in it. When I asked others about this, they said that at this company the norm was to use an electronic calendar on which others, under certain shared understandings, could write. For some reason, this person was not participating in the online calendar, but accommodated to the norm by leaving his paper calendar open.

But for me, probably the most important filter on whether or not something is interesting is to tell someone the story. This is a variation on the old saw, "I don't know what I think until I hear what I say." In the act of telling the story to someone else, you attempt to frame it in its most interesting, surprising way. And, then by seeing the reaction, you can tell whether it is truly interesting or not. Of course, the choice of whom you use in this role is important. Someone steeped in the same literature is the best, because they can see associations with others' work, and so on. I have been fortunate to have close collaborators who will listen to my stories (and I to theirs), notably Stephanie Teasley and Gary Olson.

So, now I do field work as well as lab work, because I do not want to miss out on interesting phenomena relevant to my goals of understanding how technology affects teams of individuals and designing suites of technologies to support work. Indeed, five years after reading "Learning from Notes," we wrote "Groupware in the Wild" (Olson and Teasley 1996). Four years after that came "Radical Collocation" (Teasley et al. 2000), which added surveys and daily diaries to observation and interview (I still like to count things). More recently we wrote "Distance Matters" which combines our lab and field work (Olson and Olson 2000), and we are now writing "Doing Science on the Internet" (Olson, Zimmerman, and Bos forthcoming). Although I have not given up my lab roots and even moved a bit into agent-based modeling, our whole line of field work from 1996 on wouldn't have happened if I hadn't wrestled with "Learning from Notes." I am a slow learner, but I do learn.

38

A Site for SOAR Eyes: (Re)placing Cognition

Elizabeth F. Churchill
Palo Alto Research Center (PARC), Palo Alto, California, U.S.A.

K. Beach, 1993: "Becoming a Bartender: The Role of External Memory Cues in a Work-directed Educational Activity"

One cannot mix a martini in a collins glass given society's conception of a martini.
—King Beach (1993)

"Being an academic means you will never be content," a friend said to me recently. "Just as you think you have grasped something, you will probably start challenging it. We are always looking for a new problem, a new way of looking at an old problem, or trying to pick holes in our or other people's theories."

Sometimes the impetus to rethink is initiated by a paper that is relatively unknown in one's area of research, one that is not widely regarded to be part of the canon. For me that paper was written by King Beach and published in a special issue of the *Journal of Applied Cognitive Psychology* in 1993 (Beach 1993). The paper had earlier been part of a symposium on memory and everyday life. The special issue was dedicated to cultural psychologist Sylvia Scribner, who had passed away in 1991 (for Scribner's writings, see Tobach et al. 1997).

Shifting My Perspective

The first thing that attracted me to King Beach's article was the title. This was not a title I would have expected to see in the *Journal of Applied Cognitive Psychology*. Somehow bars seem more for lay-psychologizing—not an "appropriate" place to carry out the serious work of psychological investigation. The second attractor was that a friend mentioned he'd read the paper, and thought it made some interesting points—a good example of social recommending at work. The paper was a quick read, but it "had legs"; it introduced me to new perspectives and new readings, and sparked questions that led to a personal perspective shift.

The Backdrop

Historically, HCI has been strongly influenced by cognitive information-processing models—using an understanding of cognitive processing in the design, for example, of interfaces, programming languages, and teaching aids. Some information-processing models reflect a computational model of mind; here, cognitive science and HCI overlap, with models of cognition that loosely draw inspiration from the cybernetic models of the 1950s.

This was the area of research with which I was engaged when Beach's paper was published. I had been building cognitive simulation models of people's mental models in SOAR, a production system cognitive architecture (Newell 1990). Models were crafted in the form of conditional rules for action (if *x* happens then do *y*) and were intended to show how the learning model that was built into SOAR ("chunking") mapped to human learning with practice. To make this mapping I carried out laboratory studies that charted people's performance over time on complex tasks. The overall purpose of this endeavor—simulation creation and validation—was the development of programmable user models (PUMs), models that designers could use to simulate how people were likely to comprehend, navigate, and search through information, and how people learn to do this more efficiently (more quickly) over time. PUMs could thus be used to help designers make better design choices about how to facilitate task execution.

Place Matters

What struck me about King Beach's paper? First, I was struck by where and how the work was done. Second, by implication, I was intrigued by what that meant for different conceptions of learning and knowing.

My work was based on building computer simulation models and carrying out lab-based experiments that identified some "pure" absolutes of memory and learning which could be extrapolated to the "real world" wherein those pure understandings could be extended or "contextualized." By contrast, following Scribner, Beach did not generate "ideal" models or carry out lab-based studies. He proposed the best site of study (even experimental study) to be the setting in which the activity itself takes place. Beach got out of the lab and conducted experimental science at bartending school; rather than coming up with an "analogue" of the bar in the laboratory, Beach went to the bar.

The subject of Beach's study was memory; precisely, how people remember the ingredients of complex cocktails and mix them correctly in busy, time-pressured environments. He enrolled in a commercial bartending school in New York City for a two-week course which involved lecture-demonstrations and practice sessions mixing drinks behind working bars. Bartending school graduates were expected to have the knowledge and skill to mix 100 different drinks from memory. Beach took notes while in class, notes that included some introspection but predominantly involved observation of others' activities. He also conducted structured and unstructured interviews. From his field observations he posited the issues bartenders attended to in their training—accuracy and speed—and derived an understanding of how students remembered and produced mixed drinks. He generated a set of experimental hypotheses regarding changes in memory strategies with developing experience. On-site experiments were set up with video cameras to capture what trainee and expert bartenders did; notably these experiments built on drills and tests that students were already doing in the class.

By moving out of the lab, Beach's work placed activity, knowledge, and cognitive processing in a social and material context in a way that my experimental tests and my simulations did not. By going into the field in this way, Beach established categories and actions that were meaningful to the participants themselves—he did not assume his way of mixing drinks would be the way; he did not indulge in "armchair-based ruminations and navel gazing" (as I used to call it) to generate his categories for investigation. He identified issues that drew on more general memory concepts but that were situated in the particulars of this place and these activities. Beach illustrated that one could derive one's categories for experimental work by understanding the environment itself, by carefully studying people *in situ* as they were acting on objects and evolving their understandings—by seeing what was and is meaningful to them in practice. Choosing categories to be observable, "countables," is always a delicate move of approximation; Beach's work illustrated a way in which this approximation could be grounded in the activity.

Cocktail Cognition

So how did students mix cocktails? Beach noted that novices are likely to mix drinks one at a time, following remembered recipes step by step. Experts are more likely to mix several drinks at a time, and use visual cues to remind themselves where they are in a process. Beach named these two systems of external memory cues used by the trainee and expert bartenders *verbal mnemonic symbols* (VMS) and *material mnemonic symbols* (MMS). The former are linguistic cues—names of drinks and their ingredients that are rehearsed verbally by the students as they follow recipes in the cocktail mixer guide. As these are linguistic cues, they are materially arbitrary with respect to their referents. Using a VMS strategy is time consuming and error prone in distracting situations, although it is the most obvious initial strategy for remembering drinks. By contrast, MMS are an integral part of the object to which they refer. Beach offers the example of a glass placed on the bar rail—the shape, location, and contents of the glass point to what can be added next and constrain the options for what the drink could ultimately be: *margarita, lemon drop, collins, martini, Martini . . . oops, that's not a martini, even though the glass is the same . . . it's got angostura bitters in it, so it must be a pink gin.* That is, expert bartenders actively order their working environment to scaffold memory—for example, using visually distinctive glasses, adding visible ingredients, and lining the glasses up in such a way that the drinks' list is remembered and the current state of progress easily deduced. Expert drink mixers thus tend to use methods that allow for interruption and distraction and enable them to focus on what matters—the customers. Strategies that are error prone are soon abandoned.

This experiment also revealed how trainee bartenders begin to see glasses and the bar differently through experience. They shift from selecting objects from rote memory of recipes to working with objects in the world. This move from list-memory to embodied, perceptual memory could not be achieved by my simulation models, which were effectively sightless and disembodied. In this latter view, the body is simply a convenient form of locomotion for the brain/mind; the eyes merely a means of sucking comprehensible data into the processor. Cognitive simulation models like mine would have emphasized the learning of lists of drink ingredients and the later execution of the recipe: place a dash of angostura bitters in the glass, place a measure of gin in the glass, add a lemon to the rim, goal achieved, end. The models would have predicted that drinks would be mixed in full one at a time—excellent modeling of the behavior exhibited by Beach's novices. But the models could not autonomously achieve the ontological shift to perceptual embodied memory in action that marked the move to expert bartending—the shift that Beach's paper so articulately described. The models were well designed; it was the assumptions that were built into them that suddenly seemed misguided.

Beyond the Bar

Beach's paper ends with a reflection on the experimental results using activity theory as a framework. The framework emphasizes that "internal," mental activities cannot be understood if they are analyzed separately from what is going on in the world (the "external" activities), because internal and external activities transform into each other. This allows for mental plans and simulations, and puts a great emphasis on "mediation" of internal (mental) activities and (external) actions through "tools"—in this instance the martini glass would be an example of a tool. In this study, Beach demonstrated a shift in mediation from internally driven recall to mediated recognition as the activity moved from acquiring knowledge of drink names and ingredients to a focus on accurate location- and artifact- (glass and position) cued recall which allowed the quick and accurate mixing of drinks in an interruptive environment. Activity theory also stresses that while things have objective properties that may be describable in terms of the natural sciences, they also have socially or culturally defined properties. Thus, Beach's use of activity theory points to the shared meanings of tools, their social and cultural significance—you simply wouldn't mix a martini in a collins glass. In this way tools embody and transmit social knowledge and norms.

In summary, the paper had several "aha" moments for me. First, its use of site-specific field investigations rather than generalized laboratory experiments to provide a grounded, *placed*, rather than abstracted, notion of cognition and cognitive processes; second, its demonstration of embodied cognition, that is, the active involvement of the physical artifacts and the body in considering how activities unfold; third, its concomitant acknowledgment of culturally embedded meanings as motivators and directors for action, highlighting that the laboratory itself is a culture with its own motivators for action that do not necessarily correspond to the motivators of other domains; and finally, its use of a conceptual framework that acknowledges the social, cultural, and material aspects of people's actions. As one reads the paper, cognition becomes inextricably linked to place—physically, perceptually, culturally, and theoretically. This paper made me realize that one could retain one's fascination with analytic rigor yet not give up on the enchantments of everydayness.

Relevant Today?

Beach's ideas remain relevant today. It is of course part of a larger trend of establishing the "real" world (i.e., outside the laboratory) as a legitimate setting for carrying out careful and detailed research on human cognition, action, and interaction. It is also thus part of the call to consider the situated nature of activity and the sociocultural contingencies of action. Beach's work, however, does not throw the baby out with the bathwater; it does not eschew experimentation altogether.

The method (and the paper) includes field work observation, on-site experiments and simulation experiments with the framework of activity theory. The work retains a notion of experimental investigation, even while it points to the importance of site-specific understandings.

Further, although novice and expert performance studies have largely fallen out of favor in HCI, human attention, learning, and memory are still of import in considering design decisions in the creation of interfaces, applications, products, and experiences of all kinds—from the design of personal information management tools to that of calendar tools and self-explanatory interfaces, to consideration of how we can support information indexing and tagging, and finally to the design of experiences that appropriately balance focus and interruption. These are just a few areas of current interest where attention, learning, and memory are at the core of what is being designed for, and in some ways, designed around.

39

You *Can* Go Home Again: Revisiting a Study of Domestic Computing

Allison Woodruff
Intel Research Berkeley, California, U.S.A.

M. Mateas, T. Salvador, J. Scholtz, and D. Sornsen, 1996: "Engineering Ethnography in the Home"

When I arrived at Intel Research Berkeley in 2004, Intel had a number of initiatives on the topic of the digital home. I was attracted to this topic, but my previous experience was in conducting interventions and studies in workplace environments or public spaces. I was uncertain how to approach the home, which presents unique challenges and opportunities for field-workers and designers. For example, it is a particularly private and potentially sensitive domain; participants are of diverse ages and backgrounds, and they have complex personal relationships with each other; the activities of interest are often mundane, so participants frequently have difficulty reporting them accurately; and access to the home may be limited. In facing these challenges, I was inspired by an approach described in 1996 by Intel researchers Michael Mateas, Tony Salvador, Jean Scholtz, and Doug Sorensen in their paper entitled "Engineering Ethnography in the Home" (Mateas et al. 1996).

This paper appeared in the *CHI 1996 Conference Companion* over a decade ago. It was a CHI "short paper," which according to the conventions at the time meant it was only two pages long and was not considered archival. CHI is a large conference with many tracks and a multivolume proceedings. It is easy to miss things at CHI, and I suspect that many researchers were not aware of this paper at the time it appeared.

Despite its brevity, the paper covers a great deal of material. In a sense, it is a microcosm of ethnographic investigation for design. In just two pages, this publication succinctly and clearly reports a method for investigating domestic computing, discusses findings on home life, and draws implications for design. More specifically, it introduces a method for home visits, presents important findings about domestic routines and the use of technology in the home, challenges fundamental assumptions about the design of the personal computer, and puts forward an alternative model of computing devices for the home.

Looking back, we can see that the paper was at the confluence of a number of emerging forces—a methodologically innovative paper about research in a new domain, conducted during the germination of a nascent research organization. The authors worked for Intel, in a group that helped pave the way for Intel Research, which would emerge several years later. Since the authors worked for Intel, it was natural that they were interested in the design of computing systems. More innovative (particularly at the time) was their choice of domain—the home. When the paper was published, very little indeed had been written on computing in the home (the more sociologically focused NOAH and HomeNet projects being the primary notable exceptions; see, e.g., Vitalari, Venkatesh, and Gronhaug 1985; Kraut et al. 1996).

The method used by the authors was qualitative and informed by ethnographic methods, although plainly the engagements with the participants were of short duration and did not constitute full ethnographies. At the time CHI was somewhat open to qualitative methods, although not as much as would come to be the case in subsequent years. This paper is an excellent example of the kind of work and findings that can be arrived at through qualitative methods. The authors studied the domestic activities of ten American families, visiting each home and including both parents and children in the discussion. The visits began with informal discussion over dinner, followed by a home tour, and then a "day walkthrough" using a "flannel board" (which later came to be called the "felt map"). Note that, as with many ethnographically informed inquiries, much care was taken to investigate the context (the family members, their routines, their home, etc.) rather than simply focusing on the use of technology. As an approach to doing research on technology in the home, this style of home visit, with discussion and home tours, holds up well today, as does the felt map. Much of this method is still used within many parts of Intel, and similar methods are now commonly used by researchers at other institutions as well. Of course there is a long history of researchers applying ethnographic methods in their investigations of various domains, but at the time it was fairly innovative to apply them to the study of domestic computing and home life. And the felt map was a particularly clever prompt, from which we benefited very directly.

In addition to describing this useful method, the paper also introduces a valuable model for thinking about the home, taking into account space, time, and communication in the home. For example, the authors investigated where people spent time in the home and for what purpose, and compared these findings with where the computers were positioned in the home. From these findings, the authors drew conclusions about devices that would be appropriate for the physical and temporal rhythms of the home. Specifically, they brought into question the notion of the traditional "monolithic PC" and argued that a collection of small appliances supporting multiple colocated users was likely more appropriate for domestic environments than the PCs that had historically been designed for business environments.

At Intel Research years later, one of my primary interests was to investigate how architectural layout and furniture interacted with the use of technology in the home, with an eye to designing not only better technology but better physical spaces in which to use technology. I began working with Scott Mainwaring and Ken Anderson in the People and Practices Research group at Intel Research, studying human behavior and the use of mobile technologies in the home, particularly as influenced by architectural form (see, e.g., Mainwaring and Woodruff 2005).

Mateas et al.'s previous work, with its related focus on the use of space, naturally influenced our thinking. Further, one of the authors of the 1996 paper (Tony Salvador) was at that time in the same group as my collaborators Scott and Ken. The felt map was well known within the group, although to my knowledge it had not been used since the initial study. When Scott and I were designing our protocol for our first set of home visits, Tony was kind enough to agree to meet with us to show us the felt map and tell us about his experience with it.

So it came about that, in the fall of 2004, I was lucky enough to see the actual felt map that had been reported in the 1996 paper. Tony brought in a big basket full of felt pieces and labels. He explained that the pieces of felt were used to quickly create a very rough representation of the home, with large rectangles indicating rooms and smaller pieces indicating significant objects and people. Participants and researchers then used this map to walk through the specifics of a recent day—pieces would be moved around on the map to illustrate routines and behavior.

This felt map with its movable pieces seemed like a great way to prompt participants to show us where people and devices were located in relation to each other and how they moved around in the home. I was particularly drawn to the informal nature of the felt map, which offers several advantages. For example, the felt map is obviously intended to be an abstract representation of the space, not a highly accurate one. In the spirit of informal user interfaces (Landay and Myers 1995), it encourages participants to focus on the high-level structure of the space and on their use of that space, rather than irrelevant details of the floor plan. Additionally, the felt map is playful and nonthreatening. It works well with children and with people who are not particularly comfortable with technology. Its playful and engaging nature is in tune with related techniques such as cultural probes (Gaver, Dunne, and Pacenti 1999).

Despite my enthusiasm, however, I had some reservations. When running studies, one is often confronted by a technique that sounds like a good idea but also gives one pause. Will the technique be socially awkward or intimidating for participants? Will using it make the researcher feel awkward or embarrassed in front of the participants? Will the results be "valid"? Will the technique yield results that are worth the extra effort, or will it simply be "more hassle than it's worth"? In the case of the felt map, Scott and I had some initial concerns that the population we were studying might find it a little too whimsical for their tastes, and we did not want to make participants uncomfortable. I was also concerned that participants would not actively engage with it—my intuition was that although participants might naturally reference locations on the map, it would be trickier to get them to actually move felt pieces around (and in fact Tony confirmed that this had been a challenge in the original study).

Growing as an interviewer sometimes requires reflection and a willingness to experiment, and I often have to push myself through my initial reluctance to use a new technique by working through a set of ethical and practical issues. Once I do so, my personal experience is invariably that these techniques pay off handsomely. The felt map was no exception. Inspired by the wonderful findings reported by Mateas et al. (1996), Scott and I pushed ourselves to address the issues, and we created a felt map of our own for use in our study. We were able to address perceptions of whimsicality through proper framing when we introduced the exercise, and like the authors of the original paper, we converged on a scheme in which the researchers often assisted in manipulation of the pieces. (I must say I am still not entirely satisfied regarding this latter point and hope to experiment with it more in the future.)

From the very first household we visited, we were glad we had made the effort. The felt map was a fantastic prompt for discussions with participants. Moving felt pieces around on the map proved very effective at eliciting stories about where objects and people were, and for what reasons. Walking through the day with the map brought a level of specificity to the exercise that plainly would not have been present in a more general question–answer format.

For example, in one house, the activity with the felt map uncovered that while a boyfriend was outside playing basketball with a friend, he had taken his girlfriend's laptop outside so his friend could check his email. This was an important story for our investigation of wireless laptop use, but the story probably would have been avoided in general conversation since taking the laptop outside was against the girlfriend's rules for the use of the laptop. However, the concreteness of the laptop felt piece sitting in the wrong place on the map encouraged the boyfriend to point out that the laptop had actually been outside. As another example, the map and the tokens nicely illustrated collections of objects that moved together—several participants created little stacks of devices (e.g., phone, PDA, and laptop) that would move around with them in the home.

At the time the paper was written, domestic computing was not yet an established area of research; in fact, this paper was a pioneering publication on the topic. More research has now been done in this area, but many open questions and design challenges remain. This paper is an excellent reminder of the value for design of investigating the broader context of home life, and an excellent exemplar of the results that can be achieved through the use of creative prompting materials.

40

From Gaia to HCI: On Multidisciplinary Design and Coadaptation

Wendy E. Mackay
INRIA, France

J. Lovelock, 1979: *Gaia: A New Look at Life on Earth*

In 1979, James Lovelock published a controversial book entitled *Gaia: A New look at Life on Earth*, which challenged the conventional wisdom about how the Earth evolved. He hypothesized that living organisms form a self-regulating system, named after the Greek Goddess *Gaia*, which is directly responsible for creating and maintaining the Earth's atmosphere. In other words, life did not simply evolve in response to preexisting physical conditions, but rather *coevolved*, regulating the Earth's physical conditions to create a homeostatic balance that has been maintained for eons. Although initially trained in chemistry, Lovelock worked outside and across the boundaries of "normal" science. He became a successful inventor of high-precision scientific instruments; his *electron capture detector* contributed to key discoveries including the pervasive role of pesticides in the environment. It was in his capacity as an inventor that he was hired by NASA to develop instruments to analyze extraterrestrial atmospheres and to address the question of whether or not there is life on Mars.

What, you might well ask, has this to do with human–computer interaction? For me, it is a story of the essential role of interdisciplinary research: how reaching across disciplines is essential for understanding certain kinds of phenomena and how sharing a common goal unites people across disciplinary boundaries. More specifically, it is about coevolution, but on a human scale. My doctoral dissertation, "Users and Customizable Software: A Co-adaptive Phenomenon" (Mackay 1990) is directly linked to the concept of coevolution and provides an explicit framework for showing both how technology influences the people who use it and how they in turn reinterpret it and adapt it in ways never envisioned by the original designers. To understand and create explicitly coadaptive systems requires expertise from multiple disciplines and is, I believe, essential for HCI as a field.

I first read *Gaia* in 1982, when I was a manager at Digital Equipment Corporation. I had written an authoring language that enabled nontechnical users to create educational software with text, graphics, and high-quality digital video from a videodisc. We simultaneously released IVIS, the first commercial interactive system with integrated text, graphics and video, and then produced over thirty educational software products. This was an extraordinary time and we were excited by the wealth of possibilities offered by IVIS, although I remember being severely questioned by a vice president who simply could not believe there was a market for "watching television on a computer."

One of my roles as manager was to present IVIS to potential customers, including NCAR, the National Center for Atmospheric Research, in Boulder, Colorado. They had vast quantities of multimedia climate data from around the world and hoped IVIS could help them store and visualize their data. Having just read *Gaia*, I was surprised to see it mentioned in their annual report as a driving factor behind several important discoveries. I knew that *Gaia* had been dismissed by mainstream biologists, yet here were prestigious scientists at NCAR who relied on it. Why?

A key factor was that these scientists shared a common research goal—to understand and predict the weather—that required them to work across scientific boundaries. Their inclusion of biologists in a domain previously dominated by physicists and chemists led them to fundamental insights about the impact of living organisms on the atmosphere. For example, existing physical models could not explain 20 percent of the methane in the atmosphere; their biologists traced it to huge termite mounds in South America!

I was struck by two observations: first, these scientists viewed working across disciplinary boundaries as essential for success. Like Lovelock, who teamed up with the biologist Lynn Margulies, they found that certain kinds of questions could be addressed only though shared perspectives; dogmatic focus on one discipline simply would not work. This resonated with my beliefs about software development. At that time, virtually all interactive software was being developed by people trained in engineering or math; professional organizations such as SIGCHI did not yet exist, nor were there degree programs in human–computer interaction.

I was in transition at that time; I decided to stop running a large production group and return to research on the next generation of multimedia software. Already an anomaly at DEC with my training as an experimental psychologist, I realized that even a mix of psychology and computer science was not enough. Inspired partly by Lovelock and the scientists at NCAR, I created an explicitly multidisciplinary research group, made up of one-third programmers, one-third psychologists and social scientists, and the rest a mix of designers, including a typographer, a video producer, and even an architect. We also actively included users, treating them as members of the design group throughout the design process, an early example of participatory design.

I will not pretend that it was always easy: we often had major arguments over design process, evaluation criteria, and the "ultimate design." Yet we were united in a common goal: believing sincerely that multimedia computing would change the world. We forced ourselves to articulate our underlying assumptions, to respect each others' perspectives and contributions, and to come to a shared understanding.

Multidisciplinary design is now common (or at least, given lip service) in HCI. But in those early days, seeing how multidisciplinary research helped legitimize the Gaia hypothesis at NCAR profoundly affected my own research, not just enforcing my belief in multidisciplinary teams but also encouraging me to study multidisciplinary design as a subject in itself. I continue to be fascinated by the multidisciplinary design process and how best to benefit from the insights gained across disciplines. I always work with multidisciplinary research groups and have drawn from these experiences to develop new design techniques (see Beaudouin-Lafon and Mackay 2002; Mackay 2002).

My second insight relates to a fundamental concept in the book, that of coevolution. I had been fascinated by how our customers at Digital reinvented the technology we developed, often in unexpected ways. Nardi and Miller (1991) describe a similar phenomenon among spreadsheet users; and communication technologies have often been reinvented, from email to SMS and instant messaging. (I remain surprised how often software manufacturers ignore this phenomenon, since user-driven innovation is an inexpensive source of pretested products.)

My doctoral dissertation explored how users adapt actively as well as adapt to the technology they use. I chose the term *coadaptation* to differentiate it from *coevolution*, a biological process involving changes in both DNA and the environment. Although it operates on a much smaller time scale and through different mechanisms, coadaptation is deeply influenced by the concept of coevolution. I discovered several naturally occurring examples of coadaptation during a two-year study of email use in a large corporation and in a five-month study of user customization.

In the first study, users reinvented a mail-filtering system we had introduced: they twice completely redefined it and significantly increased its adoption by others in the organization. In the second study, some users were completely overwhelmed by each new software version and were forced to completely adapt their behavior to accommodate it, while others painstakingly retrofitted and adapted the new version so it performed like the old. Every group informally designated one person who created and collected useful customizations and shared them within the group. Both studies found individual and social coadaptation: users all adapted their behavior in response to technical and social constraints, and a few also actively adapted and shared their innovations with others.

Knowing that coadaptation occurs, the interesting question for HCI is what are the implications for design? Unfortunately, although Gaia provided the initial insights, it does not tell us *how* to create successful coadaptive systems. Although multidisciplinary, the Gaia hypothesis remains squarely within the natural sciences, whose goal is to explain *existing* natural phenomena with theory and empirical evidence. Designing novel interactive systems clearly benefits from scientific disciplines, but also requires design and engineering expertise, and even that may not suffice.

So just how do we enable users to change and adapt their software in productive ways, without introducing more problems than we solve? One possibility is to lower the barriers to customization, through end-user programming (Lieberman et al. 2005) and tailoring. I have been exploring a different angle, in the context of mixed reality systems. Physical objects, particularly paper, can act both as an interface to a computer as well as objects in their own right. For example, we studied how air traffic controllers appropriated paper flight strips (Mackay 1999) which provided the insights necessary to create a highly appropriable mixed reality system called Caméléon (Mackay et al. 1998). By augmenting the physical flight strips, controllers retained their familiar functions and flexibility, but were also able to access RADAR and other on-line systems and also communicate with other controllers. Caméléon's "interaction browser" was designed to let controllers choose how their actions on these augmented strips were linked to other on-line systems and to permit them to develop new uses that we did not anticipate. Taking advantage of an existing, easily appropriable paper-based interface led us to create an interactive system that maintained the simplicity and adaptivity of the physical strips while gaining increased power through access to on-line systems and communication with other controllers.

Together with Michel Beaudouin-Lafon, I have also been exploring *generative theory* (Beaudouin-Lafon and Mackay 2000), which provides design principles for designing and integrating interaction techniques. We view interaction as a phenomenon in its own right, to be designed and modified by both designers and users. For example, the principle of *reification* turns users' previous interactions into concrete objects that they can visualize, modify, and share. Ideally, this creates a Gaia-like feedback loop whereby users can reflect on their past experience and reuse, modify, or borrow successful adaptations. In some cases, such reflection may even lead to redefining the system itself.

In rereading Lovelock's book, I thought back to the early days of HCI, when everything was new and we could draw from a wide variety of disciplines to inspire us. Over twenty-five years later, the Gaia hypothesis is taken seriously in scientific and environmental circles, multidisciplinary design has become the norm in many corporations, and HCI researchers now recognize the importance of sociotechnical systems (Suchman 1987a). The concept of coevolution (if not coadaptation!) has started to appear in the HCI literature, and I believe that the design of coadaptive systems will soon be a focus of HCI research.

41

Fun at Work: Managing HCI with the *Peopleware* Perspective

John C. Thomas
IBM Research, Yorktown Heights, New York, U.S.A.

T. DeMarco and T. Lister, 1987: *Peopleware: Productive Projects and Teams*

In 1986, I left IBM Research to start and lead an artificial intelligence laboratory at NYNEX Science and Technology. In 1987, the first edition of *Peopleware* was published, and it had a profound impact on how I approached leadership and management in the AI lab. Although I had some familiarity with all areas of AI, most of my career had focused on human–computer interaction.

Peopleware is fundamentally a book about the human aspects of software development, although the management lessons are widely applicable to any domain of knowledge work. The book should be of interest to managers of knowledge workers on a broad spectrum of topics, including personnel selection, project planning and management, motivation and reward, teamwork, and the physical and social context of work. *Peopleware* influenced me then and now to think about the relationship of HCI to work and productivity, and the broader agenda of HCI.

The style of *Peopleware* is quite different from that of a typical HCI book or journal. While the authors do present the results of some field studies, much of the writing works through the telling of stories and conversations that illustrate what worked and what did not work in real projects.

For example, one story from *Peopleware* illustrates how to demoralize a team and how to make an otherwise well-planed project late:

> During the past year, I did some consulting for a project that was proceeding so smoothly that the project manager knew she would deliver the project on schedule. She was summoned in front of the management committee and asked for a progress report. She said she could guarantee that her product would be ready by the deadline of March 1, exactly on time according to the original estimates. The upper managers chewed over that piece of unexpected good news and then called her in the next day. Since she was on time for March 1, they explained, the deadline had been moved up to January 15.

I was impressed with the effectiveness of such stories as a means to communicate their points, and this was one reason I used this approach to knowledge management later at IBM (Thomas 1999).

Probably because the authors were working consultants, they deal with various issues in a highly interdisciplinary way. Their writing continually crosses academic boundaries. They cite authors from fields as diverse as business management, architecture, psychology, programmer productivity, fiction, and creativity research.

There is also a complete lack of pretension in their writing. The breadth, depth, and length of their experience are what lend credence to their suggestions. The stylistic elements of *Peopleware* caused me to rethink my own writing style. Often HCI researchers write technical articles for other HCI researchers. This activity is no doubt valuable, but, for the field of HCI to influence real users in real contexts, it is also important to communicate with non-HCI audiences. I found the style of *Peopleware* to be a much better way to communicate important ideas and findings of HCI to managers, engineers, and operational people at NYNEX.

One main tenet of *Peopleware* is that "people" problems are more important than technical problems. Since I already had numerous management and leadership experiences, the book gave me confidence that I could manage the lab by concentrating initially on the use of people skills and gradually building up my technical expertise in artificial intelligence. To take one obvious example, it was critical to hire the very best people possible. "Best" in this context was multivalued. I wanted people who were intelligent, technically competent, and hard-working, but I also looked for people who could work well in teams, who had an entrepreneurial spirit and could help find and formulate problems as well as solve them. This was important because the AI lab was completely new, without a track record or any established ties to other parts of the organization—ties which would later prove crucial to our success. I also looked for many kinds of diversity in hiring in concert with *Peopleware*. "A little bit of heterogeneity can be an enormous aid to create a jelled team. . . . It is a clear signal that it's okay not to be a clone, okay not to fit into the corporate mold of Uniform Plastic Person" (p. 156).

Today, these hiring considerations may seem obvious, but they were viewed as unconventional in the mid-1980s. The interest in diversity as a resource also led me to co-organize two CHI workshops on cross-cultural issues in 1992 and 1993, to write several articles on accessibility, and to help organize ACM's First Conference on Universal Usability in 2000.

One of the goals of HCI is to improve productivity. As the director of the AI lab, I wanted my own people to be productive, and one major task in all areas of the

AI lab was programming. The concept of "programming productivity" is most often tied to methodologies, languages, tools, and technologies that are claimed to improve productivity. I was already somewhat skeptical about the relative importance of these approaches based on *The Mythical Man-Month* (Brooks 1975) and a linear regression study (Walston and Felix 1977), which showed that the political and social aspects of projects were much more powerful predictors of productivity than were tools and technologies. My skepticism was heavily reinforced by reading *Peopleware* as well as by the events at NYNEX Science and Technology. As is perhaps obvious, the most destructive elements to productivity are poor morale and solving the "wrong" problem.

Peopleware gives many useful and practical examples for improving and maintaining good morale and avoiding some of the common pitfalls that can lead to bad morale. These all proved useful for me personally as a manager, and my managers were also presented with these ideas and encouraged to take them seriously. One of the pitfalls to avoid is the use of phony deadlines to "motivate" people to work harder. When everyone knows that the deadline is not only impossible but arbitrary, this does not motivate people to work harder but only deepens resentment and cynicism. What does this have to do with HCI? In my *Peopleware*-expanded view, it has everything to do with HCI. What is the point of providing people with a "good user interface" to improve their productivity and lessen their frustration if the organizational and managerial climate undermine those benefits? This broader view of productivity enabled me to see a wide range of methods to improve morale and productivity. For example, at one point, when NYNEX Science and Technology had grown to about a hundred people, I got a call one day from corporate headquarters requesting that everyone in Science and Technology go to corporate headquarters to sign some forms. From a *Peopleware* perspective, it made a lot more sense to have these (two) folks from headquarters come to Science and Technology than vice versa, and that is exactly what ultimately happened.

On the positive side, there are many things management can do to make work more "fun" and increase a sense of teamwork. We had holiday parties that included satirical skits about our own foibles. We often sent teams to conferences despite a corporate mantra that strongly suggested we send only "one fireman to a fire." (Note that the fire department thankfully does not follow this rule.) Advantages of sending multiple team members to the same conference include greater coverage of potentially relevant material, greater presence and thought leadership, team-building, and the possibility of having attendees discuss their experiences with each other which this leads to greater retention and insight. The notion that a conference is merely something to be "consumed" as efficiently as possible shows a deep misunderstanding of the nature of intellectual work. *Peopleware*, through multiple examples, helps managers gain a more balanced understanding of reality: "Of course nobody ever says outright that work ought not to be fun, but the idea is there, burned into our cultural subconscious. . . . In this part we'll address the opposite premise, that work should be fun" (p. 157). This premise also led to the publication of a short article entitled "Fun" (Carroll and Thomas 1988) in the *SIGCHI Bulletin*.

The early history of HCI largely involved people originally trained in engineering and computer science trying to reach common ground with people originally trained in experimental or cognitive psychology. It is natural that the common ground that was established focused on "objective" measurements and theories that could be expressed in mathematical terms. Furthermore, early applications of HCI focused on military and industrial situations where efficiency was a key measure. Workers had little say in choosing what to work on; the implicit assumption was that they were extrinsically motivated, for instance, by pay and benefits. How they felt about their interactions with computers was perceived to be of little importance.

Over the past few decades, several important aspects of this picture have changed dramatically. First, computing power has increased tremendously along with the variety of attachable peripheral devices. As a result, computer users are exposed to a much wider variety of multimedia including video, graphics, animation, music, and sound effects. These stimuli, in turn, may provide more emotionally laden experiences. Second, the nature of the workforce has changed so that many more workers are now "knowledge workers." For these workers, it is more important that they be "effective" than that they be "efficient." Third, computers have also found their way into a large variety of consumer devices. Such users are discretionary, and much of the point of products such as video games, picture phones, and listening devices is that they produce *pleasurable experiences*, not "productivity."

As a response to these changes, the field of HCI has changed as well. It has become obvious that the social, affective, and physical contexts of use need to be understood as well as the "user interface." In 1987, this notion was less obvious, and *Peopleware* helped raise this issue. For example, the authors report on a number of field studies that show that having more space and less noise is vital to productivity: "Workers who reported before the exercise that their workplace was acceptably quiet were one-third more likely to deliver zero-defect work" (p. 55).

The authors report on another study of the impact of the auditory environment. Two sets of programmers were given a coding task. In one condition, they coded in silence. In another condition, they listened to music. The music and silence conditions were equally "productive" in terms of lines of code, but the silence condition afforded greater comprehsion: "Although the specification never said it, the net effect of all the operations was that each output number was necessarily equal to its input number. . . . Of those who figured it out, the overwhelming majority came from the quiet room" (p. 78). Thinking about the physical context of work (and not just the UI) is just one of the many ways that *Peopleware* broadened my view of HCI. In personal terms, these broader HCI concerns influenced not only the work of the HCI group, but also the work in expert systems, speech technology, and machine vision, as well as later work in robotics and software tools. One example of this broader view is illustrated in an article on ecological gaps in HCI (Thomas and Kellogg 1989).

Peopleware, though not conceived or marketed as a book on "human–computer interaction," has been very influential in my own career in HCI. It has helped transform and broaden my view of HCI to include emotional, motivational, social, and physical as well as cognitive and perceptual-motor factors. This has affected my own research in HCI as well as the way I have managed people, projects, and organizations.

42

Learning from Engineering Research

William Newman
University College London, London, U.K.

W. G. Vincenti, 1990: *What Engineers Know and How They Know It: Analytical Studies from Aeronautical History*

From time to time I get into conversations about the HCI literature that lead inexorably to a recurring question: why, notwithstanding its insightfulness, scholarship, breadth of coverage and disciplinary richness, does the literature so rarely offer up answers to the specific questions that arise during design? I am always sympathetic toward people who encounter this problem, for I often had the same experience in the late 1980s when, after a couple of decades of interactive systems research, I first began to work in an HCI lab. I now had access to shelves of books, journals, and conference proceedings to help me design experimental prototypes. Yet every time I got stuck and went to these shelves for help, I came away empty handed.

My initial reaction to these disappointments was to carry on much as before. My years at the University of Utah, Xerox PARC, and other research labs had provided opportunities to work with great researchers on a wide variety of systems, including design tools, user interface management systems, graphics editors, page description languages, integrated office systems, desktop "wallpaper," and window managers. Inspiration for these systems had come sometimes from frustration with existing software, and sometimes from opportunities presented by new technologies, foremost of which was the Xerox Alto. I saw no reason why I, now an HCI researcher, should change my ways.

I did begin to wonder, however, where this was leading me: must my entire career be spent fixing tools and exploiting new technologies? It was at about this time, in 1991, that I came across Walter Vincenti's *What Engineers Know and How They Know It* (Vincenti 1990). This is a historical study of aeronautical engineering, drawing on six case studies of research during the first half of the twentieth century. One study involves aircraft maneuverability, and the discovery by researchers at the NACA (precursor to NASA) of a parameter, stick force per *g* acceleration, determining stability in level flight. In effect, this research enabled plane builders to "design in" the stability they desired, rather than find it out by trial and error. Another study describes tests on aircraft propellers that documented how adjustments to design parameters affected overall propulsive efficiency; this helped aircraft designers to choose suitable propeller designs. I began to realize what had been missing from HCI: research driven by the specific, very practical problems of designers.

For me, *What Engineers Know* was full of fresh insights. A graduate in mechanical engineering turned computer scientist, I could only now begin to appreciate the intellectual excitement and challenge offered by engineering research. I found, for the first time, a coherent explanation of how engineers establish requirements, a topic that was not explained in textbooks on software engineering or, for that matter, on engineering of any kind. And I learned about the distinction between *normal* and *radical* technology (Constant 1980), and the need for each radical invention to be followed by periods of incremental research in order to establish it as the "normal" solution. Of these, the normal–radical distinction had the biggest initial impact on me, for I saw that I had been stuck in a cycle of inventing radical technologies, with no work on normal technologies to provide balance.

My reading and rereading of Vincenti's book established a watershed in my HCI research. From that point on I began to explore the differences between the world of engineering research that he described, and the world of HCI that I inhabited. I looked for ways to strengthen my own research by following up Vincenti's references; I drew on research methods I found in them; and I tried to build bridges between them and HCI.

One work to which Vincenti's book led me was Rogers's 1983 book, *The Nature of Engineering*. It offered a view of technology's role in society that contrasted with HCI's concern with the provision of marketable features and functions. In his introduction to *technology processes*, a term that includes technology design, Rogers points out that these processes "enable man to transform the world around him . . . by (a) increasing the efficiency of his body . . . (b) increasing the efficiency of his senses . . . , and (c) increasing the efficiency of his intellect" (p. 2). I had never considered viewing my work as a simple matter of human enhancement, despite my familiarity with Engelbart's concept of augmenting human intellect (Engelbart and English 1968). I was forced to accept, however, that Rogers's three categories accounted for most of the successful technologies I could think of at that time.

By viewing my own work in terms of human enhancement, I found it easier to deal with the thorny issue of requirements. The concept of "user requirements" had always seemed at odds with the software engineering view that requirements apply to a technology and state what that technology must do. If the role of technology was indeed to enhance people, then it seemed to me these people must have needs, possibly latent, for the said enhancements. It might be helpful to identify their needs independently, separating them from the consequent requirements on the technologies—a practice that has only recently started to find its way into HCI textbooks.

Vincenti treats requirements in aeronautics not as a topic in itself, but as part of the process of transforming needs or goals into the specifics of an aircraft's hardware. As an illustration, he describes how the Douglas DC-4 was developed to meet the needs of United Airlines, and points out that in 1936 "the economic goals of United and its associated airlines had to be translated into performance specifications for the DC-4E" (p. 211). An analogous HCI process might be to translate a need of nonspeaking people—to communicate faster—into requirements for a voice output communication aid, as described by Alm et al. (1993). Other examples include enabling conference organizers to plan their technical program more quickly, using a tangible interface (Jacob et al. 2002), and Sharlin et al.'s (2002) solution enabling assessors to measure cognitive ability faster and more simply. In each case the need leads to requirements that can be expressed in measurable terms. In contrast, the vast majority of HCI research makes no attempt to achieve measurable human enhancements that address identified needs (Newman 1997).

The challenge in pursuing the human-enhancement approach to HCI lies, therefore, in translating human needs into requirements and performance criteria. We cannot expect this translation to be a simple matter, nor its outcome to be a simple expression like the NACA's "stick force per *g*." Rather it will involve building models of the human activities that need to be enhanced (Newman 1996). It will involve tackling persistent problems in society and in the workplace, as exemplified by Salvucci's work on improving the task-switching of drivers using mobile phones (Salvucci et al. 2005), Murphy's progress in reducing search times for victims of natural disasters (Murphy 2004), and my own work with Smith into reducing the disruptive effects of introducing technologies to meetings (Newman and Smith 2006). With the aid of the resulting models, and the requirements and criteria they expose, designers may start to find answers to some of their questions, such as "Can my technology improve on what already exists?" or, "How can I predict the improvement?" or, "How have others achieved advances in meeting this need?"

HCI publications that provide answers to such questions can, I believe, provide true contributions to HCI knowledge. They can create a literature that serves the needs of practicing designers. However, this may require us to rethink what it means to make a contribution to HCI, a question that confronts everyone who writes or reviews a CHI conference submission. Here again we can discover from *What Engineers Know*, and from the more recent aeronautical history by Anderson (2004), just what it means to make a research contribution to a field of design. Some important characteristics they point out are:

Contributions should be repeatable. Vincenti describes the case of the "Davis Wing" design that was used with remarkable effectiveness in Consolidated Aircraft's B-24 bomber, but failed when used in other designs. The wing's design had no valid basis in fluid dynamics and, in Vincenti's words, "its contribution to airfoil technology was essentially nil."

Research that offers no overall enhancement may not make any contribution. Anderson mentions a finding, published by the Wright Brothers, that drag was reduced by having the pilot lie prone rather than sit erect. This made no contribution because no other designers adopted the prone-position option; the real need was to produce efficient aircraft that could be piloted from a seated position.

Contributions can consist of defining or redefining design criteria. Another of the Wrights' results, which made a fundamental contribution to aeronautics, was their restatement of the term *angle of incidence* not as the tilt of the wing in relation to the horizontal (which they showed was a worthless value), but in relation to the direction of airflow (now known as the angle of attack).

Although I had previously thought aeronautics to be far removed from HCI, my encounter with Vincenti's work marked the start of a shift in my approach to research. I realized that HCI is predisposed to focus on radical technologies, without attending to the incremental research necessary to transform these technologies into normal solutions. Furthermore, there is crucial, untapped value in the subsequent accumulation of knowledge about normal solutions, in the form of models, requirements, and performance metrics. With these added contributions, the HCI literature can be of real assistance to designers engaged in meeting the everyday needs of ordinary humans. I remain optimistic that the close examination of engineering research methods has still more to offer HCI.

43

Interaction Is the Future of Computing

Michel Beaudouin-Lafon
Université Paris-Sud, Orsay, France

P. Wegner, 1997: "Why Interaction Is More Powerful Than Algorithms"

In 1997, Peter Wegner published an article entitled "Why Interaction Is More Powerful Than Algorithms" (Wegner 1997). The word "interaction" immediately attracted my attention: I knew Wegner's work on object-oriented programming and I was curious to see what he had to say about human–computer interaction (HCI). I soon discovered that the article was not about HCI but about interaction in general, mainly among machines. Nonetheless I was struck by its relevance to my research since I have always tried to understand why programming (i.e., writing algorithms) is so similar to and yet so different from interacting with a computer. Both allow us to make the computer do something, yet they seem irreducibly different from each other.

Wegner's article is both profound and radical. Through a rare combination of theoretical, practical, and philosophical arguments, it challenges Church's thesis, the cornerstone of computer science, which states that everything a computer can do is reducible to what can be done by a finite-state Turing machine. Wegner shows that Church's thesis may hold in the closed world of an algorithm that reads its input, shuts down from the outside world while it computes its result, and then spits it out. But it cannot hold in an open system that harnesses the power of its environment by interacting with it as it runs, because the environment provides an endless stream of unpredictable events that cannot be reduced to an algorithm. This has wide implications in many areas of computer science (Goldin, Smolka, and Wegner 2006) and has attracted sharp criticism from theoretical computer scientists (few dare challenge Church's thesis), but I want to focus here on Wegner's philosophical argument and its impact on my own research in HCI.

Most modern sciences, including computer science, are strongly influenced by the rationalist and positivist belief that the workings of Nature can be completely captured by mathematical models that allow us to perfectly predict and control them. In computer science, for example, software engineering relies on formal methods to prove the correctness of large software systems; the semantic web assumes that human knowledge can be captured unequivocally by XML descriptions; and the goal of artificial intelligence is to reproduce human behavior with algorithms inside a computer.

Despite being born in the country of Descartes (or perhaps because of it), I have always thought that rationalism conveniently ignores real problems by concentrating on what can be fully understood and controlled. Indeed, all three examples above fail when confronted with the real world: formal proofs of software systems that interact with their environment are impossible unless one makes strong assumptions about the environment, typically reducing it to an algorithmic behavior; the semantic web finds it intractable to define ontologies and map them to each other when they change all the time; and artificial intelligence focuses on mental processes such as problem solving but usually ignores their tight coupling with human perception and action.

While the so-called hard sciences such as theoretical physics deal with the basic phenomena of matter and energy, the oft-despised "soft" sciences such as psychology and sociology deal with far more complex and subtle systems that clearly cannot be described by pure logic and equations. As Wegner explains, empiricists sacrifice the rationalist completeness and predictability of closed-world systems in order to address open, interactive systems in the real world. My own interpretation of this is the *myth of perfection*: under the rationalist assumption, complete and perfect control of a process is always possible; it is simply a matter of getting the model right. Wegner's notion of interaction shows that this is impossible in general, and that debunking the myth of perfection brings more power, not less.

This argument actually helped me get respect from my computer science colleagues. As a member of a hardcore computer science department, I have often felt that my work in HCI (or rather, "user interfaces," as they call it) was considered as just painting pretty pixels on the screen and giving cool demos. Telling them that interaction (what I do) is more powerful than algorithms (what they do) not only triggered interesting and controversial discussions, it also helped me analyze some of the evolutions in computer science and HCI.

Empirical approaches and interaction, in Wegner's sense, are indeed slowly becoming more common in computer science. For example, distributed systems are now ubiquitous, from the Internet to computer clusters and multicore chips. Such large and complex systems can no longer be analyzed as a single algorithm but must be seen as a set of interacting entities. Probabilistic approaches, approximate algorithms, and stochastic methods are also more widely used to deal with uncertainty, incompleteness, or simply the fact that it is better to compute a good solution in a short time rather than to wait forever for the perfect one. The latter is a feature of so-called anytime algorithms, which provide the best possible solution at any time in their execution, improving it if allowed to run longer. Such algorithms can be used to create mixed-initiative interactive systems where humans and computers take advantage of each other's expertise by running in parallel and interrupting each other (Scott, Lesh, and Klau 2002), a perfect illustration of Wegner's notion of interaction.

In HCI, the rationalist approach is less predominant but still very strong. Much research is based on the belief that we can capture human behavior formally, for example, by some task model, or that the results of controlled experiments can be taken as objective measures of the phenomena being tested. Reducing human behavior to such models is indeed tempting: it turns interactive system design into the relatively simple problem of defining the set of widgets needed to accomplish specified tasks.

I find it more interesting to design an interactive system without making unnecessary assumptions about how it will be used. I believe that an interactive system should be like a canvas for a painter, a medium to express oneself whose power comes from the freedom it gives rather than the constraints it imposes. HCI has a long tradition of considering interactive systems to be open to (re-)interpretation by their users. Informed by ethnographic work that repeatedly demonstrates that humans do not always behave in rational and predictable ways (see, e.g., Suchman 1987a), it includes such empirical approaches as participatory design (Greenbaum and Kyng 1991), end-user development (Lieberman et al. 2005) and coadaptation (Mackay 1990).

The instrumental interaction model I created (Beaudouin-Lafon 2000) stems from this same body of work, although its purpose was more operational. Instrumental interaction was inspired by the observation that humans create tools and instruments to empower themselves, to do things that they could not otherwise do, whether hammering in a nail, playing music on a piano, or putting together a budget with a spreadsheet. Instruments allow us to harness the power of the environment (here, the computer), exactly as advocated by Wegner. In fact, Wegner's paper was instrumental in making me focus on interaction rather than on the interface itself (Beaudouin-Lafon 2004), that is, on the mediation between users and computers and the capture of this mediation into interaction models.

Wegner defines interfaces as behavior specifications. This is sufficient when focusing on machine-to-machine interaction because the interaction is symmetrical: the interacting entities are similar in nature. In contrast, human–computer systems exhibit a stark asymmetry between the human means of communication and the computer's input and output devices. To resolve this asymmetry and to mediate the interaction requires the *reification* of the interaction, that is, the creation of a new object, the instrument, that translates between the languages of the two parties. Wendy Mackay and I developed this notion of reification together with other design principles in order to operationalize further the design process of interactive systems (Beaudouin-Lafon and Mackay 2000). Our goal was, and still is, to move from descriptive models of interaction to generative ones, not in the sense of automatically generating interfaces from abstract descriptions but instead by providing tools for designers to both expand and channel their creativity. Such *generative theories* are, in a sense, a tribute to Wegner's plea for empiricism over rationalism, for interaction over algorithms.

Finally, Wegner's conception of interfaces as harnesses resonates with my work on interaction techniques. Since people rely on their perceptual and motor skills to interact with computers, we need to explore how best to optimize these skills to harness the power of the computer, and vice versa. For example, my joint work with Yves Guiard on multiscale pointing and navigation (Guiard and Beaudouin-Lafon 2004) shows that Fitts's law still applies to very high indices of difficulty, that is, for pointing tasks that are inaccessible in the physical world, a clear demonstration of Wegner's concept of interface as harness.

In conclusion, I consider Wegner's article a landmark in computer science, a work that opens a window onto a new world with large areas yet to be explored. This work has often been misunderstood or dismissed, as if the new light it shed was too bright to discern anything clearly and it seemed safer after all to close the shutter. I believe that the goal of HCI is not to make pure computations somewhat more palatable for human consumption, but instead to redefine the role of information and computers in our ecology, that is, to create a paradigm shift (Kuhn 1962) from computation to interaction.

Returning to my original question about the respective natures of interaction and programming, one may draw a distinction in terms of scale. Algorithms are but building blocks in larger interactive systems, like drops of computation in a sea of interaction. Rather than trying to understand waves and currents by observing drops under a microscope, Wegner looks at the whole system on a larger scale. As with other natural and artificial systems, complexity arises from emerging behaviors and the effects of effects through a slow evolutionary process. By focusing less on algorithms and more on interaction, computing is starting to grow out of its infancy. Interaction is its future.

VIII

Seeking Common Ground

How does HCI move forward? Or at least how do we establish a firm footing? How do we keep from reinventing the wheel again and again? As a discipline we have been successful at developing a body of methods for attacking problems—but it seems clear that we need more than a set of methods that we doggedly apply to every problem we encounter. One answer is that, over time, we have developed some foundations, some areas of knowledge that all or most of the community agree on. Another answer is that, in the absence of such codified and accepted common ground, we may at least develop a discourse, a set of understood positions whose strengths and limitations we systematically explore and debate. The essays in this section examine ways in which some foundational issues have influenced the essayists.

We begin with Bill Gaver's account of the "almost illicit thrill" of reading J. J. Gibson's *The Senses Considered as Perceptual Systems*, and how Gibson's emphasis on the structure of the outside world, rather than that in the head, led him to HCI. Next, Yvonne Rogers discusses Larkin and Simon's "Why a Diagram Is (Sometimes) Worth a Thousand Words." Like Gaver, she focuses on what she sees as a shift in emphasis in HCI from what's going on inside the head to the outside world. In contrast with Rogers's dim view of the usefulness of the modeling approach, the next three essays view it in a much more positive light. Kate Ehrlich writes about Card, Moran, and Newell's groundbreaking *The Psychology of Human–Computer Interaction*, reconsidering key work on mental models, and pointing out that there may still be ways for HCI to profit from them. The essays by Gary Olson and Scott MacKenzie consider perhaps the greatest triumph of the modeling perspective: Fitts's law. Olson, in his discussion of Fitts's foundational paper, not only clearly lays out the basic work, but describes the remarkable number of nonobvious implications it had. MacKenzie discusses Card, English, and Burr's empirical comparison of pointing devices and validation of Fitts's law as a means of accounting for the results, and offers interesting reflections on the nature and power of modeling that serve as an interesting counterpoint to some of our other essayists. The essays by Giorgio De Michelis on Winograd and Flores's *Understanding Computers and Cognition*, and by Austin Henderson on Suchman's "Office Procedures as Practical Action," reengage the classic debate about situated action. This pair of essays helps us understand that strong positions can attenuate when viewed from the perspective of time. "Play, Flex, and Slop," by Paul Dourish looks at Brian Cantwell Smith's *On the Origin of Objects,* and examines a more conceptual way of thinking about the link between systems and theory.

44

A Source of Stimulation: Gibson's Account of the Environment

William Gaver
University of London, London, U.K.

J. J. Gibson, 1966: *The Senses Considered as Perceptual Systems*

In considering the problem of perception in man and animals the first question to ask should be, what is there to be perceived? And the preliminary answer would be, the environment that is common to man and animals. The senses convey information about the world, and therefore we ought to review what is known about the world that the senses detect.
—J. J. Gibson (1966, p. 7)[1]

I first read the opening lines of J. J. Gibson's *The Senses Considered as Perceptual Systems* about twenty years ago as a graduate student studying psychology. I picture myself huddled over the book, intently turning its pages, more like a kid reading an adventure story than a student reading an academic treatise. You might think this is a romantic reconstruction, but I still remember laughing with delight as I read some passages, and, looking back, I can trace a surprising number of ways that it has shaped my research ever since.

Beyond any normal intellectual enthusiasm, there was an almost illicit thrill in reading Gibson's work. This was in the heyday of the information-processing approach to psychology, when accounts of perception and cognition were a blizzard of frequencies and intensities, features and just noticeable differences, template models, semantic nets, and mental imagery. The focus of any account of perception was on what happened in the head, not what happened in the world. For if one thing was understood, it was that perception was more than a matter of the light that hits the eye, or the sounds that reach the ears. No, the stimuli reaching the sense organs were far too incomplete, intermingled, and ambiguous to allow us to see or hear in any straightforward way. In the oft-quoted words of William James, the world was a "blooming, buzzing confusion" unless one had the experience, the knowledge, and the mental capabilities to decipher it. Thus the psychology of perception may have started by characterizing light or sound, but that wasn't where the action was. What mattered was what the mind did with those lights or sounds, the exceedingly clever ways it reshaped, recombined, sorted, and categorized them to achieve a mental representation of the world.

There was a kind of seductiveness to the expertise it took to understand the theories of perception of the time. A little like joining a cult that offers the smug feeling of secret knowledge in exchange for casting off ties with the normal world of family and friends, becoming an initiate in cognitive psychology gave entrée into a realm of technical knowledge that compensated for alienating oneself from the ordinary experience of looking at or listening to the world. However much I might enjoy the mingled sounds of crickets and surf on the trail to Blacks Beach, or admire the rainbow colors of hang-gliders wheeling overhead, I was willing to accept that such things were hardly legitimate concerns for a serious student of perceptual psychology.

In this context, Gibson's suggestion that we ought to take seriously the world—*this* world, the one around us—in accounts of perception was iconoclastic to the point of sedition. Gibson turned his back on traditional accounts of the stimuli for perception and instead built his own foundation:

> The face of the earth consists of wrinkled surfaces of rock and soil along with smooth surfaces of water. The liquid surface is everywhere exactly perpendicular to the line of gravity; the solid surface is on the average perpendicular to it. . . . So the solid environment is a "support" for behavior. It is rigid. Unlike the viscous or liquid environment of mud, lava, slough or water, it permits the animal to stand and walk upon its legs, and to find his way about from place to place. This rigidity of layout puts him in danger of collision, to be sure, either with an obstacle or by falling off a cliff, but it does afford surfaces which keep the same arrangement. Rigidity gives geometrical permanence to places and constancies of shape and size to things. It therefore "supports" not only the upright stance but also locomotion, orientation, and manipulation. (Gibson 1966, pp. 8–9)

This account is so simple and lucid that at first it seems almost naive. Wrinkled surfaces, mud, lava and slough, even falling off cliffs? This sounded more like a description of my walk to the beach than the work of a perceptual psychologist. It was exciting to read, both for its bravery in describing the world from scratch, and for its transgression of the boundaries customarily imposed between science and everyday life.

Gibson's depiction is at once familiar and strange. He mixes commonplace language with a consideration of physical laws (the "line of gravity") and a seemingly obsessive attention to the obvious (the "rigidity of layout"). With hindsight, his description is skillfully crafted to provide a foundation for his later theories of perception as "pickup" of complex, ambient information, and of action as mediated by *affordances*, properties of the environment that offer possibilities to appropriately equipped animals. But for me, at the time, its primary appeal was as an account that set aside technical descriptions of insufficient stimuli, and instead took a fresh look at the world around us.

Surprisingly, Gibson's writings had the effect of leading me into human–computer interaction. Up to that point, I had turned up my nose at the field. My dismissive slogan was that real HCI problems were too complex to lead to good psychology experiments, and conversely, that good experiments could not adequately address real HCI problems.[2] Still, when my advisor Don Norman asked me to talk to his HCI group about how sound might be used in the interface, I consented.

At the time, most approaches to using sound in computer interfaces involved the auditory equivalent of data visualization. Typically, data dimensions were mapped to dimensions of sound to produce "sound-graphs" of various sorts. For example, Sara Bly (1982) mapped a data set describing the features of various species of flowers so that each flower was represented by a single tone in which, for instance, stamen height mapped to pitch, and petal width to volume. By listening to a series of the sounds, listeners could discern correlations among dimensions and classify different flower types. A number of other researchers had come up with similar ideas for using sounds; invariably, they used musical sounds and dimensions for the mappings they created.

Through my engagement with Gibson's ideas, however, I had come to realize that there was more to sound than music. Gibson concentrated almost exclusively on vision in his work, but it was apparent that his approach could be applied to hearing as well. Indeed, a section of the first chapter of *Senses* was dedicated to the environment for listening:

> A mechanical disturbance or dislocation is propagated outward from a source in accordance with the laws of wave action. Many different types of mechanical disturbance are possible: a solid may undergo shear, rupture, frictional movement, collision, or even explosion; a liquid may undergo turbulence, splashing, or even boiling; a gas may undergo vibratory flow in crevices or pipes. . . . (1966, p. 15)

Clearly, if Gibson had focused on auditory perception, he wouldn't have been concerned with music. Instead, he would have focused on what I call *everyday listening*, the experience of attending to the *sources* of sound: the shapes, sizes, and materials of objects, and the nature of the interactions that cause them to vibrate. When Norman asked me to think about sound for computer interfaces, I was already well underway exploring this new domain of perception.

With my newfound zeal for everyday listening, I speculated about how the dimensions of sources, rather than sounds themselves, might be mapped to the interface. I suggested to Don's group that perhaps it would be worthwhile thinking about an auditory equivalent to the icons, windows, and widgets that were just beginning to sweep the interface world, thanks to the newly released Macintosh and its forebears the Xerox Star and Alto. Through the use of auditory icons, sound could be used to augment basic interactions with the interface, rather than being relegated to the niche market of data exploration. Moreover, just as sound conveys information about multiple aspects of source events, auditory icons might convey multidimensional information about computer events. Thus a single sound might not only indicate that email had arrived, for instance, but also suggest its size, its type, and how much other mail was in the mailbox.

The notion of developing auditory icons was exciting enough to interest others, and the opportunities they offered me overcame my prejudices against HCI. So I pursued my ideas, first at Apple Computer and later at EuroPARC, through the creation of a number of interfaces that use auditory icons (see Gaver 1997 for a review). This perspective, so simple and yet so rich, suggested a wealth of opportunities for fruitful research and development.

Gibson's approach to perception influenced my perspective on HCI in other ways too. For instance, inspired by Gibson's account—and partially in reaction to Norman's (1988) treatment—I started to consider how Gibson's concept of affordances might be applied to technology in general. I encountered a group at Delft Technical University, led by Gerta Smets, Kees Overbeeke, and Pieter Jan Stappers, whose innovative research, both on form semantics and on the creation of depth perception from motion parallax, was also based on Gibson's ideas. Repeatedly, Gibson's perspective proved to be a source of insights into areas he himself had never considered.

Rather than describing in detail any of the work I have mentioned, let me turn to the fundamental lessons that reading Gibson's account of the environment taught me. For in addition to guiding specific aspects of my research, my encounter with Gibson's work had profound effects on my basic stance as a researcher.

First, engaging with Gibson's ideas taught me the value of entertaining ideas that initially seem implausible or wrong-headed. As I said at the start, Gibson's focus on the environment rather than the perceiver flew in the face of the basic assumptions of cognitive psychology. So misguided did his concepts of "invariants," "direct perception," and "affordances" seem, that when we received a guest lecture on the topic from a visiting professor, we were, in effect, counseled to humor the madman. But entertaining these seemingly preposterous notions turned out to be pivotal to my career. This experience makes the Queen's practice in *Alice in Wonderland,* of believing "as many as six impossible things before breakfast," seem sensible—there's nothing like having your world overthrown to get you thinking. Moreover, embracing Gibson's ideas, even provisionally, had the effect of undermining my belief in Science as the quest for one great Truth, and instead allowed me to conceive of research as the accumulation of a number of perspectives for understanding, all incomplete and many incompatible, but each shedding light on particular phenomena.

Second, Gibson's perspective shifted my attention from psychology—mental events such as perception, memory, and problem solving—toward the circumstances which contextualize psychology: the structure of the things we perceive, the kinds of events we find meaningful and memorable, the issues we typically find problematic. This is not to abandon psychology altogether, for it is the relationship between people and their environment that makes these issues potent. But stressing the world rather than the mind seems appropriate for HCI and other design-related fields, which, after all, are concerned with shaping the situations that people encounter. Certainly, this shift led me toward my current focus on practice- rather than theory-based research. Just as Gibson's emphasis on the world to be perceived underlay his account of perception, so explorations of new situations created by technologies can help us to better understand people more generally.

Perhaps most simply, and most deeply, Gibson's description of the world invited me to think for myself about the basics facts of the topics in which I later became interested. Of course, it is essential to build on the understandings achieved by those who came before us. However, it can also be useful to question assumptions. Sometimes, it is most valuable simply to relax the preconceptions inherited with learning, and look at the world afresh. To be sure, trying to find one's own way can lead to mud, lava, slough, or water—we might even risk falling off a cliff!—but the hazards seem worthwhile when one chances upon an unexpected vista. It is for this lesson that I am most grateful to Gibson.

Notes

1. Unless otherwise noted, all quotes are from Gibson (1966), *The Senses Considered as Perceptual Systems* (abbreviated *Senses* in the text).

2. To be honest, my view hasn't changed much—I just don't take psychology experiments as the only route to good research any more.

45

When the External Entered HCI: Designing Effective Representations

Yvonne Rogers
Indiana University, Bloomington, Indiana, U.S.A.

J. H. Larkin and H. A. Simon, 1987: "Why a Diagram Is (Sometimes) Worth Ten Thousand Words"

This classic is twenty years old. Its catchy title drew my attention and that of many others when it was published. According to Google Scholar, it has since been cited nearly seven hundred times. That is a lot of eyeballs. So what is the paper about, why has it been so influential, what is its relevance to HCI, and why did it have such an impact on me?

We have all heard the saying "a picture is worth a 1,000 words." In the original version, the number of words was pitched at 10,000, but somehow got reduced to 1,000 in common parlance. Even with the substantially reduced ratio, the maxim retains its potency. Why is this? What is it about a picture that says so much? And why are words claimed to be so inferior? Larkin and Simon sought to reveal the truth by examining a particular kind of picture—a diagram. Typically, a diagram is drawn to help people solve problems, particularly those relating to the grouping of certain elements. An example is a family tree that shows kinship relationships. The elements include family members, marriages, births, and deaths depicted by connecting lines and various symbols.

So how do diagrams work and why are they so appealing? Consider the following problem. "The triangle is to the right of the square. The square is to the right of the circle. What shape is in the middle?" You need to stop and think. It requires you to mentally place the objects side by side to work out the answer. It also requires you to hold in memory a partial solution (the placement of the triangle and square) before being able to move on to the next step, which is to infer the circle's location relative to the square and triangle. Considerable mental effort is required to solve even this simple problem. Now look at the diagram in figure 45.1 and see how easy it is to come to the same conclusion. It only requires us to recognize the middle

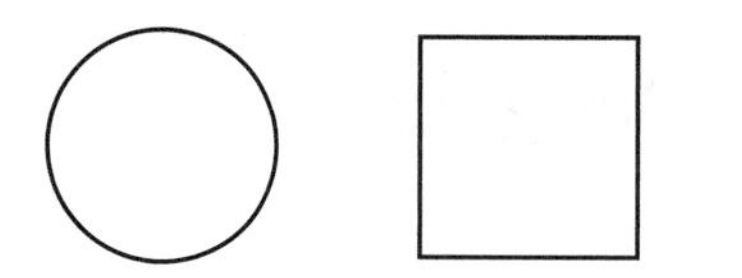
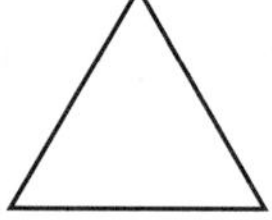

Figure 45.1
A pictorial problem solution.

shape, utilizing our well-honed perceptual skills, since it is immediately visible in the graphical representation.

From this simple example we can see how a diagram literally enables us to "read off" the solution from the representation, whereas we have to make explicit what is implicit in the sentences. In a nutshell, pictures reveal, words conceal. Though this may seem intuitive, Larkin and Simon provide an insightful theoretical account as to why this is the case. An important distinction they make is that even though diagrammatic and sentential representations are *informationally* equivalent, they are *computationally* different. That is, they contain the same information about the problem, but different amounts of cognitive effort are required to come to the solutions. In their paper, they show the effects of this on problem solving using two textbook examples taken from physics and geometry, one to do with pulleys and weights and the other with theorem proving. The problems are ones we love to hate because they are so hard and hence well suited to illustrating the benefits of diagrammatic representations. In particular, they require us to work out the ratio of weights and prove that two triangles are congruent, which entails making multiple interdependent inferences about rope lengths, angles, and the like.

I have since wondered, however, why they chose such intractable problems when they could have explained their theory using simpler ones, such as genealogy or ecosystems that use the more familiar diagrammatic forms of trees and webs. It certainly would have made it easier for the rest of us to follow. But it is often the way that to prove that you are doing "real" science you need to work on seriously hard stuff. In a similar vein, Larkin and Simon use an intricate form of computational modeling to show how the two problems are solved quite differently when using a diagram and a textual description. I found their extensive use of formalism heavy going. It was painstakingly laid out and I have to confess to glossing over a few pages of it, taking their word. So why did I like the paper?

What has stuck with me ever since was their higher-level explanation of the cognitive processes that take place when using diagrams to solve problems: we are able to readily switch our attention from one component to another of a diagram to draw our conclusions in ways that are impossible to do with a sequence of sentences. Diagrams provide simultaneous information about the location of components in a form that enables objects and their relations to be easily tracked and maintained. From this, we can deduce that the best diagrams are those that make it obvious where to look to draw conclusions.

For psychologists who were joining the field of HCI in the late 1980s, the theory provided an alternative account of the cognition that takes place when people interact with external representations. Until then, cognitive theories being imported into HCI to explain and predict user interaction were based on information-processing models that were exclusively about internal representations and had scant regard for the "external" world of artifacts, information, and representations. Best known was the human processor model whose offspring was the (now outmoded) GOMS method (Card, Moran, and Newell 1983). The former describes and the latter predicts the cognitive processes that were thought to take place inside a user's brain—how long it took to perceive a character on a screen, recognize it, decide what to do about it, and then press a key. The problem with these and other information-processing-based models, however, is that they do not represent adequately the state of affairs and can end up oversimplifying and distorting reality. Most of our cognitive activities involve interactions with external kinds of representations, such as books, documents, and computers—not to mention one another. When we are at home, we do not have to remember where everything is, because it is "out there." We decide what to eat and drink by scanning the items in the fridge, and we write lists and post-it notes to remind us of what to do. Against this backdrop of everyday psychology, I struggled (as did many others) to see how the information-processing-based methods developed for HCI were of any use to understanding how people actually interacted with computers and their environments.

Not surprisingly, these models failed miserably to be of value to interaction designers—who were primarily concerned with creating effective interfaces for displaying information, and not, say, how many words people could remember when flashed rapidly in front of them, as predicted by the well-known 7+/–2 short-term memory theory. In contrast, Larkin and Simon's concern with the external paved the way for HCI researchers to begin in earnest to theorize the role of external representations in human–computer interactions. Several followed up their claim that:

> Mental imagery—the uses of diagrams and other pictorial representations . . . held in human memory . . . play a role in problem solving quite analogous [to] external diagrams . . . and . . . this role is also played by the internal and external in concert. (Larkin and Simon 1987, p. 97)

The idea that cognition involves the interplay between internal and external representations was born.

A number of models appeared, accounting for how internal representations are combined with external ones, including Larkin's (1989) subsequent DiBs model that explained how we solve everyday problems using external displays (e.g., using the interface of a coffee machine to brew coffee) and Zhang and Norman's (1994) analysis of distributed cognitive tasks for equivalent problems represented in different external forms. Indeed, I remember during my year's sabbatical at the cognitive science department at the University of California, San Diego, in 1991, being asked by Norman's students to take part in a series of experiments on how external representations made it more or less easy to solve the "Tower of Hanoi" problem. Instead of trying to solve it in my head I was asked to balance small cups on large cups and move real oranges around on different sized plates. It got me thinking about how the physical nature of an external representation constrains the way we perceive a problem and subsequently solve it.

I spent that year immersed in the newly formed distributed cognition lab run by Ed Hutchins. He was concerned with the design of cockpits at the time and we spent countless hours analyzing how the various external representations used in the instrument panels played a critical role in the complex activity of flying planes.

There was a palpable buzz in the early '90s, as we endeavored to change the face of theorizing in HCI and psychology. O'Malley and Draper (1992) proposed a display-based account that differentiated between the knowledge users need to internalize when learning to use display-based word processors (e.g., Word) and the knowledge they can always depend on being available in the external display. Norman (1993) had a big impact, popularizing the notion that knowledge resides both in "the head" and in "the world." More recently, Wright, Fields, and Harrison (2000) developed their resource model that analyzed the information types thought to be used during human–computer interactions, both internal (e.g., memorized procedures) and external (e.g., written instructions).

Within cognitive science itself many researchers took up Larkin and Simon's seminal ideas to explore further the nature of how both static and interactive diagrams work together with how people use different and multiple external representations when solving problems. Names that spring to mind include Paul Brna, Richard Cox, Keith Stenning, Shaaran Ainsworth, Peter Cheng, Barbara Tversky, Hari Narayanan, and Mary Hegarty. A body of research has emerged that has investigated the cognitive benefits of static and interactive diagrams together with different forms of graphical representation that have proven to be of value to those in the business of designing educational software, information visualizations, and other applications.

And what lasting impact did Larkin and Simon's paper have on me? Over the years, it has made me think deeply about the design of effective external representations that can capitalize on their cognitive benefits. At first, it led me to scour the scattered literature on diagrams and other kinds of external representations. I discovered that although numerous studies had been conducted there was little mention of the rationale behind their design. Not even Larkin and Simon had any words to say on the matter. A further examination of the diagrams that educators and researchers have created (especially HCI ones) showed how a surprisingly large number of them were badly designed. The fact that not all diagrams are good made me think further about how to design more effective ones.

This line of research resulted in many fruitful years working on external representations, culminating in the external cognition framework, developed in collaboration with Mike Scaife, intended to be used for the analysis, design, and selection of advanced computer-based graphical representations, such as animations, multimedia, and virtual reality (Scaife and Rogers 1996; Rogers and Scaife 1998). In particular, we characterized a number of dimensions that could be usefully employed to determine how to design different kinds of external representations that would be of "added" cognitive value for particular users, domains, and tasks. We also explored how interactive mechanisms enabled by computer technologies could be exploited to guide and scaffold learners in knowing where to look in order to interpret and to make inferences and connections between the different elements of a graphical representation. An example is "dynalinking," where diagrammatic representations are linked with a more concrete illustration of what they stand for, such as a dynamic simulation; changes in one are matched by changes in the other, enabling a better understanding of what the abstraction means.

On reflection, Larkin and Simon's paper was timely and much needed, providing the impetus, insight, and inspiration for HCI researchers like myself, first, to conceptualize how computer–based graphical representations work and, second, to determine how to design more effective ones. But let's not get carried away; *not* all pictures are worth a 1,000 words, and, indeed, sometimes words say it all.

46

The Essential Role of Mental Models in HCI: Card, Moran, and Newell

Kate Ehrlich
IBM Research, Cambridge, Massachusetts, U.S.A.

S. K. Card, T. Moran, and A. Newell, 1983: *The Psychology of Human–Computer Interaction*

In the formative years of HCI in the early 1980s, researchers explored the idea that users form mental models of computer systems which they use to guide their interaction with the system. This was a powerful concept because it meant that if we, as interface designers, understood what kind of model the user constructed as well as the process of constructing it, we could make computers easier to use by developing systems that were consistent with that model or that made it easier to construct the model.

In this brief essay I examine a concept of mental models put forward by Card, Moran, and Newell (1983) in their book, *The Psychology of Human–Computer Interaction*, and explore its impact on the science and application of HCI. This book and subsequent papers had a strong and lasting influence on the field of HCI as an applied research discipline because it provided a testable theory that bridged the divide between psychological theories of human processing and the emerging discipline of interface design.

> Our purpose in this book is to help lay a scientific foundation for an applied psychology concerned with the human users of interactive computer systems. Although modern cognitive psychology contains a wealth of knowledge of human behavior, it is not a simple matter to bring this knowledge to bear on the practical problems of design—to build an applied psychology that includes theory, data and methodology. (Card, Moran, and Newell 1983, p. vii)

Mental Models

The concept of mental models had special meaning for me when I entered the field of HCI in the 1980s. I had recently completed my doctoral work in cognitive psychology studying language comprehension with Phil Johnson-Laird at Sussex University in England. Johnson-Laird had advanced the theory of mental models to explain how people construct internal representations of meaning from which they infer semantic relationships (see e.g., Johnson-Laird 1983). Although the theory was developed within cognitive psychology, it was influenced by cognitive science, which had been embraced by our department. Cognitive science and the funding behind it supported cross-disciplinary research at the intersection of psychology, linguistics, artificial intelligence, and philosophy.

Around the same time, another group of researchers were proposing that users form mental models of computer systems which they use to guide their interaction (see e.g., Norman 1983). In cognitive science, mental models were assumed to apply to some kind of abstract representation in people's heads. In HCI, mental models were more concrete although still representational. These models variously referred to (a) the actual model of the system; (b) the engineer's model of the system which then drives the technical design and implementation; (c) the user interface designers' model of the system; or (d) the user's model of the system.

Being steeped in theories of mental models and cognitive science I was primed to look for new ways to apply what I had learned. The opportunity came when I was a post-doc in the AI department at Yale University working with Elliot Soloway on researching expert-novice differences in programmers. We attended the 1982 Conference on Human Factors in Computing Systems in Gaithersburg, Maryland, widely regarded as the first HCI conference (although neither HCI nor CHI had yet been named). I remember the excitement of finding people from vastly different disciplines of psychology, AI, computer science, and social sciences all interested in the same set of topics about users and computer systems and the interactions among them. Although the Card et al. book was yet to be published there were several presentations and lots of hallway discussion of this new approach to human–computer interaction. I was shortly to start a career in industry, working to improve the usability of new systems and applications; a theoretically grounded approach was just what I was looking for.

From early on, mental models were used in HCI to provide a theory of the user's representation of the system as well as ways of designing a system that would influence both the content of the user's model and its construction. For Card et al., who were pursuing the goal of developing a theory of applied psychology, it was important that any concept of mental model not only be theoretically grounded but also be testable. They sought to explain and predict human–computer interaction by appealing to a type of model called GOMS, a method for describing the set of tasks the user wants to perform and his plans for performing it. In terms of the types of mental models outlined earlier, GOMS was a means to explicitly represent the user's model of the system in a way that helped to distinguish, but not direct, different design options.

GOMS stands for *goals, operators, methods, and selectional rules.*

Goals Goals represent the set of things the user wants to do using the computer, such as edit a document.

Operators Operators are the actions that belong in a user's repertoire of skills and the set of commands or operations that the system will let the user perform. At the time that GOMS was developed, operators would have been keyboard commands.

Methods Methods correspond to the sequence of subgoals and operators to achieve the goals. If the goal was to edit a document, a subgoal might be deleting a section of text. The method to achieve this goal would be described at the level of the individual actions and even keystrokes that the user would perform, beginning with placing the cursor at the beginning of the deletion point, holding down the mouse, dragging the mouse across all the text to be deleted to select it, then raising the mouse and clicking the delete key.

Selectional rules Some goals could have multiple methods. For instance, instead of using the mouse to select text for deletion, the user could use the keyboard arrows to select the text. The model included a process for selecting among the different methods.

In keeping with its goal of linking theory with research, the GOMS model was used to predict performance for "routine cognitive skills" such as text editing. The theory, which focused on skilled users, was supported by research on text editors that demonstrated that the same task took longer using the text editor with the predicted greater number of operations (Roberts and Moran 1983). A simplified version of GOMS, the Keystroke model, cast GOMS at the level of individual keystrokes to explain and predict expert error-free performance. The original model was further elaborated to provide more rigor as well as sets of tools to automate parts of the analysis process (see, e.g., John and Kieras 1996). Although the model provided testable theories it also came under a lot of criticism for its focus on low-level operations, highly skilled users, error-free performance, and an inability to take into account individual differences or effects of fatigue or motivation (see, e.g., Olson and Olson 1990). Despite some of the shortcomings there continues to be active research extensions to the GOMS model (see, e.g., John et al. 2002).

Evaluating the Influence of Card, Moran, and Newell

Although the particular details of the Card et al. theory may fall short by focusing too much on low-level tasks by skilled users, it does provide a systematic and principled set of quantitative and qualitative predictions about the ease of use of a particular interface design. It thus established much of the theoretical foundation of HCI and its place as an applied discipline, with contributions to the theory of interaction as well as to the practice of interface design and usability testing. The GOMS formulation also provided HCI researchers and practitioners with tools for building models of human behavior, many of which have found their way into areas such as usability testing with its emphasis on task modeling and performance. In fact, usability has grown from a thematic area in HCI to a separate group with its own society (Usability Professionals Association), conferences, events, and magazine.

As UI design standards and design guidelines started to infiltrate the HCI practitioner community in the early 1990s, the role of mental models as a guiding principle began to decline in favor of approaches that focused on the "look and feel" of the interface. This has not meant that an engineering approach has entirely disappeared from HCI. As recently as the 2006 Conference on Human Computer Interaction there was a panel—"Real HCI: What It Takes to Do HCI Engineering for Disasters, Driving, Disruption, and Distributed Work"—that called for an engineering approach to HCI practices including a reexamination of tasks and models to frame the design space and predict outcomes.

Looking back at what I consider to be one of the most influential bodies of work in HCI, I believe that Card, Moran, and Newell's work reinforced my commitment to HCI. They demonstrated that there was a set of interesting problems that required a deep understanding of people combined with an appreciation of the opportunities of new innovative technology for the solution. They convinced me that we could advance our theoretical understanding of technology and interfaces but also contribute to the practical design and implementation of new products and services.

But the role of mental models, including the work of Card et al., has not advanced without controversy. There is an inevitable tension between the psychologists, computer scientists, engineers, and designers who make up the HCI field. Discussion of mental models brings up the lingering debate over whether science, engineering, or design drives HCI. Do theoretical concepts such as mental models as representation really contribute to the practical issues of interface design or system engineering, or are they a distraction? Where is the real "science" in HCI? Can science and design coexist? These are questions that the next generation of HCI will continue to ponder.

47

A Most Fitting Law

Gary M. Olson
University of Michigan, Ann Arbor, Michigan, U.S.A.

P. M. Fitts, 1954: "The Information Capacity of the Human Motor System in Controlling the Amplitude of Movement"

The field of human–computer interaction does not have much in the way of laws. The practice of doing user-centered design relies heavily on heuristics, checklists, surveys, interviews, and iterative testing. Though some quantitative methods are used (some number of controlled experiments, some modeling efforts like GOMS), the science of HCI is based heavily on qualitative methods. Nonetheless, there is at least one law that has had considerable prominence in HCI: Fitts's law.

Paul M. Fitts was a psychologist who was very interested in practical as well as theoretical problems of human performance. He got his Ph.D. in 1938 at the University of Rochester and was on the faculty of the University of Tennessee until 1941. At that point he went to Washington, D.C., to work on the war effort. He worked with the U.S. Army Air Forces on problems of selection and training of pilots. In 1945 he became director of the Psychology Branch of the AAF Aero Medical Laboratory at Wright Field in Dayton, Ohio. He left active military service in 1949, and reopened a Laboratory of Aviation Psychology at Ohio State University. In 1958 he moved to the University of Michigan, where he remained until his untimely death at the age of 53 in 1965.

Paul was known as a founding spokesperson for engineering psychology, whose goal was to understand how to design equipment so that it would work well with the characteristics of human behavior. He wrote an influential review of engineering psychology (Fitts 1951) in the classic *Handbook of Experimental Psychology*. He strongly believed that basic research and applications could proceed hand in hand, an idea at the heart of Donald Stokes's thesis on Pasteur's quadrant (Stokes 1997), a point of view that has influenced me a lot. (Further details about Fitts's life and work are available in Pew 1994.)

His well-known law was published in the *Journal of Experimental Psychology* in 1954 (it was later reprinted in the *Journal of Experimental Psychology: General* in 1992 as a classic paper). It is a relatively brief paper, reporting three experiments which provided the data for a formulation of the mathematical expression of the law itself. The law can be summarized quite succinctly:

$$MT = a + b \log_2 (2A/W)$$

where MT = movement time, a and b = empirically determined constants (regression coefficients), A = distance (or amplitude) of the movement, and W = width of the target. In words, the law states that the time it takes to move to a target is a function of the length of the movement and the size of the target. This law has been verified for many kinds of situations (see Welford 1968).

When exposed to this law, many HCI designers and researchers say "So what?" It seems intuitive and unremarkable. But two things must be kept in mind. First of all, it is a quantitative law, not a qualitative one. The law states a precise prediction about how movement and target characteristics are related quantitatively. As noted in the previous paragraph, these quantitative predictions have been verified for a wide range of cases. Second, it has led to a number of interface innovations that are both surprising and interesting. I turn to these next.

This law became interesting to HCI folks when devices to control the cursor on a windowed interface came into being. Card, English, and Burr (1978) used the Fitts's law framework to analyze a number of different selection devices. But the law can also be used as a framework for design. Here are a number of design ideas that come specifically from an understanding of Fitts's law.

The value of the edge of the screen Walker and Smelcer (1990) showed that putting a to-be-selected item on the edge of the screen is highly effective for minimizing selection time. This is because the edge of the screen is virtually of infinite size. No matter how slow or fast you move the cursor, when you get to the edge it stops. A nice practical illustration of this is the contrast between the standard Mac and Windows interfaces. In the Mac the main menu is at the top of the screen, along an edge. In Windows the menu items are near the top of a window, but they are not on the edge of the screen, even when the window is maximized, and are therefore harder to select. An interesting corollary of this point is that the optimal location for a to-be-selected item is the corner of the screen, as it is essentially infinite in two dimensions.

The value of pop-up menus A menu that pops up when you click is another excellent design idea based on Fitts's law. Whereas the edge idea just discussed makes the target of infinite size, a pop-up menu makes the movement zero, at least to get to the menu itself. After that, of course, a movement is needed to make a selection.

Selecting from a pop-up menu If you get to the menu with no movement, then ideally the items on the menu to be selected should minimize the distance you have to move. This can be done in one of two ways:

1. *Centering on a linear menu.* This is where, when you click to get the menu, your cursor is in the middle of the menu at the start.
2. *Pie menus.* Here, the menu items are arrayed around a circle. A movement of only one pixel gets you to an item, though of course a movement to any point in the wedge for an item works. A side benefit: the farther you move your cursor in the menu, the bigger the wedge becomes, making the target bigger.

Fittsizing a menu A good design for a linear pull-down menu is to have the size of the target for items get larger the farther down the list the items get. Of course, as the targets get larger the distance to be traversed gets longer. But Walker and Smelcer (1990) showed that Fittsizing with a 20 percent increase in size per item improves the speed of selection.

Organization of walking menus Walking menus are hierarchical menus, where selecting an item opens up another menu alongside it. In some complex systems such walking menus can go several levels deep. Walker and Smelcer (1990) showed that Fittsizing and aligning key portions of the menu at the edge of the screen can help with the selection of items in walking menus. Tognazzini (1999) discusses how the Macintosh interface uses a V-shaped buffer zone to help avoid drifting to an item on the higher-level menu as one moves laterally.

Expanding items as you move toward them The task bar at the bottom of the OS X interface on the Macintosh has items that expand as you move over them. This momentarily gives one a larger target, making rapid selection easier. McGuffin and Balakrishnan (2005) studied this phenomenon in some detail, showing benefits for expanding targets as one moves toward them. However, they note that if there are targets close to each other, the design gets more complicated.

These are interesting examples, but there are a number of movement phenomena for which Fitts's law is too simple. Fitts's law focuses on one-dimensional movements, that is, linear movements from a starting point to a target. But there can be two-dimensional movements on a screen, and three-dimensional movements in virtual or real spaces. MacKenzie and Buxton (1992) looked at two-dimensional movements, and explored some extensions of the model that provide a better fit to data on two-dimensional selections. The law also applies only to rapid movements aimed at a target. It does not apply to slower kinds of movements on the screen, such as drawing.

Thinking about Fitts's law and its implications for interface design brings home how important it is to use multiple methods in thinking about good design. The extent to which Fitts's law is ignored in common interfaces suggests that there is nothing apparently intuitive about the law, despite its simplicity. So knowledge of the law is an important element of good design. But it is obviously only one element of what goes in to good design. The features of good interfaces come from many sources. Whether it's on the science side or the design side, HCI must fundamentally use multiple methods. Quantitative laws, and their qualitative interpretations, have a role in the field.

Finally, some personal notes. Like Fitts, I first was immersed in applied problems during a tour in the military. After graduate school I spent three years in the U.S. Navy, assigned to a human factors group at the Naval Submarine Medical Research Center in Groton, Connecticut. Fresh from being caught up in the exciting controversies of psycholinguistics and the new emerging cognitive science, I found ways to use both the concepts and the methods I had learned to explore problems in submarine and diving tasks. This blending of basic and applied work resurfaced later when I got involved in problems of human–computer interaction in the early 1980s.

Several years ago the School of Information at the University of Michigan decided to honor me with a named collegiate chair, with a name of my choice. The rules of this honor are that the name must be a distinguished University of Michigan faculty member who was retired. My immediate choice was Paul M. Fitts, for I had long admired his work, and his legacy at the University is still evident. His wife, Mary, lives in the same neighborhood as we do. So I explored with her whether this would be acceptable to her, and she was delighted. I had some years earlier chaired the annual Paul M. Fitts lectures in the Department of Psychology, so Mary already knew about my connection to her husband. As a result, I am now the Paul M. Fitts Collegiate Professor of Human–Computer Interaction, a designation of which I am very proud.

48

Reflections on Card, English, and Burr

I. Scott MacKenzie
York University, Toronto, Ontario, Canada

S. K. Card, W. K. English, and B. J. Burr, 1978: "Evaluation of Mouse, Rate-Controlled Isometric Joystick, Step Keys, and Text Keys for Text Selection on a CRT"

About twenty years ago, I was a graduate student at the Ontario Institute for Studies in Education at the University of Toronto. The acronym, HCI, for human–computer interaction, meant little to me at the time, but there was a course with "Human–Computer Interaction" as the title. It seemed interesting, so I enrolled. Today, I consider HCI my field of research, and this is in large part due to that course. In fact, it is due to one paper I read during that course.

The course readings included a textbook (I will not name it here) and a dozen or so papers. Overall, I was not very excited. Many of the readings were a tad thin on substance, in my view at least. This feeling changed completely when I read the paper to which this essay is directed: "Evaluation of Mouse, Rate-Controlled Isometric Joystick, Step Keys, and Text Keys for Text Selection on a CRT," by Card, English, and Burr. Now, it might not seem a must-read paper from the title, but don't be fooled. I read the paper because I had to for the course. And I'm glad I did, because it changed my life. That's an overstatement, I suppose, but it is true that this paper was a tipping point for me. I read it. I liked it. I liked it a lot. I was inspired and motivated to dig deeper. Before I knew it, I was hooked. HCI was for me!

The paper is important because it was the first detailed comparative evaluation of the mouse. Card, English, and Burr established, beyond dispute, that the mouse was a superior input device for selecting objects on a display. They compared it to a joystick and to two key-based methods for selecting text. Their three conclusions say it all. Briefly:

The positioning time of the mouse is significantly faster than . . .
The error rate of the mouse is significantly lower than . . .
The rate of movement with the mouse is nearly maximal . . .

The number of follow-on papers on pointing devices in HCI is likely in the hundreds, and all are guided by this seminal work by Card, English, and Burr.

The 1970s was an exciting time for computing. Bitmapped graphics displays were replacing character-mapped displays, and researchers were investigating new ways for humans to interact with computers. About ten years earlier, Douglas Englebart had invented the mouse (See English, Engelbart, and Berman 1967). Researchers at Xerox, including Card, English, and Burr, were looking to improve the design (eventually putting a rolling ball inside it) and to evaluate and compare the mouse in new paradigms of interaction.

The paper presents what we in HCI often call a "user study." Unbeknownst to me at the time, the study was, in fact, an empirical experiment with human participants conforming to the standards for such as refined over many decades in experimental psychology. Card, English, and Burr's paper is a representative and guiding example. The study was thorough. They tested four devices while systematically varying the distance to move, the size of the targets, and the angle of movement. They practiced participants to a clearly described criterion of expertise. Throughout, the paper is an exemplar of sound research and concise reporting. Of course, I read it again in preparing this essay. Terrific, still. Take a moment to read the abstract:

Four devices were evaluated with respect to how rapidly they can be used to select text on a CRT display. The mouse is found to be fastest on all counts and also to have the lowest error rates. It is shown that variations in positioning time with the mouse and joystick are accounted for by Fitts's Law. In the case of the mouse, the measured Fitts's Law slope constant is close to that found in other eye-hand tasks leading to the conclusion that positioning time for this device is almost the minimal achievable. Positioning time for the key devices is shown to be proportional to the number of keystrokes which must be typed.

Why copy the abstract here? First, to convey the content. But let me add: I review a lot of submissions to conferences and journals. It is extraordinary how often I am compelled to criticize the abstract in my reviews. Not here. This abstract delivers in 112 words exactly what it should. It tells the reader "what was done" and "what was found." No more, no less. Researchers too often treat an abstract as an introduction to the paper, and fail to convey the most salient findings. The rest of Card, English, and Burr is crafted just as well: carefully executed and succinctly delivered.

But there is more. Card, English, and Burr went beyond a typical user study. Here are the first are two sentences in the discussion section (p. 608):

> While these empirical results are of direct use in selecting a pointing device, it would obviously be of greater benefit if a theoretical account of the results could be made. For one thing, the need for some experiments might be obviated; for another, ways of improving pointing performance might be suggested.

This is an inspired preamble to their discussion on building models—models of interaction that (a) embed a theoretical account of the underlying human processes and (b) can serve as prediction tools for *a priori* analyses of alternative design scenarios. The remainder of the paper is about modeling using Fitts's law. They build and compare Fitts's law models for the mouse and joystick. This snagged me. The idea and mechanics of building a predictive model were new to me. It was empirical; it was built on established theory; it combined this theory with direct measurements of human behavior. The result is an equation predicting the time to select a target based on the distance (D) to the target and the target size (S). Although the form is usually different today, Card, English, and Burr give the equation as

$$T = a + b\log_2(D/S + 0.5)$$

The log term is the "index of difficulty," in bits. It has been the subject of considerable research and debate in the more than fifty years since Fitts's original paper. But that's another story.

One of the most provocative aspects of Fitts's law—and it is elaborated in detail by Card, English, and Burr (1978)—is that the slope coefficient in its reciprocal form ($1/b$) carries the units "bits per second." This term, called "throughput" today, is a performance measure representing the rate of information processing exhibited by users while performing point-select tasks. Wow! Are we humans mere channels for information transmission? Of course not, but the analogy works extraordinarily well, as the correlations for Fitts's law models are often well above $r = .900$. Clearly, this was fertile ground for further research.

Before I knew it, I was reading the original papers by Fitts (1954) and others and chipping away at a few problems and issues that were apparent to me, such as the need to include accuracy in the model, ways to apply the model to two-dimensional tasks, and the benefits of a more theoretically correct formulation for index of difficulty (MacKenzie 1992). Needless to say, Card, English, and Burr (1978) showed the first use of Fitts's law in human–computer interaction. Many dozens of Fitts's law papers have followed.

Card, English, and Burr's call for modeling in human–computer interaction was the seed for what today is a major component of research in our field. Not everyone in HCI accepts the benefits of models of interaction, however; so, let me finish by making a case for modeling.

A model is a simplification of reality. Consider an architect's scale model of a building or a physicist's equation for the trajectory of a tossed ball. Both are reductions or simplifications of more complex phenomena. They are useful because they allow us to explore the phenomena, think about them, make changes, and so on—without actually constructing the building or throwing the ball. A great many problems in HCI have been explored in this manner over the years. A recent example is the Fitts-digraph model for text entry. It combines Fitts's law with a language model. The language part is a set of letter pairs (digraphs) and their frequencies in a language corpus. The Fitts-digraph model yields a prediction of text entry speed, for example, using a finger on a small keyboard (e.g., RIM's *Blackberry*) or a stylus on a virtual keyboard on a PDA's display. Fitts's law gives the time to tap each key given the size of the key and the distance from the previous key, and the language model tells us the relative occurrence of each movement. Combine the two and you have a prediction of text entry speed for a given keyboard in a given language. That's not the main point, though. In an effort to design a better keyboard, we might consider some changes, such as resizing some of the keys, rearranging the letters, reducing the number of keys by placing two or more letters on each key, or adding extra interactions for word completion, and so on. These changes can be explored, each accompanied by a predicted entry speed, without actually building anything. This is a powerful way to explore the text entry problem, and, indeed, there has been considerable work in this vein in recent years in HCI (MacKenzie and Soukoreff 2002). I hope, in some way, you are convinced that models are great tools for HCI research. It all began with Card, English, and Burr.[1]

Note

1. The course where I first read Card, English, and Burr was taught by Robert S. MacLean, who later supervised my Ph.D. research on Fitts's law. Many thanks are offered to Dr. MacLean for the many inspiring conversations I enjoyed under his guidance. Thanks are also extended to my Ph.D. committee members William Buxton, Nishi Nishisato, and George Tracz, and to external examiner Stu Card. Thanks as well to Janet Read who first drew my attention to the "HCI Remixed" initiative, and to Tom Erickson who provided thorough comments and suggestions on an early draft of this essay.

49

The Contribution of the Language-Action Perspective to a New Foundation for Design

Giorgio De Michelis
University of Milano–Bicocca, Milano, Italy

T. Winograd and F. Flores, 1986: *Understanding Computers and Cognition*

Understanding Computers and Cognition appeared in 1986, the same year as the first Conference on Computer Supported Cooperative Work (CSCW). Drafts of the book, however, had circulated in the research community some years before. At the same time, the first CSCW conference was in preparation and laid the ground for the emergence of CSCW as a research field. Terry Winograd was both coauthor of the book and among the early promoters of the conference, where he presented a paper on the same theme as the book (Winograd 1986): it was natural for the CSCW community, therefore, to recognize *Understanding Computers and Cognition* as a reference point and to discuss it passionately.

The debate began immediately: the journal *Artificial Intelligence* published a review of it by Lucy Suchman (Suchman 1987b), who strongly argued against the book's effort to create abstract models of human conversation. The critique was corroborated by her book *Plans and Situated Actions* (Suchman 1987a), which contained a revised version of her Ph.D. thesis. *Plans and Situated Actions* also had a very deep influence on the emerging field of CSCW and, beyond that, it influenced the larger human–computer interaction community.

Many scholars read the two books as champions of two opposing perspectives: *language-action*, characterizing human conversations from the action viewpoint and proposing a new type of computer-based system, the Coordinator, to support the network of commitments the former creates; and *situated action*, emphasizing the irreducibility of human actions and interactions to any formalized model and arguing against the intrinsic authoritarian objective of building computer-based systems derived from those formal models.

Other scholars saw the two books as complementary as if they, together, indicated a new perspective to be criticized or discussed and further developed. Let me recall, on this point, the paper by Vera and Simon (1993), which discussed both perspectives in a radical critique of the situated action and cognition perspective.

The debate was reopened by Lucy Suchman in 1993 at the European Conference on CSCW in Milano, where she presented her reconsideration of the language-action perspective. Suchman argued that human action is intrinsically situated, and that producing models of it leads to undue discipline when it is applied in practice. Her paper has been republished in the *CSCW Journal* (Suchman 1994), together with a reply by Terry Winograd (Winograd 1994) where he clarifies the difference between formal, comprehensive models of behavior and formal structures used in communication and recording, and recalls that speech act theory, like any explicit accounting procedure, enforces a kind of uniformity that is necessary in any routinized communication. Later, the *CSCW Journal* hosted a debate in which several scholars commented on the controversy.

My personal research trajectory has been deeply influenced by *Understanding Computers and Cognition* and in these twenty years I had several occasions to return to it and to the work of its authors (see, e.g., De Cindio et al. 1986; De Michelis 1994; De Michelis and Grasso 1994), so it's for me a pleasure and a challenge to review it, again.

Twenty years is enough time to look back at a book with new eyes, discriminating what is no longer of interest from that which remains relevant.

There are a few ideas whose time has passed. The speech acts classification, proposed by John R. Searle as a way to characterize the pragmatic dimension of the language experience (Searle 1969), has proven to be ineffective in classifying human utterances. While listening to what someone is saying, we can recognize in it an illocutionary point—but, if we recall that utterance again, we can attribute to it a different illocutionary point. That is, illocutionary points arise from the interpretation process by the listener and can't be considered as an attribute of the utterance itself. If we attribute the illocutionary point to the utterance itself, we reify human communication, missing the creative role of listening and the fact that any utterance opens up innumerable interpretational possibilities. Even if some studies in artificial intelligence still make use of speech acts, and the scholars participating in the language-action conferences don't see this point, I think that this part of the critique of Flores and Winograd's work has been largely accepted.

The Coordinator, as a system supporting cooperative work, as well as its successor, Action Workflow, have been interesting prototypes. But although they allow us to understand the dynamics of human interaction within work processes, they have become neither best-selling systems nor widely diffused standards in the larger domain of information systems. The Coordinator's structuring of human communication, which assumes that utterances have a unique, unambiguous illocutionary point, just doesn't produce more effective communication. And in the case of Action Workflow, although making commitments explicit helps to deal with breakdowns, it appears unnecessary when the action flows as expected. The discussion about their features has not resulted in any significant new ideas that have come to be seen as part of the core knowledge of CSCW and HCI. Most of the younger scholars in these fields probably have had no occasion to see or study these systems.

Despite the fact that some key aspects of *Understanding Computers and Cognition* had only ephemeral or minor impact on the field, many of its themes remain important. Let us consider a few of them.

Winograd and Flores dedicate one chapter of their book to hermeneutics, in particular to the contributions to it by Martin Heidegger and Georg Gadamer. In this chapter, they bring the reader to a new understanding of human experience and of the role of computers in it. It's a radical shift from the dominant naive acceptance of a rationalistic and realistic approach to knowledge of modern science. Contrary to the common perception of computer work, they suggest that the design of computer-based applications must embody the relational and pragmatic understanding of human condition that emerged in twentieth-century European philosophy. In no other scientific discipline, even when naive realism was discussed, had anyone proposed such a radical shift. In computer science, the widely diffused common understanding was, and still is, that science couldn't possibly learn anything from phenomenology and antirationalistic philosophies: Edward Feigenbaum, to cite just one example, once defined phenomenology as "cotton candy" (quoted in Mc Corduck 1979, p. 197). After the publication of *Understanding Computers and Cognition*, a growing number of researchers and designers in the areas of CSCW, ubiquitous computing, and interaction design have begun to study and discuss philosophers like Edmund Husserl, Martin Heidegger, Hans Georg Gadamer, Ludwig Wittgenstein, and Jean Luc Nancy. In these works, it is clear that grounding the design of usable applications in a deep understanding of the human condition is not a superficial and transitory fashion.

The language-action perspective, characterizing the interplay of conversing with acting in human experience, opened a new horizon for the study of computer-based systems. If our experience gets its sense from the coupling of actions with conversations, then we must assume that all information is communication (Winograd 2006,

p. 72). The ideas of Austin (1962), retain, I think, their validity. Despite the weakness of the classification built on his ideas by John Searle, Austin has shown that the illocutionary point of any utterance links it with (future, present, and past) actions. Our conversations create the social space of our lives: as human beings, we are immersed in a network of commitments that define our agendas. Even the situated action perspective must look, therefore, beyond the spatial context of human experience to its pragmatic dimension: the network of a person's commitments is, in fact, the logical space from which her future derives its sense.

Another important idea in the book is that conversations, instead of messages or speech acts, are the atomic elements of communication. What a person says in a conversation makes reference to what has been said before and in fact is not understandable out of its conversational context. Systems that support human communication should, therefore, link all the messages within a conversation, so that users can easily situate any message or speech act within its context.

Finally, *Understanding Computers and Cognition* proposes a critique of artificial intelligence that goes beyond moralistic caveats and ill-founded prejudices about technology and offers new research terrains. It's not the inadequacy of computers that condemns the most ambitious (and sometimes arrogant) artificial intelligence programs to failure; rather, it's the irreducibility of human behavior to any model. We can't develop a realistic simulation of human intelligence that isn't embodied in a "living system," but we can dedicate our efforts to create "intelligent" applications for systems that support situatedness.

The discussion about *Understanding Computers and Cognition* declined after the mid-1990s, but its influence has continued, as shown by two books—Paul Dourish's *Where the Action Is* (Dourish 2001) and Claudio Ciborra's *The Labyrinths of Information* (Ciborra 2002). Dourish proposes a phenomenological foundation for embodied interaction, offering new insights into the interplay between language and action. The book not only begins its presentation of embodied interaction by drawing on the contributions of *Understanding Computers and Cognition*, but continues in line with the theoretical style of that book, grounding its discourse on analysis and design of computer-based technologies in a careful reading of texts of the phenomenological/hermeneutical school of European philosophy.

Claudio Ciborra uses the customer–performer cycle, proposed for the first time in *Understanding Computers and Cognition* and later developed in Action Workflow, to explain the Customer Relationship Management (CRM) strategy at IBM (where Flores and Winograd's ideas were taken into account). He also pays tribute to them for inspiring him to study Heidegger's philosophy.

In conclusion, the greatest contribution that Terry Winograd and Fernando Flores have given to CSCW, HCI, and interaction design is that of proposing a new research style, bringing with it new insights into human relationships and the role of technologies. It combines direct observation of human behavior, avoiding any preconceptions or prejudices about it, with a careful reading of phenomenological and hermeneutical philosophy, providing a well-founded theoretical framework for understanding the relational nature of human experience.

50

Following Procedures: A Detective Story

Austin Henderson
Pitney Bowes, Shelton, Connecticut, U.S.A.

L. Suchman, 1983: "Office Procedures as Practical Action: Models of Work and System Design"

In the summer of 1965, I was a recent mathematics graduate doing contract programming through IBM on the automation of the manufacturing operations of Avon Products outside Montreal. I was talking to a contract manager about whether the quantity of, say, perfume bottles outstanding on a contract could ever go negative. The systems department for whom I worked (the IT of the time) had declared it never would, and that I should not worry about it. Concerned that the world might be a little more complex than systems had noticed—or chosen to notice—I had found my way via the loading dock to the contracts department. John, the contract manager, then gave me at least five reasons why we systems folk were naive to think that such a thing would never happen, and I indicated that I would take this news back to the systems department and build it into the program. At this point, John said something that changed my life: "Stop! Don't build all that into the program. Tomorrow the world will come up with a sixth reason, and the day after another; you'll never stay ahead of the world. Just make the program so the contract balance is allowed to go negative, but let *me* be able to adjust balances to match reality, and transfer quantities from one contract to another, to fix things up." Now, after forty years of experience and theorizing about building systems for people, what I hear John as having said was this: "Don't try to make the program model the world; instead, make it into a tool that helps *me* do my work, including modeling the world however *I* want."

By the early 1980s, I had found my way to Xerox PARC, and was surrounded by the aftermath of the first stages of the PC revolution. Xerox had challenged PARC to figure out how computing could improve work in offices (the strategic form of "What does a digital copier look like?"). To address this, we now had personal machines, connected by networks, supported by laser printers. However, almost everyone was acting in a way that I now see as very much like my systems friends at Avon. They were saying that because people in offices had to follow office procedures, we should build tools that modeled the office procedures and that would support people in following them. And besides, they felt, computers are good at following procedures, so that should make them well suited to the job.

I say "almost" everyone. I was aware that Lucy Suchman had been looking into the underlying assumption of what is meant by "following procedures." I had also been working with Lucy in studying how people operate copiers, which involved following instructions. I was aware that Lucy had spent time in the summer of 1979 with the people at PARC who dealt in office procedures as a central part of their primary job, the folks on the third floor, the accounting office. As at Avon, I was uncomfortable with the easy alignment of the senses of "following procedures." We were seeing what that meant on copiers, so I knew there was a difference between what computers did and what people did in following procedures. And as everyone now knows, Lucy helped us all understand operating machines in a new way. I was very interested to see what Lucy would find in the accounting office.

And then I saw an early draft of a paper entitled "Office Procedures as Practical Action: Models of Work and System Design" (Suchman 1983). I read it—with considerable difficulty—and then read it again. I talked about it at PARC, and when it was published in 1983, I talked about it with anybody who would listen. And I have been talking about it ever since.

Lucy's paper tells a story that clearly challenges the office information systems view of procedures—and in very much the same way that John at Avon challenged the systems office's assumptions about contracts. The difference was that at Avon I had tripped over the problem. At Xerox, Lucy had gone looking for it, analyzed what she saw, and then developed a clear yet wonderfully nuanced account.

The issue was this: the action on the ground was different from the idealized view of the action held by the system's builders. Lucy proposed that there were three different models of following procedures: the first model was the computer scientist's view, where procedures are made up of instructions, the meaning of the instructions is crisp and well defined, a machine is built to act precisely according to that definition, and there is no room for, or interest in, any action other than exactly what the instructions are defined to mean. Made sense to me; I was a computer scientist.

The second model was the manager's view: here people carry out the instructions (processes, procedures), but because meanings are not precisely defined, the actions that follow are the result of interpreting the instructions in the context of their work. People do what the instructions say, but some interpretation is needed so that the actions are appropriate to the circumstances. Made sense to me; I had created maps to my house with instructions, and heard people's tales of woe about what happened when they tried to use them; I had watched people following the instructions for clearing jams in copiers and seen the resulting triumphs and disasters.

However, the third model was a complete surprise. In the accounting office, Lucy found that the relationship between people's actions and the procedures they were following was distinctly more indirect. She found that people were acting to create a record that showed that the office procedure had been carried out. That record has to satisfy those who judge such records (managers, auditors, etc.) as a proxy for judging the activity. The procedure is linked to the action through the making of a record. In an office, following procedures is about creating records!

As I said, understanding this took effort, because it was one level more indirect than I had been prepared for. And for that reason, over the years, as I give this paper to almost every person I work with and tell them to read it, I tell them they will have to work at it. If prepared to work hard, they are set up for a really wonderful surprise. For rather than try to simply explain the matter, Lucy tells a detective story. It is the story of a single case of paying an invoice. The arrival of the invoice occasions an amazing amount of detective work on the part of the office workers, in order to make sense of the world and the records as they find them, and then alignment work, to bring the invoice into coordination with the world, the records, and the payment procedures. Lucy's paper leads you through the experience of the worker. The worker is a detective. Something in the case is seriously wrong, but what? And what to do about it? I won't spoil the story for you; go read it yourself.

In the end, from the paper I came to understand that the world is richer than our simple accounts like to tell. We hope things are simple; we try to press them into being simple by using words and concepts loosely—even metaphorically. But in fact things are much richer than that, and our stories better reflect that fact. Because that richness is precisely what allows the world to change and grow and respond to new and diverse situations. You might be able to fool yourself into believing the simple story in a static and unchanging world, but such accounts will fall apart in the diverse, changing, open-ended world that we all really live in.

When you have understood that, you are in a position to start to address how computers might help. Because the actual activity of people "following" procedures in the real world is far from simple, it takes great care to make computers supportive of real people following procedures. This is a message that needs to be carried to all those companies who make office systems—either social or software—and all those layers of experts—including the functional (e.g., HR, finance, service) and IT departments—who deploy office systems in businesses. It is a message that needs to be carried to managers who have to get work done, and to the business process people who try to get all the kinks out of the processes so that all the actions of following procedures are without "defects." It is a message that needs to be carried to those who make laws (e.g., Sarbanes-Oxley) that assume that companies get things done by making procedures and then "simply" following them. The message is that the actions of real people in carrying out procedures are much richer than their laws, or their management, or their systems currently embrace. The message is that we need to get real: real work is often done despite the system, not by way of it. There are millions of dollars and untold amounts of people's time being wasted for lack of getting this right.

I also find that Lucy's third view of following procedures makes me cautious: following procedures is central to our work and to our stories of working and is generally regarded as pretty simple. Yet the understandings produced in Lucy's paper are rich and, to me, surprising. If something as simple as following instructions isn't so simple, what other naive assumptions am I making and, as a consequence, using to build systems inappropriately? Where else am I still being the "systems guy" from Avon? Lucy's story suggests that the role of systems may be even more richly related to work processes than I learned in 1965: systems are not a model by which controllers control the work, not a tool for helping the workers model their processes, but a workspace within which the work can be shaped, carried out, and reflected on.

Over the years, I have shared Lucy's paper with everyone I work with. There are three reasons for this: First, I am greatly concerned with the ways computers are deployed in supporting work and this paper directly addresses a root cause of that concern. I, and many others, have been fighting this battle for years. We believe that our systems are being built wrong, and that our management and lawmakers are working with inadequate and sometimes dangerous views of working and the world. Lucy helped us understand work better, and we have yet to make really good use of that understanding. It is about time we did so, and the paper helps make the case.

The second reason for sharing this paper is that it makes the day-to-day work of an anthropologist accessible. For in studying the accounting office, Lucy too was doing detective work: she was trying to understand what the office workers were doing. If in the end they were solving problems, and making records, and aligning with procedures, then that is what Lucy needed to understand. Both detectives engage the same material—the office workers to understand and take actions to make their world coherent, the anthropologist to understand what the office workers have understood and to tell a story about it.

The third reason I share the paper is that, delightfully, Lucy accomplishes the telling of these two detective stories in the same account. And further, she does so by enabling you to be yet a *third* detective, struggling to have your own understandings emerge as the story evolves. As participants you are engaged with Lucy in understanding what the office workers are understanding about this payment; and as Lucy's audience you are engaged in understanding what Lucy is coming to understand about procedures. The paper gives us three aligned and dependent journeys of discovery.

So this great paper carries an important message about office procedures and office work, one that I think still needs to be learned today. And it provides a revealing glimpse into the practice of an anthropologist. And it delivers a damn good story, damn well told. I have profited by using this paper to powerfully deliver its important messages to adversaries and colleagues alike. And I have enjoyed reading its story for years. Thanks, Lucy, for telling it.

51

Play, Flex, and Slop: Sociality and Intentionality

Paul Dourish
University of California, Irvine, California, U.S.A.

B. C. Smith, 1996: *On the Origin of Objects*

In the period between 1993 and 1996, I was living a complicated, privileged, and very enjoyable intellectual life. I was technically on leave of absence from the Rank Xerox Research Centre in Cambridge, England, but I continued to spend much time there with an inspiring group of colleagues. My leave was to conduct research toward my Ph.D. in the Department of Computer Science at University College London (UCL), a second, equally engaging intellectual environment. Finally, I was also spending time at Xerox's Palo Alto Research Center in Palo Alto, California (where I later worked full time.) At these three places, I was involved in a series of interrelated projects. At Cambridge, I had come to be deeply concerned with the nature of the relationship between technical and social phenomena in collaborative systems. At UCL, my Ph.D. work involved technological developments in support of this relationship, drawing particularly on work in computational reflection, an approach that had most extensively been applied to programming language design, but which I was attempting to repurpose for collaborative system development. At PARC, these projects came together in a different configuration, where a group of researchers assembled by Annette Adler were attempting to think about the relationship between the technical and the social at an architectural level. One member of this group was Brian Cantwell Smith, who was circulating drafts of a book in progress, published in 1996 under the title "On the Origin of Objects."

It is a rich and complex book, and marks a waypoint in a long-term intellectual project in which Smith has been engaged for several decades. The project is essentially to understand what computational "stuff" is, in a way that both is philosophically rigorous and does justice to the complex role that computational artifacts and processes have in our everyday lives. Of course, we have theories of computation, of which the Church-Turing account is the best known, but these fail to satisfy

Smith's criteria. The lambda calculus or Turing machines fail to account, say, for Microsoft Word or World of Warcraft, not only because these systems are large and complex enough to become intractable within those formal structures, but also because the structure and meaning of those systems extends beyond the mathematical world and into the physical and social as well.

Smith's approach is part of the broader program in the philosophy of mind that undergirds much work in cognitive science, but his approach is a radically alternative one. Cognitivism rests on the claim that cognition is a computational process, so that cognitive function and behavior can be understood in computational terms, leading to a program that strives to understand how the computational features of cognition arise. This founders, Smith suggests, because we do not really have an understanding of what computation might be. In this book, he explores the metaphysics of representation that provides a foundation for the broader enterprise; a new approach to intentionality that, in his words, "aims to steer a path between the Scylla of pure realism and the Charybdis of pure constructionism."

The model that emerges is one of intentional reference as a mutual achievement of subject and object, one that must be continually maintained and supported. It is a highly contingent form of intentionality, but indeed, as he shows, this very contingency—the flex or play in representational practice—is critical to its effectiveness.

Now as then, my work in HCI lies at the intersection of computer science and social science. Computation appears in Smith's book primarily in its motivation; and the social, while implicit throughout, rarely appears explicitly. Nonetheless, in rereading *Objects* lately along with a group of my students, I was struck by the extent to which, in both its content and approach, its influence on my own subsequent work has been profound. Let me draw attention here to three considerations—one methodological, and two substantive—that I draw from Smith but that remain central in my research.

The first methodological concern is simply that the sort of foundational inquiry that Smith conducts is not just feasible but consequential and necessary. HCI is typically approached as a practical matter, but in its constitution of both the objects and subjects of interaction, it relies on a range of philosophical and epistemological commitments that we rarely subject to much scrutiny. This is not simply a matter of theoretical hygiene, although that is important; it also affects both what we think the subject matter of HCI might be, and under what auspices we might form a range of disciplinary alliances to conduct that work. Interactive system design is, after all, a process of theorizing about social life, expectations, needs, and activities;

understanding just what commitments are caught up in those, and in the relationship between empirical investigation and technological representation, is of paramount importance. *Objects* provides a telling example of the importance of taking foundations seriously, and a model of how to do so productively.

The first substantive concern is one of the key themes of the book—that active work is required to maintain the alignments of intentional structures with their referents. In looking for a middle ground between naive realism and pure constructionism, Smith outlines a model of intentionality in which the intentional relationship requires the active participation of both parties. In doing so, he also provides an important account of computational reference as an intersubjective experience. Computer systems are thoroughly intentional phenomena; representational from the metaphors of the user interface to the imposition of one and zero as an account of the world of continuous voltage. By focusing on representational practice as a process not of mechanical translation but of continuous and precarious alignment, Smith places the intentional subject firmly in the picture. Representational practice depends on a form of manufactured complicity between subject and object.

In my own work, which depends on seeing computational artifacts not only as technological objects but also as sites of social and cultural production, this turn to the active maintenance of a representational relationship is a critical one. This view underwrites a shift away from thinking simply about the social "impact" of technologies and toward thinking, instead, about how people produce and enact cultural phenomena by means of information technology. In recent work, for example, I have been thinking about privacy not as something that people have, but as something that people do; the patterns by which people share, attend to, and orient to objects and activities as informative is a way that the social organization of groups is produced. The ways in which information is shared, produce and demonstrate social ties; the ways in which secrets are mutually recognized are means by which cultural values and meanings are reproduced.

The second substantive issue that I want to note here is the importance that Smith places on flex, slop, and play, and the fact that this flexibility in how systems of reference operate is critical to their success. To draw on one of his examples, imagine a computer system (or a paper ledger) in which numbers are presented twice in order to detect accidental errors. From one perspective, the multiple representations of the "same" number are intentionally linked; they represent the same thing. From another, though, the effectiveness of the system as a means to detect errors depends on their being disconnected; if the two numbers were so tightly linked that a spontaneous error in one of them caused the other to change too, then the power of the double-entry system would be lost. Making representations effective requires some flexibility in how we manage the boundaries of the categories and the effective reach of representations. Again, this speaks to the work involved in maintaining alignment between representations and the world, but it also speaks to the importance of flexibility in the creation of new forms of representational practice and the emergence of meaning in situations that are structured not just technically but also socially. It turns our attention away from a mechanistic account of representation and meaning and toward an account that is inherently open, subject to interpretation and reinterpretation, in which meaning is always contingent, partial, and bounded. Our ability to work within a system of partial connection and disconnection is fundamental. This insight is central to the account of coupling in embodied interaction as developed in *Where the Action Is* (Dourish 2001).

Smith's concern is with computation both as a phenomenon to be unpacked and as a site at which to reimagine metaphysical problems. Computation is only tangentially his topic in *Objects* (although it takes up a much more central role in the follow-on work to which he teasingly alludes several times in the course of the book). Human–computer interaction is not a topic of his direct attention at all. Nonetheless, whenever I return to *Objects*, I am struck anew by the relevance of the arguments, and by the profound impact it has had on my own work, in many ways.[1]

Note

1. I owe a great deal to those people with whom I have read Smith's book and whose understandings have helped to shape mine: first at PARC: Annette Adler, Austin Henderson, David Levy, Gene McDaniel, Bob Printis, and Vijay Saraswat; later at Apple: Dave Curbow, Tom Erickson, Jed Harris, and Austin Henderson again; and most recently at UC Irvine: Johanna Brewer, Judy Chen, Paul DiGioia, Mads Ingstrup, Carolina Johansson, Charlotte Lee, David Nguyen, Jennifer Rode, and Amanda Williams. Not to mention Brian himself.

References

Abowd, G. D. 1999. Classroom 2000: An Experiment with the Instrumentation of a Living Educational Environment. *IBM Systems Journal, 38* (4), 508–530.

Abowd, G. D., Atkeson, C., Hong, J., Long, S., Kooper, R., and Pinkerton, M. 1997. Cyber-Guide: A Mobile Context-Aware Tour Guide. *Wireless Networks, 3* (5), 421–433.

Ackerman, M. S., and McDonald, D. W. 1996. Answer Garden 2: Merging Organizational Memory with Collaborative Help. In *Proceedings of the 1996 ACM Conference on Computer-Supported Cooperative Work*, 97–105. New York: ACM Press.

Alm, N., Todman, J., Elder, L., and Newell, A. F. 1993. Computer Aided Conversation for Severely Impaired Non-Speaking People. In *Proceedings of the SIGCHI Conference on Human Factors in Computing System*, 236–241. New York: ACM Press.

Anderson, J. D. 2004. *Inventing Flight: The Wright Brothers and Their Predecessors.* Baltimore: Johns Hopkins University Press.

Aoki, P. M., Romaine, M., Szymanski, M. H., Thornton, J. D., Wilson, D., and Woodruff, A. 2003. The Mad Hatter's Cocktail Party: A Mobile Social Audio Space Supporting Multiple Simultaneous Conversations. In *Proceedings of the SIGCHI Conference on Human Factors in Computing Systems*, 425–432. New York: ACM Press.

Austin, J. L. 1962. *How to Do Things with Words.* Cambridge, Mass.: Harvard University Press.

Baecker, R. M. 1969. Picture-Driven Animation. In *Proceedings 1969 Spring Joint Computer Conference*, 273–288.

Baecker, R. M. 1981. *Sorting out Sorting.* 30-minute color sound film, Dynamic Graphics Project, University of Toronto. (Excerpted in *SIGGRAPH Video Review* 7, 1983.) Retrieved from http://www.utoronto.ca/ic/media/vidcol/price95.html/.

Baecker, R. M. 1993. *Readings in Groupware and Computer Supported Cooperative Work: Software to Facilitate Human-Human Collaboration.* San Francisco: Morgan Kaufmann.

Baecker, R. M. 2003. A Principled Design for Scalable Internet Visual Communications with Rich Media, Interactivity, and Structured Archives. In *Proceedings of the 2003 Conference of the Centre for Advanced Studies on Collaborative Research*, 83–96. Indianapolis: IBM Press.

Baecker, R. M. 2006. Designing Electronic Memory Aids: A Research Framework, Workshop on Designing for People with Cognitive Impairments. In *CHI '06 Extended Abstracts on Human Factors in Computing Systems*, 1635–1638. New York: ACM Press.

Baecker, R. M., and Buxton, W. 1987. *Readings in Human Computer Interaction: A Multidisciplinary Approach*. San Francisco: Morgan Kaufmann.

Baecker, R. M., Grudin, J., Buxton, W., and Greenberg, S. 1995. *Readings in Human Computer Interaction: Toward the Year 2000*. San Francisco: Morgan Kaufmann.

Baecker, R. M., and Marcus, A. 1990. *Human Factors and Typography for More Readable Programs*. Reading: Addison-Wesley.

Baecker, R. M., Rosenthal, A., Friedlander, N., Smith, E., and Cohen, A. 1996. A Multimedia System for Authoring Motion Pictures. In *Proceedings of the Fourth ACM International Conference on Multimedia*, 31–42. New York: ACM Press.

Baltes, B. B., Dickson, M. W., Sherman, M. P., Bauer, C. C., and LaGanke, J. 2002. Computer-mediated Communication and Group Decision Making: A Meta-analysis. *Organizational Behavior and Human Decision Processes*, *87* (2), 156–179.

Bannon, L. 1992. From Human Factors to Human Actors: The Role of Psychology and Human Computer Interaction Studies in System Design. In *Design at Work: Cooperative Design of Computer Systems*, ed. J. Greenbaum and M. Kyng. Mahwah, N.J.: Lawrence Erlbaum.

Bannon, L., and Bødker. S. 1997. Constructing Common Information Spaces. In *Proceedings of the Fifth European Conference on Computer-Supported Cooperative Work*, 81–96. Dordrecht: Kluwer Academic.

Bannon, L., and Kuutti, K. 2002. Shifting Perspectives on Organizational Memory: From Storage to Active Remembering. In *Managing Knowledge: An Essential Reader*, 190–210, ed. S. Little, P. Quintas, and T. Ray. Thousand Oaks, Calif.: Open University/Sage Publications. (Initially published in *The Proceedings of the 29th Annual Hawaii International Conference on System Sciences*, IEEE Computer Society Press, 1996.)

Bass, S. 1959. *Opening Credits to "North by Northwest."* Alfred Hitchcock (dir.), MGM, 1959. Retrieved June 2006, http://www.twenty4.co.uk/on-line/issue001/project01/clips/nbynwest.rm/.

Bass, S. 1960. *Opening Credits to "Psycho."* Alfred Hitchcock (dir.), Universal, 1960. Retrieved June, 2006, from http://www.twenty4.co.uk/on-line/issue001/project01/clips/psycho.rm/.

Beach, K. 1993. Becoming a Bartender: The Role of External Memory Cues in a Work-Directed Educational Activity. *Journal of Applied Cognitive Psychology*, 7 (3), 191–204.

Beaudouin-Lafon, M. 2000. Instrumental Interaction: An Interaction Model for Designing Post-WIMP User Interfaces. In *Proceedings of the SIGCHI Conference on Human Factors in Computing Systems*, 446–453. New York: ACM Press.

Beaudouin-Lafon, M. 2004. Designing Interaction, not Interfaces. In *Proceedings of the Working Conference on Advanced Visual Interfaces*, 15–22. New York: ACM Press.

Beaudouin-Lafon, M., and Mackay, W. E. 2000. Reification, Polymorphism, and Reuse: Three Principles for Designing Visual Interfaces. In *Proceedings of the Working Conference on Advanced Visual Interfaces*, 102–109. New York: ACM Press.

Beaudouin-Lafon, M., and Mackay, W. E. 2002. Prototyping Development and Tools. In *Handbook of Human-Computer Interaction*, ed. J. A. Jacko and A. Sears, 1006–1031. Mahwah: Lawrence Erlbaum.

Berlin, L. M., Jeffries, R., O'Day, V., Paepcke, A., and Wharton, C. 1993. Where Did You Put It? Issues in the Design and Use of a Group Memory. In *Proceedings of the SIGCHI Conference on Human Factors in Computing Systems*, 23–30. New York: ACM Press.

Bewley, W. L., Roberts, T. L., Schroit, D., and Verplank, W. L. 1983. Human Factors Testing in the Design of Xerox's 8010 "Star" Office Workstation Interface Design 3—Experimental Evaluation. In *Proceedings of SIGCHI Conference on Human Factors in Computing Systems*, 72–77. New York: ACM Press.

Beyer, H., and Holtzblatt, K. 1996. *Contextual Design*. San Francisco: Morgan Kaufmann.

Bier, E. A., and Stone, M. C. 1986. Snap-dragging. In *Proceedings of the 13th Annual Conference on Computer Graphics and Interactive Techniques*, 33–240. New York: ACM Press.

Bjerknes, G., Ehn, P., and Kyng, M., eds. 1987. *Computers and Democracy: A Scandinavian Challenge*. Aldershot: Gower.

Bly, S. 1982. Presenting Information in Sound. In *Proceedings of the 1982 Conference on Human Factors in Computer Systems*, 371–375. New York: ACM Press.

Bly, S. 1988. A Use of Drawing Surfaces in Different Collaborative Settings. In *Proceedings of the 1998 ACM Conference on Computer-Supported Cooperative Work*, 250–256. New York: ACM Press.

Bly, S., Harrison, S., and Irwin, S. 1993. Media Spaces: Bringing People Together in a Video, Audio, and Computing Environment. *Communications of the ACM*, *36* (1), 28–45.

Boardman, R., and Sasse, M. A. 2004. Stuff Goes in the Computer But it Doesn't Come Out. In *Proceedings of the SIGCHI Conference on Human Factors in Computing Systems*, 583–590. New York: ACM Press.

Bødker, S., Ehn, P., Kammersgaard, J., Kyng, M., and Sundblad, Y. 1987. A Utopian Experience. In *Computers and Democracy—A Scandinavian Challenge*, ed. G. Bjerknes, P. Ehn, and M. Kyng, 251–278. Aldershot: Avebury Press.

Borning, A. 1981. The Programming Language Aspects of ThingLab, a Constraint-Oriented Simulation Laboratory. *ACM Transaction on Programming Languages and Systems*, *3* (4), 353–387.

Boslaugh, D. L. 1999. *When Computers Went to Sea: The Digitization of the United States Navy*. Piscataway, N.J.: IEEE Computer Society Press.

Bossen, C. 2002. The Parameters of Common Information Spaces: The Heterogeneity of Cooperative Work at a Hospital Ward. In *Proceedings of the 2002 ACM Conference on Computer Supported Cooperative Work*, 176–185. New York: ACM Press.

Brooks, F. 1975. *The Mythical Man-Month*. Reading: Addison-Wesley.

Brown, B., and Laurier, E. 2005. Designing Electronic Maps: An Ethnographic Approach. In *Map-Based Mobile Services—Theories, Methods, and Implementations*, ed. A. Zipf, L. Meng, and T. Reichenbacher. New York: Springer.

Brown, T. 2005. Strategy by Design. *Fast Company*, 95, 52–54.

Bruckman, A. 1998. Community Support for Constructionist Learning. *Computer Supported Cooperative Work*, 7 (1–2), 47–86.

Buchenau, M., and Suri, J. F. 2000. Experience Prototyping. In *Proceedings of the Conference on Designing Interactive Systems*, 424–433. New York: ACM Press.

Burtnyk, N., and Wein, M. 1976. Interactive Skeleton Techniques for Enhancing Motion Dynamics in Key Frame Animation. *Communications of the ACM, 19* (10), 564–584.

Bush, V. 1945. As We May Think. *Atlantic Monthly*, *76* (1), 101–108.

Buxton, W. 2004. Forward into the Past. *Time Magazine*, *164* (15), 53.

Buxton, W. 2005a. Interaction at Lincoln Laboratory in the 1960's: Looking Forward—Looking Back. Panel Introduction. In *CHI '05 Extended Abstracts on Human Factors in Computing Systems*, 1162–1167. New York: ACM Press.

Buxton, W. 2005b. Piloting Through the Maze. *Interactions Magazine*, *12* (6), November–December, 10.

Card, S. K., English, W. K., and Burr, B. J. 1978. Evaluation of Mouse, Rate-Controlled Isometric Joystick, Step Keys, and Text Keys for Text Selection on a CRT. *Ergonomics*, *21*, 601–613.

Card, S. K., Moran, T., and Newell, A. 1983. *The Psychology of Human–Computer Interaction.* Mahwah: Lawrence Erlbaum.

Carroll, J. M., and Thomas, J. C. 1988. Fun. *SIGCHI Bulletin*, *19* (3), 21–24.

Carstensen, P. H., and Nielsen, M. 2001. Characterizing Modes of Coordination: A Comparison between Oral and Artifact Based Coordination. In *Proceedings of the 2001 ACM SIGGROUP Conference on Supporting Group Work*, 81–90. New York: ACM Press.

Chandler, A. D. 1977. *The Visible Hand: The Managerial Revolution in American Business.* Cambridge, Mass.: Harvard University Press.

Charny, B. 2002. New Cell Feature Helps Find Friends. *CNET News.com.* Retrieved from http://news.com.com/2100-1033-946224.html/2100-1033-946224.html.

Cherny, L. 1999. *Conversation and Community: Chat in a Virtual World.* Stanford: CSLI Publications.

Cherny, L. 2006. *Jobs on BayCHI.* Retrieved from http://www.ghostweather.com/blog/2006/06/jobs-on-baychi.html/.

Ciborra, C. 2002. *The Labyrinths of Information: Challenging the Wisdom of Systems.* Oxford: Oxford University Press.

Clarke, S. 1997. Encouraging the Effective Use of Contextual Information in Design. Ph.D. thesis, University of Glasgow.

Cockton, G. 2006. Focus, Fit, and Fervour: Future Factors Beyond Play with the Interplay. *International Journal of Human-Computer Interaction, 21* (2), 239–250.

Constant, E. W. 1980. *The Origins of the Turbojet Revolution.* Baltimore: Johns Hopkins Univeristy Press.

Conway, M. E. 1968. How Do Committees Invent? *Datamation*, *14* (4), 28–31.

Cringley, R. X. 2004. *Out of School: Doug Engelbart's Experience Shows That Even The Best Technology Can Be Ignored If It Is Difficult to Classify.* I, Cringley. Retrieved August 26, 2004, from http://www.pbs.org/cringely/pulpit/pulpit20040826.html/.

Cypher, A. 1993. *Watch What I Do: Programming by Demonstration.* Cambridge, Mass.: MIT Press.

De Cindio, F., De Michelis, G., Simone, C., Vassallo, R., and Zanaboni, A. M. 1986. CHAOS as a coordination technology. In *Proceedings of the 1986 ACM Conference on Computer-Supported Cooperative Work*, 325–342. New York: ACM Press.

DeMarco, T., and Lister, T. 1987. *Peopleware: Productive Projects and Teams.* New York: Dorset.

De Michelis, G. 1994. Categories, Debates, and Religion Wars. *Computer Supported Cooperative Work: an International Journal, 3* (1), 69–72.

De Michelis, G., and Grasso, M. A. 1994. Situating Conversations within the Language/Action Perspective: The Milan Conversation Model. In *Proceedings of the 1994 ACM Conference on Computer Supported Cooperative Work*, 89–100. New York: ACM Press.

Dennis, A. R., and Reinicke, B. A. 2004. Beta Versus VHS and the Acceptance of Electronic Brainstorming Technology. *MIS Quarterly, 28* (1), 1–20.

Dewey, J. 1938. *Experience and Education.* New York: Macmillan.

Dey, A. K., Salber, D., and Abowd, G. D. 2001. A Conceptual Framework and a Toolkit for Supporting the Rapid Prototyping of Context-Aware Applications. *Human-Computer Interaction, 16*(2–4), 97–166.

Dourish, P. 2001. *Where the Action Is: The Foundations of Embodied Interaction.* Cambridge, Mass.: MIT Press.

Dourish, P., Edwards, W. K., LaMarca, A., Lamping, J., Petersen, K., Salisbury, M., Thornton, J., and Terry, D. B. 2000. Extending Document Management Systems with Active Properties. *ACM Transactions on Information Systems, 18* (2), 140–170.

Dreyfuss, H. 1955. *Designing for People.* London: Simon and Schuster.

Dreyfuss, H. 1960. *The Measure of Man: Human Factors in Design.* New York: Whitney Library of Design.

Dubrovsky, V. J., Kiesler, S., and Sethna, B. N. 1991. The Equalization Phenomenon: Status Effects in Computer-Mediated and Face-to-Face Decision-Making Groups. *Human-Computer Interaction, 6* (2), 119–146.

Dumais, S., Cutrell, E., Cadiz, J., Jancke, G., Sarin, R., and Robbins, D. C. 2003. Stuff I've Seen: A System for Personal Information Retrieval and Re-use. In *Proceedings of the 26th Annual International ACM SIGIR Conference on Research and Development in Information Retrieval*, 72–79. New York: ACM Press.

Dundes, A., ed. 1998. *Cinderella: A Casebook.* Madison: University of Wisconsin Press.

Edwards, W. K. 1997. Flexible Conflict Detection and Management in Collaborative Applications. In *Proceedings of the 8th Annual International Conference on Mobile Computing and Networking*, 139–148. New York: ACM Press.

Edwards, W. K., Newman, M. W., Sedivy, J. Z., Smith, T. F., and Izadi, S. 2002. Challenge: Recombinant Computing and the Speakeasy Approach, 271–278. *Proceedings of the 8th*

Annual International Conference on Mobile Computing and Networking. New York: ACM Press.

Ehn, P., and Kyng, M. 1991. Cardboard Computers: Mocking-it-up or Hands-on the Future. In *Design at Work: Cooperative Design of Computer Systems*, ed. J. Greenbaum and M. Kyng. Mahwah: Lawrence Erlbaum.

Ehrlich, S. F. 1987a. Social and Psychological Factors Influencing the Design of Office Communications Systems. In *Proceedings of the SIGCHI/GI Conference on Human Factors in Computing Systems and Graphics Interface*, 323–329. New York: ACM Press.

Ehrlich, S. F. 1987b. Strategies for Encouraging Successful Adoption of Office Communication Systems. *ACM Transactions on Information Systems, 5* (4), 340–357.

Electronic Frontier Foundation. 1994. Third Annual EF Pioneer Awards. Retrieved April 16, 2007, from http://www.eff.org/awards/pioneer/1994.php/.

Engelbart, D. C. 1962. *Augmenting Human Intellect: A Conceptual Framework*. Stanford: Stanford Research Institute.

Engelbart, D. 1968. The oNLine System (NLS) demo. *The American Federation of Information Processing Societies' Fall Joint Computer Conference*. Retrieved from http://unrev.stanford.edu/.

Engelbart, D. C., and English, W. K. 1968. A Research Center for Augmenting Human Intellect. In *Fall Joint Computer Conference: Proceedings*, 395–410, American Federation Information Processing Societies. Washington, D.C.: Thompson Books.

English, W. K., Engelbart, D. C., and Berman, M. L. 1967. Display Selection Techniques for Text Manipulation. *IEEE Transactions on Human Factors in Electronics, 8* (1), 5–15.

Erickson, T. 1997. Social Interaction on the Net: Virtual Community as Participatory Genre. In *Proceedings of the Thirtieth Hawaii International Conference on Systems Sciences*, 13–21. Los Alamitos, Calif.: IEEE Computer Society.

Erickson, T. 2000. *Theory Theory: A Designer's View*. Retrieved from http://www.visi.com/~snowfall/theorytheory.html/.

Erickson, T. 2006. From PIM to GIM: Personal Information Management in Group Contexts. *Communications of the ACM, 49* (1), 74–75.

Erickson, T., and Kellogg, W. A. 2003. Social Translucence: Using Minimalist Visualizations of Social Activity to Support Collective Interaction. In *Designing Information Spaces: The Social Navigation Approach*, ed. K. Höök, D. Benyon, and A. Munro, 17–42. New York: Springer.

Erickson, T., Smith, D. N., Kellogg, W. A., Laff, M. R., Richards, J. T., and Bradner, E. 1999. Socially Translucent Systems: Social Proxies, Persistent Conversation, and the Design of "Babble." In *Proceedings of the SIGCHI Conference on Human Factors in Computing Systems*, 64–71. New York: ACM Press.

Faaborg, A., and Lieberman, H. 2006. A Goal-Oriented Browser. In *Proceedings of the SIGCHI Conference on Human Factors in Computing Systems*, 751–760. New York: ACM Press.

Fano, R. M. 1998. Joseph Carl Robinett Licklikder. In *Biographical Memoirs, 75*. Washington, D.C.: National Academy Press.

Fitts, P. M. 1951. Engineering Psychology and Equipment Design. In *Handbook of Experimental Psychology*, ed. S. S. Stevens, 1287–1340. New York: Wiley.

Fitts, P. M. 1954. The Information Capacity of the Human Motor System in Controlling the Amplitude of Movement. *Journal of Experimental Psychology*, *47*, 381–391. (Reprinted in *Journal of Experimental Psychology: General*, *121*, 1992, 262–269.)

Fitzpatrick, G. 2003. *The Locales Framework: Understanding and Designing for Wicked Problems*. New York: Springer.

Fitzpatrick, G., Kaplan, S., and Mansfield, T. 1998. Applying the Locales Framework to Understanding and Designing. In *1998 Australasian Computer Human Interaction Conference, OzCHI '98*, 122–129. Los Alamitos, Calif.: IEEE Computer Society.

Foldes, P. 1974. *Hunger/La Faim*. 16 mm computer animated film. National Film Board of Canada. Available at http://www.nfb.ca/animation/objanim/en/films/.

Ford, S., Forlizzi, J., and Ishizaki, S. 1997. Kinetic Typography: Issues in Time-based Presentation of Text. *CHI '97 Extended Abstracts on Human Factors in Computing Systems*, 269–270. New York: ACM Press.

Forsythe, D. 1995. Ethics and Politics of Studying "Up" in Technoscience. Paper presented at the American Anthropology Association annual meeting, Washington, D.C. (Published as Forsythe, D. 1999. Ethics and Politics of Studying Up in Technoscience. *Anthropology of Work Review*, *20* [1], 6–11.)

Forsythe, D. 1998. "It's Just a Matter of Common Sense": Ethnography as Invisible Work. *Computer-Supported Cooperative Work*, *8* (1–2), 127–145.

Francik, E., Rudman, S. E., Cooper, D., and Levine, S. 1991. Putting Innovation to Work: Adoption Strategies for Multimedia Communication Systems. *Communications of the ACM*, *34* (12), 52–63.

Furnas, G. W. 1986. Generalized Fisheye Views. In *Proceedings of the SIGCHI Conference on Human Factors in Computing Systems*, 16–23. New York: ACM Press.

Furnas, G. W. 2006. A Fisheye Follow-Up: Further Reflections on Focus + Context. In *Proceedings of the SIGCHI Conference on Human Factors in Computing Systems*, 999–1008. New York: ACM Press.

Galloway, K., and Rabinowitz, S. 1980. *Hole in Space*. Mobile Image Videotape.

Gaver, B., Dunne, T., and Pacenti, E. 1999. Cultural Probes. *Interactions*, 6 (1), 21–29.

Gaver, W. 1997. Auditory Interfaces. In *Handbook of Human-Computer Interaction*, ed. M. G. Helander, T. K. Landauer, and P. Prabhu. Amsterdam: Elsevier Science.

Gellersen, H., ed. 1999. *Handheld and Ubiquitous Computing: First International Symposium, HUC '99*. New York: Springer.

Gemmell, J., Bell, G., and Lueder, R. 2006. MyLifeBits: A Personal Database for Everything. *Communications of the ACM*, *49* (1), 88–95.

Gemmell, J., Bell, G., Lueder, R., Drucker, S., and Wong, C. 2002. MyLifeBits: Fulfilling the Memex Vision. In *Proceedings of the Tenth ACM International Conference on Multimedia*, 235–238. New York: ACM Press.

Gibson, J. J. 1966. *The Senses Considered as Perceptual Systems*. London: George Allen and Unwin.

Gibson, J. J. 1979. *The Ecological Approach to Visual Perception.* Boston: Houghton Mifflin.

Giddens, A. 1986. *The Constitution of Society: Outline of the Theory of Structuration.* Berkeley: University of California Press.

Goffman, E. 1959. *The Presentation of Self in Everyday Life.* New York: Anchor.

Golder, S. A., and Huberman, B. A. 2006. The Structure of Collaborative Tagging Systems. *Journal of Information Science*, *32* (2), 198–208.

Goldin, D. Q., Smolka, S. A., and Wegner, P. 2006. *Interactive Computation: the New Paradigm.* Berlin: Springer-Verlag.

Gould, J., Conti, J., and Hovanyecz, T. 1983. Composing Letters with a Simulated Listening Typewriter. *Communications of the ACM*, *26* (4), 295–308.

Greenbaum, J., and Kyng, M. 1991. *Design at Work: Cooperative Design of Computer Systems.* Mahwah: Lawrence Erlbaum.

Greenberg, S., Hayne, S., and Rada, R., eds. 1995. *Groupware for Real-Time Drawing: A Designer's Guide.* New York: McGraw-Hill.

Greenberg, S., and Marwood, D. 1994. Real-Time Groupware as a Distributed System: Concurrency Control and Its Effect on the Interface. In *Proceedings of the 1994 ACM Conference on Computer Supported Cooperative Work*, 207–217. New York: ACM Press.

Greenberg, S., Roseman, M., Webster, D., and Bohnet, R. 1992. Human and Technical Factors of Distributed Group Drawing Tools. *Interacting with Computers*, *4* (1), 364–392.

Grinter, R. E. 1996. Supporting Articulation Work Using Software Configuration Management Systems. *Computer Supported Cooperative Work*, *5* (4), 447–465.

Grinter, R. E. 1998. Recomposition: Putting It All Back Together Again. In *Proceedings of the 1998 ACM Conference on Computer Supported Cooperative Work*, 393–403. New York: ACM Press.

Grudin, J. 1994. Groupware and Social Dynamics: Eight Challenges for Developers. *Communications of the ACM*, *37* (1), 92–105.

Grudin, J. 2004. Return on Investment and Organizational Adoption. *Proceedings of the 2004 ACM Conference on Computer Supported Cooperative Work*, 274–277. New York: ACM Press.

Grudin, J. 2005. Three Faces of Human-Computer Interaction. *IEEE Annals of the History of Computing*, *27* (4), 46–62.

Guiard, Y., and Beaudouin-Lafon, M. 2004. Target Acquisition in Multiscale Electronic Worlds. *International Journal of Human Computer Studies*, *61* (6), 875–905.

Gutwin, C., and Greenberg, S. 2002. A Descriptive Framework of Workspace Awareness for Real-Time Groupware. *Computer Supported Cooperative Work*, *11* (3–4), 411–446.

Guy, M., and Tonkin, E. 2006. Folksonomies: Tidying up Tags? *D-Lib Magazine*, *12* (1).

Hackman, J. R. 1985. Doing Research That Makes a Difference. In *Doing Research That Is Useful for Theory and Practice*, ed. E. E. Lawyer, A. M. Mohrman, S. A. Mohrman, G. E. Ledfgord, T. G. Cummings, et al. New York: Wiley/Jossey-Bass.

Harper, R. H. R., and Hughes, J. A. 1992. "What a F-ing System! Send 'Em All to the Same Place and Then Expect Us to Stop 'Em Hitting": Making Technology Work in Air Traffic Control. In *Technology in Working Order: Studies of Work, Interaction and Technology*, ed. G. Button, 127–144. London: Routledge.

Harrison, S., Bly, S., Anderson, S., and Minneman, S. 1997. The Media Space. In *Video-Mediated Communication*, ed. K. Finn, A. Sellen, and S. Wilbur, 273–300. Mahwah: Lawrence Erlbaum.

Harrison, S., and Dourish, P. 1996. Re-Placing Space: The Roles of Place and Space in Collaborative Systems. In *Proceedings of the 1996 ACM Conference on Computer Supported Cooperative Work*, 67–76. New York: ACM Press.

Heath, C., and Luff, P. 1992. Collaboration and Control: Crisis Management and Multimedia Technology in London Underground Line Control Rooms. *Computer Supported Cooperative Work*, *1* (1–2), 69–94.

Herbsleb, J. D., and Grinter, R. E. 1999. Splitting the Organization and Integrating the Code: Conway's Law Revisited. In *Proceedings of the 21st International Conference on Software Engineering*, 85–95. New York: ACM Press.

Hiltz, S. R., and Turoff, M. 1978. *The Network Nation: Human Communication via Computer*. Reading: Addison-Wesley.

Hiltz, S. R., and Turoff, M. 1993. *The Network Nation: Human Communication via Computer*, revised edition. Cambridge, Mass.: MIT Press.

Hindus, D., Ackerman, M. S., Mainwaring, S., and Starr, B. 1996. Thunderwire: A Field Study of an Audio-Only Media Space. In *Proceedings of the 1996 ACM Conference on Computer Supported Cooperative Work*, 238–247. New York: ACM Press.

Hollan, J., and Stornetta, S. 1992. Beyond Being There. In *Proceedings of the SIGCHI Conference on Human Factors in Computing Systems*, 119–125. ACM Press.

Irby, C., Bergsteinsson, L., Moran, T., Newman, W., and Tesler, L. 1977. *A Methodology for User Interface Design*. Xerox Corporation, Systems Development Division. Internal Report.

Ishii, H., and Kobyashi, M. 1993. Integration of Interpersonal Space and Shared Workspace: Clearboard Design and Experiments. *ACM Transactions on Information Systems*, *11* (4), 349–375.

Jacob, R. J. K., Ishii, H., Pangaro, G., and Patten, J. 2002. A Tangible Interface for Organizing Information Using a Grid. In *Proceedings of the SIGCHI Conference on Human Factors in Computing Systems*, 339–346. New York: ACM Press.

Jacobs, J. 1961. *The Death and Life of Great American Cities*. New York: Random House.

Johansen, R., Valle, J., and Collins, K. 1977. Learning the Limits of Teleconferencing: Design of a Teleconferences Tutorial. In *Evaluating New Telecommunication Services*, ed. M. C. J. Elton, W. A. Lucas, and E. W. Conrath, 385–398. London: Plenum Press.

John, B. E., and Kieras, D. E. 1996. The GOMS Family of User Interface Analysis Techniques: Comparison and Contrast. *ACM Transactions on Computer Human Interaction (ToCHI)*, 3 (4), 320–351.

John, B. E., and Mashyna, M. M. 1997. Evaluating a Multimedia Authoring Tool. *Journal of the American Society for Information Science*, *48* (11), 1004–1022.

John, B. E., Vera, A., Matessa, M. Freed, M., and Remington, R. 2002. Automating CPM-GOMS. In *Proceedings of the SIGCHI Conference on Human Factors in Computing Systems*, 147–154. New York: ACM Press.

Johnson, J., Roberts, T. L., Verplank, W., Smith, D. C., Irby, C., Beard, M., and Mackey, K. 1989. The Xerox Star: A Retrospective. *In Computer*, *22* (9), 11–29.

Johnson-Laird, P. N. 1983. *Mental Models: Towards a Cognitive Science of Language, Inference, and Consciousness*. Cambridge: Cambridge University Press.

Kelley, D., and VanPatter, G. K. 2005. Design as Glue: Understanding the Stanford d.school. *NextD Journal*, *7.3*.

Kidd, A. 1994. The Marks are on the Knowledge Worker. In *Proceedings of the ACM SIGCHI Conference on Human Factors in Computing Systems*, 186–191. New York: ACM Press.

Kiesler, S., Siegel, J., and McGuire, T. W. 1984. Social Psychological Aspects of Computer-Mediated Communication. *American Psychologist*, *39* (10), 1123–1134.

Kingsolver, B. 1989. *Holding the Line: Women in the Great Arizona Mine Strike of 1983*. Ithaca, N.Y.: ILR Press.

KMDI. 2006. Retrieved from http://www.kmdi.utoronto.ca/.

Kraut, R., Scherlis, W., Mukhopadhyay, T., Manning, J., and Kiesler, S. 1996. The HomeNet Field Trial of Residential Internet Services. *Communications of the ACM*, *39* (12), 55–65.

Krippendorff, K. 2006. *The Semantic Turn: A New Foundation for Design*. Boca Raton, Fla.: CRC Press.

Kruger, J., Epley, N., Parker, J., and Ng, Z. 2005. Egocentrism Over E-mail: Can We Communicate as Well as We Think? *Journal of Personality and Social Psychology*, *89* (6), 925–936.

Kruger, R., Carpendale, S., Scott, S., and Greenberg, S. 2004. Roles of Orientation in Tabletop Collaboration: Comprehension, Coordination, and Communication. *Computer Supported Collaborative Work*, *13* (5–6), 501–537.

Krupat, A. 1992. *Ethnocriticism: Ethnography, History, Literature*. Berkeley: University of California Press.

Kuhn, T. S. 1962. *The Structure of Scientific Revolutions*. Chicago: University of Chicago Press.

Landay, J. A., and Myers, B. A. 1995. Interactive Sketching for the Early Stages of User Interface Design. In *Proceedings of the SIGCHI Conference on Human Factors in Computing Systems*, 43–50. New York: ACM Press.

Larkin, J. H. 1989. Display-Based Problem-Solving. In *Complex Information Processing: The Impact of Herbert Simon*, ed. D. Klahr and K. Kotovsky, 319–341. Mahwah, N.J.: Lawrence Erlbaum.

Larkin, J. H., and Simon, H. A. 1987. Why a Diagram Is (Sometimes) Worth Ten Thousand Words. *Cognitive Science*, *11*, 65–99.

Lave, J., and Wenger, E. 1991. *Situated Learning: Legitimate Peripheral Participation.* Cambridge: Cambridge University Press.

Lavery, D., Cockton, G., and Atkinson, M. P. 1997. Comparison of Evaluation Methods Using Structured Usability Problem Reports. *Behaviour and Information Technology*, *16* (4), 246–266.

Levy, S. 1984. Of Mice and Men. *Popular Computing*, *4* (5), 70–78.

Licklider, J. C. R. 1960. Man–Computer Symbiosis. *IRE Transactions on Human Factors in Electronics HFE-1 (1)*, 4–11. (Reprinted in *In Memoriam: J. C. R. Licklider: 1915–1990*, ed. R. W. Taylor. Digital Systems Research Center Reports 61, 1990.)

Licklider, J. C. R. 1965. *Libraries of the Future*. Cambridge, Mass.: MIT Press.

Licklider, J. C. R. 1968. Man–Computer Communication. *Annual Review of Information Science and Technology*, *3*, 201–240.

Licklider, J. C. R. 1970. Social Prospects of Information Utilities. In *The Information Utility and Social Choice*, ed. H. Sackman and N. H. Nie. Montvale, N.J.: AFIPS Press.

Licklider, J. C. R., and Clark, W. 1962. On-Line Man–Computer Communication. *AFIPS Conference Proceedings*, *21*, 113–128.

Licklider, J. C. R., and Taylor, R. W. 1968. The Computer as a Communications Device. *Science and Technology*, *76*. (Reprinted in *In Memoriam: J.C.R. Licklider: 1915–1990*, ed. R. W. Taylor. Digital Systems Research Center Reports 61, 1990.)

Lieberman, H. 2001. *Your Wish Is My Command: Programming by Example*. San Francisco: Morgan Kaufmann.

Lieberman, H., Paternó, F., Klann, M., and Wulf, V. 2005. *End-User Development: An Emerging Paradigm*. Dordrecht: Kluwer Academic.

Lipkie, D. E., Evans, S. R., Newlin, J. K., and Weissman, R. L. 1982. Star Graphics: An Object-Oriented Implementation. *ACM Computer Graphics*, *16* (3), 115–124.

Lovelock, J. 1979. *Gaia: A New Look at Life on Earth*. Oxford: Oxford University Press.

Löwgren, J. 1995. Applying Design Methodology to Software Development. In *Proceedings of the Conference on Designing Interactive Systems*, 87–95. New York: ACM Press.

Löwgren, J. 2002. How Far Beyond Human-Computer Interaction Is Interaction Design? *Digital Creativity*, *13* (3), 186–189.

Löwgren, J. 2006. Articulating the Use Qualities of Digital Designs. In *Aesthetic Computing*, ed. P. Fishwick, 383–403. Cambridge, Mass.: MIT Press.

Lynch, K. 1960. *The Image of the City*. Cambridge, Mass.: MIT Press.

Mackay, W. E. 1990. Users and Customizable Software: A Co-Adaptive Phenomenon. Ph.D. thesis, Massachusetts Instititute of Technology.

Mackay, W. E. 1999. Is Paper Safer? The Role of Paper Flight Strips in Air Traffic Control. *ACM Transactions on Computer-Human Interaction*, 6 (4), 311–340.

Mackay, W. E. 2002. *Using Video to Support Interaction Design*. CHI'02 Tutorial DVD. Retrieved from http://stream.cc.gt.atl.ga.us/hccvideos/viddesign.htm/.

Mackay, W. E., Fayard, A-L., Frobert, L., and Médini, L. 1998. Reinventing the Familiar: Exploring an Augmented Reality Design Space for Air Traffic Control. In *Proceedings of the*

SIGCHI Conference on Human Factors in Computing Systems, 558–565. New York: ACM Press.

MacKenzie, I. S. 1992. Fitts' Law as a Research and Design Tool in Human–Computer Interaction. *Human–Computer Interaction*, *7* (1), 91–139.

MacKenzie, I. S., and Buxton, W. 1992. Extending Fitts' Law to Two Dimensional Tasks. In *Proceedings of the SIGCHI Conference on Human Factors in Computing Systems*, 219–226. New York: ACM Press.

MacKenzie, I. S., and Soukoreff, R. W. 2002. Text Entry for Mobile Computing: Models and Methods, Theory and Practice. *Human–Computer Interaction*, *17* (2), 147–198.

Mainwaring, S. D., and Woodruff, A. 2005. Investigating Mobility, Technology, and Space in Homes, Starting with "Great Rooms." *Proceedings of the Ethnographic Praxis in Industry Conference*, 188–195. Arlington, Virginia: American Anthropological Association.

Malone, T. W., Yates, J., and Benjamin, R. I. 1987. Electronic Markets and Electronic Hierarchies. *Communications of the ACM*, *30* (6), 484–497.

Marx, M., and Schmandt, C. 1996. MailCall: Message Presentation and Navigation in a Non-Visual Environment. In *Proceedings of the SIGCHI Conference on Human Factors in Computing Systems*, 165–172. New York: ACM Press.

Mateas, M., Salvador, T., Scholtz, J., and Soresen, D. 1996. Engineering Ethnography in the Home. In *Conference Companion on Human factors in Computing Systems*, 283–284. New York: ACM Press.

McCarthy, J., and Wright, P. 2004. *Technology as Experience*. Cambridge, Mass.: MIT Press.

McCorduck, P. 1979. *Machines Who Think*. San Francisco: W. H. Freeman.

McDonald, D. W. 2001. Evaluating Expertise Recommendations. In *Proceedings of the 2001 International ACM SIGGROUP Conference on Supporting Group Work*, 214–223. New York: ACM Press.

McDonald, D. W. 2003. Recommending Collaboration with Social Networks: A Comparative Evaluation. In *Proceedings of the SIGCHI Conference on Human Factors in Computing Systems*, 593–600. New York: ACM Press.

McDonald, D. W., and Ackerman, M. S. 2000. Expertise Recommender: A Flexible Recommendation System and Architecture. In *Proceedings of the 2000 ACM Conference on Computer-Supported Cooperative Work*, 231–240. New York: ACM Press.

McGrath, J. E. 1991. Time, Interaction, and Performance (TIP): A Theory of Groups. *Small Group Research*, *22* (2), 147–174.

McGuffin, M. J., and Balakrishnan, R. 2005. Fitts' Law and Expanding Targets: Experimental Studies and Designs for User Interfaces. *ACM Transactions on Computer–Human Interaction*, *12* (4), 388–422.

McLuhan, M. 1994. *Understanding Media: The Extensions of Man*. Cambridge, Mass.: MIT Press.

Milgram, S., Sabini, J., and Silver, M. eds. 1992. *The Individual in a Social World: Essays and Experiments*, 2nd edition. New York: McGraw-Hill.

Muller, M. J. 1992. Retrospective on a Year of Participatory Design Using the PICTIVE Technique. In *Proceedings of the SIGCHI Conference on Human Factors in Computing Systems*, 455–462. New York: ACM Press.

Muller, M. J. 1997. Ethnocritical Heuristics for Reflecting on Work with Users and Other Interested Parties. In *Computers and Design in Context*, ed. M. Kyng and L. Mathiassen. Cambridge, Mass.: MIT Press.

Muller, M. J. 1999. Translation in HCI: Toward a Research Agenda. Available as TR 99-05. Retrieved July 16, 2006, from http://www.research.ibm.com/cambridge/.

Muller, M. J. 2003. Participatory Design: The Third Space in HCI. In *Handbook of HCI*, ed. J. Jacko and A. Sears. Mahwah: Lawrence Erlbaum.

Muller, M. J., Tudor, L. G., Wildman, D. M., White, E. A., Root, R. W., Dayton, T., Carr, R., Diekmann, B., and Dykstra-Erickson, E. A. 1995. Bifocal Tools for Scenarios and Representations in Participatory Activities with Users. In *Scenario-Based Design for Human-Computer Interaction*, ed. J. Carroll. New York: Wiley.

Mumford, E., and Weir, M. 1979. *Computer Systems in Work Design—The Ethics Method*. New York: Wiley.

Murphy, R. R. 2004. Human–Robot Interaction in Rescue Robotics. *IEEE Transactions on Systems, Man and Cybernetics, Part C, 34* (2), 138–153.

Nardi, B., and Miller, J. 1991. Twinkling Lights and Nested Loops: Distributed Problem Solving and Spreadsheet Development. *International Journal of Man-Machine Studies, 34* (2), 161–184.

Needham, R. 2003. Computer Security? *Philosophical Transactions of the Royal Society A, 361* (1808), 1549–1555.

Nelson, H., and Stolterman, E. 2003. *The Design Way: Intentional Change in an Unpredictable World*. Englewood Cliffs, N.J.: Educational Technology Publications.

Nelson, T. 1974. *Computer Lib/Dream Machines*. Self-published. (Republished in 1987 by Microsoft Press, Redmond, Wash.)

Newell, A. 1990. *Unified Theories of Cognition*. Cambridge, Mass.: Harvard University Press.

Newman, W. M. 1996. Models of Work Practice: Can They Support the Analysis of System Designs? In *Conference on Human Factors in Computing Systems*, 216. New York: ACM Press.

Newman, W. M. 1997. Better or Just Different? On the Benefits of Designing Interactive Systems in Terms of Critical Parameters. In *Proceedings of the Conference on Designing Interactive Systems*, 239–245. New York: ACM Press.

Newman, W. M., and Smith, E. L. 2006. Disruption of Meetings by Laptop Use: Is There a 10-Second Solution? In *CHI '06 Extended Abstracts on Human Factors in Computing Systems*. New York: ACM Press.

Newman, W. M., and Sproull, R. 1979. *Principles of Interactive Computer Graphics*. New York: McGraw-Hill.

Nielsen, J. 1989. *CHI '89 Trip Report*. Retrieved May 22, 2006, from http://www.useit.com/papers/tripreports/chi89.html/.

Noble, Douglas D. 1991. In the Cage with the Smart Machine. *Science as Culture*, *10* (2.1), 131–140.

Norman, D. A. 1983. Some Observations on Mental Models. In *Mental Models*, ed. D. Gentner and A. Stevens. Mahwah: Lawrence Erlbaum.

Norman, D. A. 1988. *The Design of Everyday Things*. New York: Currency-Doubleday.

Norman, D. A. 1993. Cognition in the Head and in the World: An Introduction to the Special Issue on Situated Action. *Cognitive Science: A Multidisciplinary Journal*, *17* (1), 1–6.

Norman, D. A. 2003. *Emotional Design: Why We Love (or Hate) Everyday Things*. New York: Basic Books.

NRC. 1970. From Handel to Haydn to the Headless Musician. *Science Dimension*, *2* (3). Retrieved from http://ieee.ca/millennium/electronic_music/em_headless.html/.

NRC. 1971a. *Keyframe Animation*. 7 min., 45 sec. 16 mm film, produced by the National Research Council of Canada. Available at http://www.billbuxton.com/.

NRC. 1971b. *The Music Machine*. 11 min. 16 mm film, produced by the National Research Council of Canada. Available at http://www.billbuxtion.com/.

Nunamaker, J., Briggs, R. O., Mittleman, D. D., Vogel, D. R., and Balthazard, P. A. 1997. Lessons from a Dozen Years of Group Support Systems Research: A Discussion of Lab and Field Findings. *Journal of Management Information Systems*, *13* (3), 163–207.

Olson, G. M., and Olson, J. S. 2000. Distance Matters. *Human Computer Interaction*, *15* (2–3), 139–179.

Olson, G. M., Olson, J. S., Carter, M. R., and Storrosten, M. 1992. Small Group Design Meetings: An Analysis of Collaboration. *Human Computer Interaction*, *7* (4), 347–374.

Olson, G. M., Zimmerman, A., and Bos, N., eds. In press. *Science on the Internet*. Cambridge, Mass.: MIT Press.

Olson, J. S., and Olson, G. 1990. The Growth of Cognitive Modeling in Human-Computer Interaction Since GOMS. *Human–Computer Interaction*, *5* (2–3), 221–265.

Olson, J. S., and Teasley, S. 1996. Groupware in the Wild: Lessons Learned from a Year of Virtual Collocation. In *Proceedings of the 1996 ACM Conference on Computer Supported Cooperative Work*, 419–427. New York: ACM Press.

O'Malley, C., and Draper, S. 1992. Representation and Interaction: Are Mental Models All in the Mind? In *Models in the Mind*, ed. Y. Rogers, A. Rutherford, and P. Bibby. Amsterdam: Kluwer Academic.

Orlikowski, W. J. 1992. Learning from Notes: Organizational Issues in Groupware Implementation. In *Proceedings of the 1992 ACM Conference on Computer-Supported Cooperative Work*, 362–369. New York: ACM Press.

Palen, L. 1999. Social, Individual, and Technological Issues for Groupware Calendar Systems. In *Proceedings of the SIGCHI Conference on Human Factors in Computing Systems*, 17–24. New York: ACM Press.

Palen, L., and Dourish, P. 2003. Unpacking "Privacy" for a Networked World. In *Proceedings of the SIGCHI Conference on Human Factors in Computing Systems*, 129–136. New York: ACM Press.

Papert, S. 1980. *Mindstorms*. New York: Basic Books.

Parnas, D. L. 1972. On the Criteria to Be Used in Decomposing Systems into Modules. *Communications of the ACM*, *15* (12), 1053–1058.

Paulos, E., and Goodman, E. 2004. The Familiar Stranger: Anxiety, Comfort, and Play in Public Places. In *Proceedings of the SIGCHI Conference on Human Factors in Computing Systems*, 223–230. New York: ACM Press.

Paulos, E., and Jenkins, T. 2005. Urban Probes: Encountering Our Emerging Urban Atmospheres. In *Proceedings of the Conference on Human Factors in Computing Systems*, 341–350. New York: ACM Press.

Pew, R. W. 1994. Paul Morris Fitts, 1912–1965. In *Division 21 Members Who Made Distinguished Contributions to Engineering Psychology*, ed. H. L. Taylor, 23–44. Washington, D.C.: The American Psychological Association.

Pinelle, D., Gutwin, C., and Greenberg, S. 2003. Task Analysis for Groupware Usability Evaluation: Modeling Shared-Workspace Tasks with the Mechanics of Collaboration. *ACM Transactions on Human Computer Interaction*, *10* (4), 281–311.

Poltrock, S. E., and Grudin, J. 2005. Videoconferencing: Recent Experiments and Reassessment. In *Proceedings of the 38th Hawaii International Conference on System Sciences*, CD-ROM.

Postmes, T., and Brunsting, S. 2002. Collective Action in the Age of the Internet: Mass Communication and Online Mobilization. *Social Science Computer Review*, *20* (3), 290–301.

Postmes, T., Spears, R., Lee, A. T., and Novak, R. J. 2005. Individuality and Social Influence in Groups: Inductive and Deductive Routes to Group Identity. *Journal of Personality and Social Psychology*, *89* (5), 747–763.

Potter, M. 1984. Rapid Serial Visual Presentation (RSVP): A Method for Studying Language Processing. In *New Methods in Reading Comprehension Research*, ed. D. E. Kieras and M. A. Just, 91–118. Mahwah, N.J.: Lawrence Erlbaum.

Prante, T., Streitz, N., and Tandler, P. 2004. Roomware: Computers Disappear and Interaction Evolves. *Computer*, *37* (12), 47–54.

Preece, J. 2000. *Online Communities: Designing Usability, Supporting Sociability*. New York: Wiley.

Price, B. A., Baecker, R. M., and Small, I. S. 1993. A Principled Taxonomy of Software Visualization. *Journal of Visual Languages and Computing*, *4* (3), 211–266.

Pruitt, J., and Grudin, J. 2003. Personas: Practice and Theory. In *Proceedings of the 2003 Conference on Designing for User Experiences*, 1–15. New York: ACM Press.

Pulfer, J. K. 1968. Digital Display Hardware for Man–Machine Communication Studies. *Canadian Information Processing Society Quarterly Bulletin*, *8* (6), 18–23.

Pulfer, J. K. 1971. Man–Machine Interaction in Creative Applications. *International Journal of Man-Machine Studies*, *3*, 1–11.

Raccoon, L. B. S. 1997. Fifty Years of Progress in Software Engineering. *ACM SIGSOFT Software Engineering Notes*, *22* (1), 88–104.

Resnick, P., and Virzi, R. 1995. Relief from the Audio Interface Blues: Expanding the Spectrum of Menu, List, and Form Styles. *ACM Transactions on Computer-Human Interaction*, *2* (2), 145–176.

Roberts, T., and Moran, T. 1983. The Evaluation of Computer Text Editors: Methodology and Empirical Results. *Communications of the ACM*, *26* (4), 265–283.

Rogers, E. 1995. *Diffusion of Innovations*. New York: Free Press.

Rogers, G. F. C. 1983. *The Nature of Engineering: a Philosophy of Technology*. New York: Macmillan.

Rogers, Y., and Scaife, M. 1998. How Can Interactive Multimedia Facilitate Learning? In *Intelligence and Multimodality in Multimedia Interfaces: Research and Applications*, ed. J. Lee. Menlo Park, Calif.: AAAI Press.

Roof, J., and Wiegman, R., eds. 1995. *Who Can Speak? Authority and Critical Identity*. Urbana and Chicago: University of Illinois Press.

Russell, D. M., Moran, T., and Jordan, D. 1988. The Instructional Design Environment. In *Intelligent Tutoring Systems: Lessons Learned*, ed. J. Psotka, D. Massey, Jr., and S. Mutter. Mahwah, N.J.: Lawrence Erlbaum.

Salvucci, D. D., Zuber, M., Beregovaia, E., and Markley, D. 2005. Distract-R: Rapid Prototyping and Evaluation of In-Vehicle Interfaces. In *Proceedings of the SIGCHI Conference on Human Factors in Computing Systems*, 581–589. New York: ACM Press.

Scaife, M., and Rogers, Y. 1996. External Cognition: How Do Graphical Representations Work? *International Journal of Human-Computer Studies*, *45* (2), 185–213.

Schmandt, C., and Davis, J. 1989. Synthetic Speech for Real Time Direction-Giving. *IEEE Transactions on Consumer Electronics*, *35* (3), 649–653.

Schmidt, K., and Bannon, L. 1992. Taking CSCW Seriously: Supporting Articulation Work. *Computer Supported Cooperative Work*, *1* (1), 7–40.

Schmidt, K., and Simone, C. 1996. Coordination Mechanisms: Towards a Conceptual Foundation of CSCW Systems Design. *Computer Supported Cooperative Work*, *5* (2–3), 155–200.

Schön, D. 1987. *Educating the Reflective Practitioner: Toward a New Design for Teaching and Learning in the Professions*. San Francisco: Jossey-Bass.

Schuler, D., and Namioka, A., eds. 1993. *Participatory Design: Principles and Practices*. Mahwah, N.J.: Lawerence Erlbaum.

Scott, S. D., Lesh, N., and Klau, G. W. 2002. Investigating Human-Computer Optimization. In *Proceedings of the SIGCHI Conference on Human Factors in Computing Systems*, 155–162. New York: ACM Press.

Searle, J. R. 1969. *Speech Acts*. Cambridge: Cambridge University Press.

Shankar, T. 2005. Speaking on the Record. Ph.D. dissertation, Massachusetts Institute of Technology.

Sharlin, E., Itoh, Y., Watson, B., Kitamura, Y., Sutphen, S., and Liu, L. 2002. Cognitive Cubes: A Tangible User Interface for Cognitive Assessment. In *Proceedings of the SIGCHI Conference on Human Factors in Computing Systems*, 347–354. New York: ACM Press.

Sherman, E. 2004. *Geocaching: Hike and Seek with Your GPS.* Berkeley, Calif.: Apress.

Shneiderman, B., Card, S., Norman, D. A., Tremaine, M., and Waldrop, M. M. 2002. Fighting Our Way from Marginality to Power. Panel at CHI@20. Minneapolis, Minnesota.

Small, D., Ishizaki, S., and Cooper, M. (1994). Typographic Space. In *Proceedings of the ACM Conference on Human Factors in Computing Systems (CHI'94) Conference Companion*, 437–438.

Smith, B. C. 1996. *On the Origin of Objects.* Cambridge, Mass.: MIT Press.

Smith, B. K., Frost, J., Albayrak, M., and Sudhakar, R. 2007. Integrating Glucometers and Digital Photography as Experience Capture Tools to Enhance Patient Understanding and Communication of Diabetes Self-Management Practices. *Personal and Ubiquitous Computing, 11* (4), 273–286.

Smith, D., Irby, C., Kimball, R., and Harslem, E. 1982. The Star User Interface: An Overview. In *Proceedings of the AFIPS 1982 National Computer Conference*, 515–528. Arlington, Virginia: AFIPS Press.

Smith, D., Irby, C., Kimball, R., Verplank, B., and Harslem, E. 1982. Designing the Star User Interface. *Byte, 7* (4), 242–282.

Smith, D. C. 1975. *Pygmalion: A Creative Programming Environment.* AI Memo 260, Computer Science Department, Stanford University. Stan-CS-75-499.

Smith, D. C. 1977. *Pygmalion: A Creative Programming Environment.* Basel: Birkhäuser-Verlag.

Sproull, L., and Kiesler, S. 1991. *Connections: New Ways of Working in the Networked Organization.* Cambridge, Mass.: MIT Press.

Stage, J., and Hornbæk, K. 2006. The Interplay between Usability Evaluation and User Interaction Design. *International Journal of Human–Computer Interaction, 21* (2), 117–123.

Star, S. L. 1999. The Ethnography of Infrastructure. *American Behavioral Scientist, 43* (3), 377–391.

Stokes, D. E. 1997. *Pasteur's Quadrant: Basic Science and Technological Innovation.* Washington, D.C.: Brookings Institution Press.

Strauss, A. 1988. The Articulation of Project Work: An Organizational Process. *Sociological Quarterly, 2* (29), 163–178.

Strauss, A. 1993. *Continual Permutations of Action.* Berlin: Aldine de Gruyter.

Streitz, N. 1986. Cognitive Ergonomics: An Approach for the Design of User-Oriented Interactive Systems. In *Man-Computer Interaction Research: MACINTER I*, ed. F. Klix and H. Wandke, 21–33. Amsterdam: North-Holland.

Streitz, N. 2001. Augmented Reality and the Disappearing Computer. In *Proceedings of the 9th International Conference on Human-Computer Interaction (HCI International 2001).* Mahwah, N.J.: Lawrence Erlbaum.

Streitz, N., Geißler, J., Haake, J., and Hol, J. 1994. DOLPHIN: Integrated Meeting Support across LiveBoards, Local and Remote Desktop Environments. In *Proceedings of the 1994 ACM Conference on Computer Supported Cooperative Work*, 345–358. New York: ACM Press.

Streitz, N., Geißler, J., and Holmer, T. 1998. Roomware for Cooperative Buildings: Integrated Design of Architectural Spaces and Information Spaces. In *Cooperative Buildings—Integrating Information, Organization, and Architecture: Proceedings of the First International Workshop, CoBuild '98*, 4–21, ed. N. Streitz, S. Konomi, and H. Burkhardt. Heidelberg: Springer-Verlag.

Streitz, N., Geißler, J., Holmer, T., Konomi, S., Müller-Tomfelde, C., Reischl, W., Rexroth, P., Seitz, P., and Steinmetz, R. 1999. i-LAND: An Interactive Landscape for Creativity and Innovation. In *Proceedings of the SIGCHI Conference on Human Factors in Computing Systems*, 120–127. New York: ACM Press.

Streitz, N., Haake, J., Hannemann, J., Lemke, A., Schuler, W., Schütt, H., and Thüring, M. 1992. SEPIA: A Cooperative Hypermedia Authoring Environment. In *Proceedings of the ACM Conference on Hypertext*, 11–22. New York: ACM Press.

Streitz, N., Kameas, A., and Mavrommati, I. (eds.). 2007. *The Disappearing Computer: Interaction Design, System Infrastructures, and Applications for Smart Environments.* LNCS volume 4500. Heidelberg: Springer.

Streitz, N., Konomi, S., and Burkhardt, H. 1998. Cooperative Buildings—Integrating Information, Organization, and Architecture. In *Proceedings of the First International Workshop, CoBuild '98.* Heidelberg: Springer-Verlag.

Streitz, N., and Nixon, P. 2005. The Disappearing Computer. *Communications of the ACM, 48* (3), 33–35.

Streitz, N., Röcker, C., Prante, T., van Alphen, D., Stenzel, R., and Magerkurth, C. 2005. Designing Smart Artifacts for Smart Environments. *Computer, 38* (3), 41–49.

Streitz, N., Tandler, P., Müller-Tomfelde, C., and Konomi, S. 2001. Roomware: Towards the Next Generation of Human–Computer Interaction Based on an Integrated Design of Real and Virtual Worlds. In *Human-Computer Interaction in the New Millennium*, ed. J. Carroll, 553–578. Reading: Addison-Wesley.

Stults, R. 1986. *Media Space.* Systems Concepts Lab Technical Report. Palo Alto: Xerox PARC.

Suchman, L. 1983. Office Procedures as Practical Action: Models of Work and System Design. *ACM Transactions on Information Systems, 1* (4), 320–328.

Suchman, L. 1987a. *Plans and Situated Actions: The Problem of Human–Machine Interaction.* Cambridge: Cambridge University Press.

Suchman, L. 1987b. Review of "Understanding Computer and Cognition" by T. Winograd and F. Flores. *Artificial Intelligence, 31*, 227–232.

Suchman, L. 1994. Do Categories Have Politics? The Language/Action Perspective Reconsidered. *Computer Supported Cooperative Work*, 2 (3), 177–190.

Sutherland, I. 1963. Sketchpad: A Man–Machine Graphical Communication System. In *Proceedings of the Spring Joint Computer Conference*, 329–345.

Swann, J., Chartre, E., and Ludwig, D. 2003. Galileo: Benefits for Location Based Services. *Journal of Global Positioning Systems, 1* (2), 57–66.

Tang, J. 1989. Listing, Drawing, and Gesturing in Design: A Study of the Use of Shared Workspaces by Design Teams. Ph.D. thesis, Department of Mechanical Engineering, Stanford University. Also published as Report SSL-89-3, Xerox PARC.

Tang, J. 1991. Findings from Observational Studies of Collaborative Work. *International Journal of Man–Machine Studies*, *34* (2), 143–160.

Tang, J., and Minneman, S. 1990. VideoDraw: A Video Interface for Collaborative Drawing. In *Proceedings of the ACM SIGCHI Conference on Human Factors in Computing Systems*, 313–320. New York: ACM Press.

Tang, J., and Minneman, S. 1991. VideoWhiteboard: Video Shadows to Support Remote Collaboration. In *Proceedings of the SIGCHI Conference on Human Factors in Computing Systems*, 315–322. New York: ACM Press.

Tang, A., Neustaedter, C., and Greenberg, S. 2006. VideoArms: Embodiments for Mixed Presence Groupware. In *Proceedings of the 20th BCS-HCI British HCI 2006 Group Conference*.

Tanner, P. 1971. Polyphonic Composition. In *Proceedings of the 2nd Canadian Man–Computer Computer Communications Conference*. Ottawa: National Research Council, Radio and Electrical Engineering Division.

Tanner, P. 1972a. MUSICOMP: An Experimental Aid for the Composition and Production of Music. ERB-869. Ottawa: National Research Council, Radio and Electrical Engineering Division.

Tanner, P. 1972b. Some Programs for the Computer Generation of Polyphonic Music. ERB-862. Ottawa: National Research Council, Radio and Electrical Engineering Division.

Teasley, S., Covi, L., Krishnan, M. S., and Olson, J. S. 2000. How Does Radical Collocation Help a Team Succeed? In *Proceedings of the 2000 ACM Conference on Computer Supported Cooperative Work*, 339–346. New York: ACM Press.

Thomas, J. C. 1999. Narrative Technology and the New Millennium. *Knowledge Management Journal, 2* (9), 14–17.

Thomas, J. C., and Kellogg, W. A. 1989. Minimizing Ecological Gaps in Interface Design. *IEEE Software*, *6* (1), 78–86.

Thompson, L. F., and Coovert, M. D. 2006. Understanding and Developing Virtual CSCW Teams. In *High-Tech Teams: Making Effective Work Teams with People, Machines, and Networks*, ed. C. A. Bowers and E. Salas. Washington, D.C.: American Psychological Association.

Tobach, E., Farlane, R., Parlee, M., Martin, L., and Kapelman, A., eds. 1997. *Mind and Social Practice: Selected Writings of Sylvia Scribner*. Cambridge: Cambridge University Press.

Tognazzini, B. 1999. Ask Tog: A Quiz Designed to Give You Fitts. Retrieved June 15, 2006, from http://www.asktog.com/columns/022DesignedToGiveFitts.html/.

Tufte, E. R. 1990. *Envisioning Information*. Cheshire: Graphics Press.

Turoff, M. 1972. Delphi Conferencing: Computer-Based Conferencing with Anonymity. *Technological Forecasting and Social Change*, *3*, 159–204.

Valente, T. W. 1995. *Network Models of the Diffusion of Innovations*. Cresskill, N.J.: Hampton Press.

Vera, A. H., and Simon, H. A. 1993. Situated Action: A Symbolic Interpretation. *Cognitive Science*, *17*, 7–48.

Vincenti, W. G. 1990. *What Engineers Know and How They Know It: Analytical Studies from Aeronautical History*. Baltimore: Johns Hopkins University Press.

Vitalari, N. P., Venkatesh, A., and Gronhaug, K. 1985. Computing in the Home: Shifts in the Time Allocation Patterns of Households. *Communications of the ACM*, *28* (5), 512–522.

Waldrop, M. M. 2001. *The Dream Machine: J. C. R. Licklider and the Revolution That Made Computing Personal*. London: Penguin Books.

Walker, N., and Smelcer, J. B. 1990. A Comparison of Selection Times from Walking and Pull-Down Menus. In *Proceedings of the SIGCHI Conference on Human Factors in Computing Systems*, 221–225. New York: ACM Press.

Walston, C. E., and Felix, C. P. 1977. A Method of Programming Measurement and Estimation. *IBM Systems Journal*, *16* (1), 54–73.

Want, R., Hopper, A., Falcao, V., and Gibbons, J. 1992. The Active Badge Location System. *ACM Transactions on Information Systems*, *10* (1), 91–102.

Watts, J. C., Woods, D. D., Corban, J. M., Patterson, E. S., Kerr, R. L., and Hicks, L. C. 1996. Voice Loops as Cooperative Aids in Space Shuttle Mission Control. In *Proceedings of the 1996 ACM Conference on Computer Supported Cooperative Work*, 48–56. New York: ACM Press.

Wegner, P. 1997. Why Interaction Is More Powerful Than Algorithms. *Communications of the ACM*, *40* (5), 80–91.

Weiser, M. 1991. The Computer for the 21st Century. *Scientific American*, *265* (3), 66–75.

Weiser, M. 1993. Some Computer Science Issues in Ubiquitous Computing. *Communications of the ACM*, *36* (7), 75–84.

Weiser, M., and Brown, J. S. 1996. Designing Calm Technology. *PowerGrid Journal*, *1* (1).

Welford, A. T. 1968. *Fundamentals of Skill*. London: G. B. Methuen.

Whiteside, J., Bennett, J., and Holtzblatt, K. 1988. Usability Engineering: Our Experience and Evolution. In *Handbook of Human-Computer Interaction*, ed. M. Helander, 791–817. Amsterdam: Elsevier North-Holland.

Whittaker, S. Bellotti, V., and Gwizdka, J. In press. Email as PIM. In *Personal Information Management*, ed. W. Jones and J. Teevan.

Whittaker, S., and Hirschberg, J. 2001. The Character, Value, and Management of Personal Paper Archives. *ACM Transactions on Computer-Human Interaction*, *8* (2), 150–170.

Whyte, W. H. 1980. *The Social Life of Small Urban Spaces*. New York: Project for Public Spaces.

Whyte, W. H. 1988. *City: Return to the Center*. New York: Anchor Books.

Williams, G. 1997. Task Conflict and Language Differences: Opportunities for Videoconferencing. In *Proceedings of the Fifth European Conference on Computer Supported Cooperative Work*, 97–108. Amsterdam: Kluwer Academic.

Wilson, S. 2002. *Information Arts: Intersections of Art, Science, and Technology*. Cambridge, Mass.: MIT Press.

Winograd, T. 1986. A Language/Action Perspective on the Design of Cooperative Work. In *Proceedings of the First Conference on CSCW*, 203–220. New York: ACM Press.

Winograd, T. 1994. Categories, Disciplines, and Social Coordination. *Computer Supported Cooperative Work, 2* (3), 191–197.

Winograd, T., ed. 1996. *Bringing Design to Software*. Reading: Addison-Wesley.

Winograd, T. 1997. The Design of Interaction. In *Beyond Calculation: The Next 50 Years of Computing*, ed. P. Denning and B. Metcalfe. Heidelberg: Springer-Verlag.

Winograd, T. 2006. Designing a New Foundation for Design. *Communications of the ACM, 49* (5), 71–74.

Winograd, T., and Flores, F. 1986. *Understanding Computers and Cognition*. Westport, Conn.: Ablex Publishing.

Wixon, D., Holtzblatt, K., and Knox, S. T. 1990. Contextual Design: An Emergent View of System Design. In *Proceedings of the SIGCHI Conference on Human Factors in Computing Systems*, 329–336. New York: ACM Press.

Wixon, D., and Wilson, C. 1997. The Usability Engineering Framework for Product Design and Evaluation. In *Handbook of Human-Computer Interaction*, 2nd edition,, 653–688, ed. M. Helander, T. K. Landauer, and P. Prabhu. Amsterdam: Elsevier.

Woodruff, A., and Aoki. P. M. 2004. Push-to-Talk Social Talk. *Computer Supported Cooperative Work, 13* (5–6), 409–441.

Wright, P., Fields, R., and Harrison, M. 2000. Analyzing Human–Computer Interaction as Distributed Cognition: The Resources Model. *Human Computer Interaction, 15* (1), 1–41.

Wroblewski, D. 1991. The Construction of Human–Computer Interfaces Considered as a Craft. In *Taking Software Design Seriously: Practical Techniques for Human-Computer Interaction Design*, ed. J. Karat, 1–19. New York: Press.

Xerox Corporation. 1981. *Xerox Red Book, The: Star Functional Specification, Revision 5.3 for Star-1*. Systems Development Division, Xerox Corporation.

Yates, J. 1989. *Control Through Communication: The Rise of System in American Management*. Baltimore: Johns Hopkins University Press.

Zagal, J., and Bruckman, A. 2005. From Samba Schools to Computer Clubhouses: Cultural Institutions as Learning Environments. *Convergence, 11* (1), 88–105.

Zhang, J., and Norman, D. A. 1994. Representations in Distributed Cognitive Tasks. *Cognitive Science, 18*, 87–122.

Zuboff, S. 1988. *In the Age of the Smart Machine*. New York: Basic Books.

Index